REFLEXIVE GOVERNANCE

Reflexive governance offers a theoretical framework for understanding modern patterns of governance in the European Union (EU) institutions and elsewhere. It offers a learning-based approach to governance, but one which can better respond to concerns about the democratic deficit and to the fulfillment of the public interest than the currently dominant neo-institutionalist approaches. The book is composed of one general introduction and eight chapters. Chapter one introduces the concept of reflexive governance and describes the overall framework. The following chapters of the book then summarise the implications of reflexive governance in major areas of domestic, EU and global policy-making. They address in turn: Services of General Interest, Corporate Governance, Institutional Frames for Markets, Regulatory Governance, Fundamental Rights, Healthcare Services, Global Public Services and Common Goods. While the themes are diverse, the chapters are unified by their attempt to get to the heart of which concepts of governance are dominant in each field, and what their successes and failures have been: reflexive governance then emerges as one possible response to the failures of other governance models currently being relied upon by policy-makers.

Volume 22 in the series Modern Studies in European Law

Modern Studies in European Law

Reflexive Governance

Redefining the Public Interest in a Pluralistic World

Edited by

Olivier De Schutter

and

Jacques Lenoble

·HART·
PUBLISHING

OXFORD AND PORTLAND, OREGON
2010

Published in the United Kingdom by Hart Publishing Ltd
16C Worcester Place, Oxford, OX1 2JW
Telephone: +44 (0)1865 517530
Fax: +44 (0)1865 510710
E-mail: mail@hartpub.co.uk
Website: http://www.hartpub.co.uk

Published in North America (US and Canada) by
Hart Publishing
c/o International Specialized Book Services
920 NE 58th Avenue, Suite 300
Portland, OR 97213–3786
USA
Tel: +1 503 287 3093 or toll-free: (1) 800 944 6190
Fax: +1 503 280 8832
E-mail: orders@isbs.com
Website: http://www.isbs.com

British Library Cataloguing in Publication Data

Data Available

ISBN: 978-1-84946-068-2

Typeset by Columns Ltd, Reading
Printed and bound in Great Britain by
CPI Antony Rowe Ltd, Chippenham, Wiltshire

Contents

3 Reflexive Governance, Regulation and Meta-Regulation: Control or Learning?

Colin Scott

PART II BEYOND NEO-INSTITUTIONALISM

4 Neo-Institutionalist and Collaborative-Relational Approaches to Governance in Services of General Interest: The Case of Energy in the UK and Germany

Tony Prosser, Helen Adlard, Burkard Eberlein, Gabriele Britz and Karsten Herzmann

5 Reflexive Approaches to Corporate Governance: The Case of Heathrow Terminal 5   97

Simon Deakin and Aristea Koukiadaki

6 The Democratic Experimentalist Approach to Governance: Protecting Social Rights in the European Union   115

Olivier De Schutter

PART III   TOWARDS 'GENETIC' REFLEXIVE GOVERNANCE

7   From Collaborative to Genetic Governance: The Example of Healthcare Services in England   147

Peter Vincent-Jones and Caroline Mullen

8   The Contribution of Network Governance in Overcoming Frame Conflicts: Enabling Social Learning and Building Reflexive Abilities in Biodiversity Governance   179

Tom Dedeurwaerdere

List of Contributors

Helen Adlard is a lawyer with the Infrastructure Planning Commission, Bristol. She was previously a solicitor and partner in a city law firm, and has law lecturing and research experience. She has an MA in French from Edinburgh University, and is a Legal Associate of the Royal Town Planning Institute and a member of the Law Society's Planning Law Accreditation Scheme.

Gabriele Britz is Professor of Public Law and European Law at the Justus-Liebig-Universität in Giessen, Germany. She holds a PhD in law from the Johann Wolfgang Goethe-Universität in Frankfurt/Main, Germany.

Eric Brousseau, PhD in Economics from the University of Paris, is Professor of Economics at the University Paris Ouest. He is the Director of EconomiX, a Joint Research Center of the CNRS and the University Paris Ouest. He also coordinates the CNRS's Research Consortium 'Information and Communication Technologies and the Society' (GDR TICS). At the international level he is the founder and the director of the European School for New-Institutional Economics, and is the secretary of the International Society for New-Institutional Economics. His research agenda focuses on the economics of institutions, contracts and multi-level governance with three main fields of application: Intellectual Property Rights, the Internet and digital activities, and the environment. He has edited several books on these subjects and has published more than 50 papers in referred journals.

Olivier De Schutter is Professor at the University of Louvain (UCL) and at the College of Europe, and is a Member of the Centre for Philosophy of Law. A visiting professor at Columbia University and a member of the Global Law School Faculty at New York University, he has, since 2008, been the UN Special Rapporteur on the Right to Food. His publications are in the areas of international human rights and governance.

Simon Deakin is Professor of Law in the Faculty of Law and Corporate Governance Programme Director at the Centre for Business Research, University of Cambridge. He has held visiting professorships at Nantes, Melbourne, Columbia and Doshisha Universities, and at the EUI, Florence. He was elected a Fellow of the British Academy in 2005.

Tom Dedeurwaerdere is Research Director of the Biodiversity Governance Unit of the Centre for the Philosophy of Law and Professor at the Faculty of Philosophy, Université catholique de Louvain. He is a graduate in engineering and philosophy, with a PhD in philosophy. His main research focus is on the institutional analysis of the governance of genetic resource commons and the global knowledge commons.

Burkard Eberlein, MSc (Public Administration, LSE), MA and PhD (Political Science, University of Konstanz, Germany). He is currently Assistant Professor of Policy, Schulich School of Business and Graduate Coordinator and Associate Director at The Canadian Centre for German and European Studies (CCGES), York University (Toronto, Canada).

Jean-Michel Glachant, PhD in economics at La Sorbonne University, is Professor in European energy policy at the Loyola de Palacio Chair, and Director of the Florence School of Regulation at European University Institute in Florence.

Karsten Herzmann, is Research Assistant to the Chair for Public Law and European Law at the Justus-Liebig Universität, Giessen. He was educated at the Universität Giessen, the Universiteit Gent and the European University Institute in Florence. He holds a law degree from the Universität Giessen.

Aristea Koukiadaki is Leverhulme Trust Fellow at Warwick Business School (University of Warwick) and Research Associate at the Centre for Business Research (University of Cambridge). She holds a law degree from Greece, an LL.M (University of Manchester) and a PhD (University of Warwick). Her research interests are in comparative labour law and industrial relations, EU law and governance.

Jacques Lenoble is Professor of Philosophy of Law at the Université catholique de Louvain (Louvain-la-Neuve) and Director of the University's Centre for Philosophy of Law. The research projects conducted jointly with Marc Maesschalck relate to philosophy of law, theory of the norm and theory of governance. They have numerous publications to their credit, including *Toward A Theory of Governance – The Action of Norms* (London, Kluwer Law International, 2003) and more recently, *Democracy, Law and Governance* (Aldershot, Ashgate, 2010).

Marc Maesschalck is Professor of Philosophy of Law at the Université catholique de Louvain (Louvain-la-Neuve) and the Facultés universitaires Saint-Louis (Brussels). He is also responsible for the Philosophy Unit at the Centre for Philosophy of Law. His research projects conducted jointly with Jacques Lenoble relate to philosophy of law, theory of the norm, and theory of governance. They have numerous publications to their credit, including *Toward A Theory of Governance – The Action of Norms* (London, Kluwer Law International, 2003) and more recently, *Democracy, Law and Governance* (Aldershot, Ashgate, 2010).

Caroline Mullen is a Research Officer at the Centre for European Law and Legal Studies, School of Law, University of Leeds, and works on the Reflexive Governance in the Public Interest project. She has previously worked at the University of Birmingham. Her research interests are in governance and citizenship, especially deliberative democracy and reflexive governance; ethics of risk; conceptions of equality and distributive fairness. She gained her PhD 'Sustaining life, enabling activity and inflicting death: What risk and physical harm caused by transport is morally defensible?' from the Centre for Social Ethics and Policy, School of Law at the University of Manchester.

Tony Prosser is Professor of Public Law at the University of Bristol and Visiting Professor at the College of Europe, Bruges. He was formerly John Millar Professor of Law at the University of Glasgow and Jean Monnet Fellow at the European University Institute, Florence. He has an LLB from the University of Liverpool.

Colin Scott is Professor of EU Regulation and Governance at University College London. He holds an LLB (First Class Hons) from the London School of Economics and an LLM from Osgoode Hall Law School of York University, Toronto.

Peter Vincent-Jones is Professor of Law at the Centre for European Law and Legal Studies, School of law, University of Leeds. He holds a BA (Hons) in Law and Social and Political Sciences from the University of Cambridge; an MA in Socio-Legal Studies from the University of Sheffield; and a PhD in Law from the University of Sheffield.

Introduction

Institutions Equipped to Learn

OLIVIER DE SCHUTTER AND JACQUES LENOBLE

T HE GLOBAL FINANCIAL and economic crisis of 2008–09 confirms the fall of the neo-liberal state, which already was under severe critique since the mid 1990s (Harvey 2005, Mirowski and Plehwe 2009, Plant 2009). This fall in turn followed the demise of the Welfare State in the late 1970s and 1980s. Impressive as they are, these successive defeats have not deprived us of any viable alternative with which to rethink the future of regulation and the role of the state in market mechanisms. On the contrary, they have opened up new possibilities: they are a source not of intellectual stalemate, but of political and institutional imagination. It is the objective of this book to outline some of the possible scenarios. We hope to test these scenarios in the light of what we know, against the background of past failures and, sometimes, successes. We also hope to convince the reader that what we do *not* know matters, to the same degree as lessons learned from past experiences: only theories of governance that take seriously the limits of our ability to anticipate on all the uncertainties of a complex and fast-changing world have some chances of succeeding.

Our core intuition is that the crisis of the pre-existing, ready-made models is not simply due to the fact that these models were wrong. The crisis runs deeper: it is attributable to the fact that these models believed they were correct — that they could provide answers to the need to manage complexity. It is the very idea of a 'model' that should now be questioned. The crisis of the Welfare State ran much deeper than its symptoms, in particular unsustainably high levels of public deficit, in the context of changing demographics and economic globalisation. Also, the demise of the neo-liberal state stems not simply from a failure to recognise the reality of market failures and to provide public goods at an acceptably high level. Rather, both models failed also because of their inability to rethink the mental image of the norm on which they were premised. They failed not simply because they were ill-adapted to a dynamic reality: they failed because their representation of what adaptation means was deeply inadequate.

I.   LEARNING-BASED GOVERNANCE

The research programme in which this collection of essays originates[1] is based on the hypothesis that, by examining which new forms of governance are emerging in a variety of fields, and how these different forms of governance succeed in establishing institutions or mechanisms equipped to learn, we can achieve a better understanding of the way forward. Two premises underlie such a research programme. First, we submit, by relating different substantive domains to one another — by establishing links, say, between debates on corporate governance and on health care reform, or between the protection of social rights in the European Union (EU) and the management of global commons — we should make it easier to identify, within each of these domains, certain blindspots: unquestioned assumptions or routines, and in particular, theories of governance on which reforms in each of these domains seem to rely, without a clear understanding of the limits of what each of these theories has to offer. The idea was, in other terms, one of mutual check and control: progress in each substantive field, we believed, could only be achieved through comparison with other fields, in order to uncover the limitations of the range of perspectives competing in each domain.

Secondly, we take as a departure point that governance today should be conceived so as to provide the actors involved with an opportunity for learning. Tools such as monitoring and evaluation, benchmarking of best practices, consultation and participation, or feedback mechanisms, have come to play a central role in many of what are currently the most influential theories of governance. This is not by accident. Rather, these theories of governance share a common diagnosis about what may have gone wrong in the past. More or less explicitly, they all recognise that both decentralised coordination through prices and command-and-control regulation have failed. Market-based solutions appear most often unable to fill the gap between individual and social costs, leaving open the problem of externalities and leading to sub-optimal solutions; and even when appropriate incentive sets are devised to overcome this difficulty, these solutions do not allow for transformative actions that can change the framework in which the actors are placed: they leave unresolved, in other terms, the problem of collective action. As to the regulatory approaches that have been typical of much of the policies associated with the Welfare State, they too are seen as inefficient, insufficiently flexible, and lacking sensitivity to the context in which they are applied; they also are premised on a definition of the public interest that is based on compliance with certain institutional procedures, and which in that sense is formalistic and top-down, rather than deliberative and bottom-up.

Learning-based theories of governance seek to move beyond the current impasse. However, they too confront a dilemma. On the one hand, the formalistic

[1]   The Reflexive Governance (REFGOV) project (no CIT3-CT-2005–513420) is funded under the 6th EC Framework Programme on Research and Development. It is coordinated by the Centre for Philosophy of Law of the Catholic University of Louvain (CPDR-UCL).

models of rule application have failed. Such models presupposed the possibility of a clear separation between the principal and the agent, and they were ultimately based on an ideal of the transparency of the norm. These models therefore underestimated the difficulties of maintaining the distinction between rule-making and rule-following in pluralistic societies, in which the contexts are dynamic and increasingly diverse, to the point even that the idea of setting up rules in order to limit the freedom of the actors in local settings strikes us as naive at best, and certainly as anachronistic. Yet, on the other hand, we cannot satisfy ourselves with purely decentralised solutions, uncoordinated with each other, or linked only through market-based interactions. Not only must we ensure that such solutions will be identified according to procedures that take into account the various interests at stake and provide a genuine opportunity for each of the stakeholders to be heard; we also must allow for the possibility of collective action, in order for the collectivity to be able to transform itself and to choose the direction in which to move. Although we may have to renounce the revolutionary ideas of grand meta-narratives and of rebuilding societies brick by brick according to one master plan, we nevertheless must leave open the possibility of history and democratic self-determination. The final destination may be unknown, yet we cannot escape the need to make choices at each crossing point, where different paths depart from — and to explore the widest number of paths possible.

The current attempts to redefine governance on the basis of the learning imperative move in different directions. Among economists, neo-institutionalist approaches seek to escape a definition of learning as a natural selection process, exemplified for instance in the evolutionary branch of economics, in which the most appropriate solutions emerge from being tested against the environment, that will reward some and penalise others. Neo-institutionalists recognise the role of institutions: as Douglass North once put it bluntly, a purely 'individualistic calculus of costs and benefits would suggest that cheating, shirking, stealing, assault and murder should be everywhere evident' (North 1981: 1). They recognise the role of institutions in shaping expectations and in solving coordination problems; and they seek to alert us to the need to conceive of 'choice' between different options as having to be guided, and as something radically different from a blind process of selection. They fail, however, to explain how what is in the general interest — and deserves to be considered as a desirable outcome — can be imposed or defined from some position external to the actors themselves. Carl Menger, in many ways the founder of evolutionary economics, famously asked 'How can it be that institutions which serve the common welfare and are extremely significant for its development come into being without a common will directed towards establishing them?' (Menger (1883) 1995: 146). To this question, the answer of neo-institutionalists is to reject the presupposition of such a perfect match: they assert that the common will must be restored and rehabilitated, and given a central place in directing the evolution of society.

However, they fail to define who is to define this common will, and in the name of which privileged access to what is in the general interest it should be recognised primacy.

Within current political science, the dominant approaches to learning-based governance are collaborative-relational. Such approaches often rely, more or less explicitly, on Habermas' theory of communicative action. They situate 'learning' in the organisation of a dialogue between various constituencies or actors: each of these participants will 'learn', it is hoped, by being obliged to provide good reasons for the positions they defend, and by having to engage with the views of the other participants. Communication here is not 'blind', it is not understood simply as feedback from the environment and it does not function only through price signals. But nor is it top-down, and nostalgic of a Rousseauist conception of the general will: instead, it is seen as organised deliberation, in which the widest possible spectrum of viewpoints should be heard, and in which consensus should be attained between the participants on the basis of rational argument (see for instance, Freeman 1997). This view, however, fails to make a clear distinction between an argument that is *acceptable* from a rational point of view, and an argument that is *accepted in fact* in the course of the deliberation. Because the wedge is not recognised between acceptability in theory and acceptation in fact, no distinction is made between the idealised community of listeners and the existing community of participants. It is in other terms presupposed that the actors involved have access to a 'rational point of view' that will emerge through a discussion from which coercion and rhetorical tricks will be banished. Within this understanding of learning, the actors recognise that they do not know, before entering into the discussion, where the most desirable solution lies. However, their apparent modesty is short-lived, for they also believe that by joining their efforts, by confronting their views, they can arrive at the solution that will be most desirable for all. Not only do they act as if disembodied, detached from time, space and context, they also act as if there were no perspective inaccessible to them: they believe, or they want to believe, that they possess within them all the possible perspectives, as if they were just pieces of a hologram — each piece projecting the entire image, although viewed from a smaller subset of angles.

Pragmatist approaches to governance represent an advance on both neo-institutional and collaborative-deliberative approaches, because they take seriously the reality that all knowledge is provisional and radically contextualised. They do not simply recognise this in theory: they organise institutions in order to take this into account. In one version, best represented in the work of Charles Sabel, institutions should favour decentralised problem-solving, combined with the pooling of results in order to facilitate and accelerate collective learning, based on such local experimentalism (Sabel and Zeitlin 2008; Sabel and Zeitlin 2010; Sabel and Cohen 1997; Gerstenberg and Sabel 2002). In another version, typified by authors such as Donald Schön, Martin Rein, and Chris Argyris (Argyris and Schön 1974; Argyris and Schön 1978; Schön and Rein 1994; Argyris 1993), actors engaged in collective action and negotiation should be made aware of the fact that when they engage controversies, they select the relevant 'facts' differently, depending on their respective biases and backgrounds, and that progress can only be made if they agree to question the very 'framing' of the problem they seek to address (Schön and Rein 1994: 4–5).

Both these approaches are genuinely pragmatic, in three different and complementary meanings of the expression. First, they accept that innovation — the emergence of new solutions to apparently intractable problems that cannot be resolved by a simple appeal to 'the facts' — can only emerge from actors' engagement with concrete controversies. Learning is therefore not a theoretical enterprise, and it is not an abstract calculation of the pros and the cons of different scenarios. It is necessarily embedded: linked to problem-solving in specific settings. Secondly, they acknowledge the open-ended nature of the inquiry: 'the policy dialectic', Schön and Rein write, 'is inherently open-ended. New solutions tend to generate new problems. The pragmatic resolution of existing controversies tends to set the stage for new controversies' (Schön and Rein 1994: 81). In that sense, learning is a continuous process, and theories therefore are permanently revised and tested. Thirdly, and most crucially, they posit that true learning can only occur by a revision of the very presuppositions that guide us in action, and those we fall back upon and make explicit when we have to defend our choices against external critiques. True learning, or 'double loop' learning in the vocabulary of Argyris and Schön, must be distinguished from mere adaptation of policies to changing environments, without questioning our background assumptions or mental maps: it occurs 'when error is detected and corrected in ways that involve the modification of an organization's underlying norms, policies and objectives' (Argyris and Schön 1978: 2–3). Encouraging learning, in that sense, means encouraging actors becoming aware of their tacit assumptions and the frames guiding their engagement in action, in order to provide them with an incentive to revise them.

The genetic approach to governance, as developed within the Centre for Philosophy of Law (see in particular Lenoble and Maesschalck 2010), builds on these advances in the theory of governance. It is pragmatist in the sense which has just been referred to. Its specific contribution is to ask how the actors involved in collective action and problem-solving can be supported in operating a revision of the assumptions guiding both their description of the problem, and their choice of solutions. It posits that such revision can be triggered by requesting from these actors both an exercise in reconstruction and an exercise in political imagination. The necessity of an exercise in reconstruction appears clearly once we recognise that our desires and expectations, including the evaluation of possible alternatives, are shaped by our past history and by the existing social norms which we have internalised to a more or less important degree (da Cunha and Junho Pena 1997), as well as on the psychological tendency to adapt one's preferences to one's situation (Elster 1982 and 1983). These psychological mechanisms imply that individual or collective 'choices', made on the basis of subjective preferences, cannot be trusted blindly. Instead, we have to create the background conditions that will ensure both that the 'preferences' expressed will be questioned, by an explicit examination of their genesis; and that the role each actor seeks to play for himself is open to question. For this reason, learning-based theories of governance may have to be complemented by an approach focused on the capacities of the actors. For the ability of actors to engage in such processes cannot be merely postulated: it must be affirmatively created. This can only occur from within: it requires not simply an environment that is empowering and facilitative, but also a transformation in the understanding of the actors themselves of how they should redefine their roles.

The first characteristic of the genetic approach to reflexive governance that distinguishes it from other, competing versions of reflexive governance, is best explained if we seek to contrast our approach to that made popular under the label of 'capabilities'. Considered superficially, there seem to be strong similarities between the genetic approach to governance and the capabilities approach, pioneered in the work of Sen and Nussbaum (Sen 1985 and 1987, Nussbaum 2000). But there are in fact also important differences that deserve highlighting. The capabilities approach recognises both the need to ensure that individuals have the resources required to effectively take part in collective action, and that they may differ widely in their ability to use the resources that are available to them, depending on their specific situation (for one attempt to ground public action on the idea of capabilities enhancement in European social policies, see Salais and Villeneuve 2004). It also leads to insist on the fact that, due in particular to the tendency of individuals to adapt to their situation, their subjective 'happiness' cannot be trusted as a reliable guide of their wellbeing. This constitutes one of the cornerstones of Sen's or Nussbaum's critiques of utilitarianism, which is based on the premise that social choices should be guided by the need to maximise the 'utilities' of individuals, understood as their subjective degree of happiness. It is a welcome antidote to the view that adaptive preferences present also certain positive sides (Kahneman et al 1999) and, indeed, could be treated as a 'capability' of some sort — the ability of individuals to 'make the best' of the set of circumstances which they are confronted with (Teschl and Comim 2005).

The genetic version of reflexive governance recognises the need to create the background conditions required to ensure that such preferences will not be dependent on context-dependent baselines (or, more realistically, will be less dependent on such baselines). However, the genetic approach departs from the capabilities approach in two important respects. First, it is sceptical of the 'basic needs' approach such as pioneered by Nussbaum and (reluctantly) endorsed, in certain respects, by Sen (Drèze and Sen 1995). While it recognises the need for individuals and organisations to be equipped to learn — and thus to have access to the required normative and organisational resources — the genetic approach to governance therefore does not believe in the possibility of listing those resources, as some sort of minimum set of entitlements that would ensure the success of collective action. Those resources can only be identified in particular contexts, and the list must necessarily be open to revision; although a failure to ask whether the conditions are appropriate to allow for learning to take place in any particular setting is a guarantee of failure, no predefined set of conditions can form a guarantee of success. Secondly, in addition, what actors need is not just to be equipped with the required capabilities: they must be prepared to question their very representation of their role and, ultimately, of their identity. The problem is therefore not simply to provide these actors with resources, and to enhance their ability to influence the processes in which they are engaged: the problem is for these actors to perceive that they may change their understanding of how they may contribute to identifying solutions to new problems, for which it not just their past knowledge that is inadequate, but also their past 'positioning', or what they understood were their 'preferences'. In order terms, while a 'capabilities' approach seeks to equip actors from the outside (with more or less attention being paid to the context in which the actors are placed), the genetic approach insists on the need to empower actors in a very specific way: by encouraging them to exercise power also on the existing identities and traditional definition of interests.

The genetic approach to reflexive governance is also specific in a second sense. Turning its attention to the future — the actors' expectations, rather than their inherited preferences, identities or representations — it emphasises the need to broaden political imagination. It does so by encouraging actors to reflect upon possible futures by getting rid of institutional fetishism: by re-imagining ways to act collectively that are not constrained by the existing institutional frameworks and by the narrow range of possibilities such frameworks allow. In a complex and fast-changing world, realism commands to broaden this inventive capacity, and it is unrealistic to expect that all problems can be solved appropriately within institutions as they are given. Whether, politically, certain scenarios will be feasible, is a different matter. However, we would be conceding defeat at too early a stage if we were to renounce exploring certain possibilities before testing them.

II. COMPARING DIFFERENT VERSIONS OF LEARNING-BASED GOVERNANCE

The previous section has distinguished among different attempts to develop reflexive governance, the new institutionalist *démarche*, the collaborative-relational (or deliberative) model, or various pragmatist approaches. All these versions of governance recognise the limits of formal models, and the inability of theory to guide the practice of institutions. They are all, in that basic sense, institutional and holistic, rather than formal and prone to reduce the complex reality into simple schemes or grand narratives. But they draw different conclusions from the fact that we don't know. They all acknowledge that we must learn — and they are all, in that sense, reflexive. However, these different versions of governance organise mechanisms for learning that are based on different assumptions, more or less heroic, and that equip institutions, more or less well, to deal with contexts which are increasingly diverse, unpredictable, and dynamic. This book offers to explore these different answers, and to provide the reader with the tools that will allow him or her to compare their respective insufficiencies and merits. While various criteria can be used for such an evaluation, we suggest that three criteria in particular may play an important role in the future.

First, theories of governance are more or less attentive to the concrete possibilities of actors to become active participants in decision-making processes that seek to include them. Learning-based theories of governance posit that learning should take place without teaching: the solutions are not to be imposed from above, they must emerge from below. However, that is not to say that the actors should not be supported in their ability to learn. The lack of information, power imbalances, the inability to translate intuitions about desired outcomes into concrete policy proposals, or the lack of access to networks — all this matters, and even the best institutional frameworks will fail to result in the formulation of innovative and optimal solutions unless these questions are addressed. Indeed, this is something approaches based on the notion of capabilities adequately point out. Whether these approaches provide the best answer may be questioned, but the problem at least seems to us difficult to ignore. The test for us, however, is not simply whether each of the various models pay sufficient attention to this problem: it is also whether, beyond equipping the actors to learn, they will succeed in triggering a revision of actors' self-representation, ie of their understanding of the role they are to play.

Secondly, theories of governance may be more or less capable of offering answers to the regulatory needs of a world that is increasingly economically globalised and interdependent. On the one hand, this globalisation and this interdependency can be seen as an opportunity: particularly as transnational networks develop, this facilitates benchmarking on the basis of the best practices identified through comparison, and mutual evaluation. Accountability and collective learning can improve as a result, and each actor's ideologies and representations may have to be questioned in the light of a fast-changing environment. But, on the other hand, the increasingly global nature of the problems confronting societies — ranging from preserving the environment and managing natural resources to protecting workers' rights and regulating financial markets — require collective action at a scale that far exceeds the nation-state, or even that of regional integration organisations. This confronts the theory of collective action to new and largely unprecedented challenges: how to develop collective action in the absence of fora that are sufficiently integrative to allow for trade-offs between different issues, and in which actors meet that only share a minimal sense of solidarity? In addition, in the context of globalisation, responses may be given within each local constituency, based primarily on the need to improve the competitiveness and efficiency of the local economic actors, in disregard of other, equally important values — particularly social and environmental sustainability. How the two can be reconciled, and how, in particular, collective learning can be orientated towards the fulfilment of aims other than improving performance on increasingly global markets, is a question addressed in a number of contributions to this book.

Thirdly, the different theories of governance discussed in this volume differ in their ability to generate truly novel solutions to regulatory problems. 'New' cannot automatically emerge from the 'old': to make real progress, and to do so at the required speed, questioning and re-examining past routines may not be enough. But if innovation doesn't happen by chance, can it happen by design? Can it be 'generated', for instance, by comparison between different answers given to similar problems — in the hope, perhaps, that the transposition into one situation of a response tested elsewhere will be sufficiently distorted to develop into something new and untested? As we have seen, one of the disabilities of the neo-institutionalist and collaborative-deliberative models of governance is that these models posit that innovation can emerge from within existing panoplies, as if solutions currently in use were necessarily capable of redefining themselves and mutating into something new. Pragmatist models offer alternative answers to this problem. Democratic experimentalism posits that exchanges between different constituencies can result in innovation, as each constituency will have to redefine its policies, and improve on them, in the light of the successes and failures of others. Organisational learning as pioneered by Argyris locates the source of innovation in the dialectic between theory-in-use (guiding action in practice) and espoused theory (professed by the actor when asked to justify choices), since the tension between what we do in fact and what we profess to do leads to permanent correction and improvement. The genetic approach insists on the need to challenge not just the policies we implement nor just our mental maps, or 'frames', but also the very sources of our preferences and orientations, and the definition of our identities, by a genealogical approach seeking to locate where they originate from.

III.   THE STRUCTURE OF THE BOOK

We could have sought to address these questions by a theoretical discussion of each of the models of reflexive governance distinguished above. Alternatively, we could have aligned a set of case studies, without any theoretical framework, but with a comparative chapter trying to draw the lessons from the different examples surveyed and attempting to reconstruct, from the outside as it were, what has been at stake in each of the developments. We chose instead a method that faithfully replicates what has characterised the research programme on 'Reflexive governance' from the outset.

Each of the authors is a member of one of the research networks involved in this collective endeavour. These teams have been exploring a variety of areas, through a variety of disciplines — including in particular law, political science, economics, and philosophy. They were asked to map the positions adopted in the different substantive fields under study, and to criticise these positions in the light of alternative, emerging of theories of governance that might challenge whichever approaches are dominant in the particular area concerned. The method is at once reconstructive, reflexive, and prospective. It is reconstructive in that it seeks to examine the theories of governance (and associated understandings of collective learning) mobilised in the debates conducted within each substantive area of study. It is reflexive insofar as it seeks to criticise the way these debates are conducted, by highlighting their blindspots and limitations in the light of alternative theories available — thus exposing the fragility and, sometimes, the poverty of the background theories mobilised in current debates. It is also prospective, in that the researchers sought to propose new ways of addressing the challenges facing regulators, on the basis of the insights gained from the first two steps of the method outlined. One advantage of this approach, we believed, was that it could create bridges between jurists, political scientists, economists, and philosophers, obliging all the researchers involved to identify the dependency of the various positions adopted within their respective disciplines on what represents in fact a very limited set of theories of governance, if compared to the wide spectrum of alternative theories available.

This book is arranged with a view both to introduce the reader to the theoretical debates on different theories of governance, and to examine how these debates are played out in a number of substantive areas.

Chapter one, by Jacques Lenoble and Marc Maesschalck, reviews the different versions of 'reflexive governance' that currently coexist under this label. They show how this coexistence is fragile, and how the label is therefore ambiguous when used too loosely. Indeed, each of these theories is based (albeit most often implicitly) on a distinct view of collective learning. But the different views of collective learning that these theories espouse are more or less plausible, in that they make more or less strong assumptions about the ability of social actors to 'learn', ie to revise their framing of the situation and the adequacy of the answers they provide to the question of regulation. Lenoble and Maesschalck are particularly suspicious of theories of governance that presuppose a natural capacity of actors to adapt to the feedback from the environment, as in biological theories of natural selection. Instead, they insist on the need to affirmatively create the conditions required for this 'capacity to learn' to emerge. The 'genetic' approach to reflexive governance is defined as one that satisfies this condition: it is 'genetic' in the sense that it seeks to 'generate' this capacity, or to 'produce' it, rather than simply presupposing it or ignoring the question. This introductory chapter therefore elaborates on the content of the 'genetic' approach to reflexive governance, and situates it in comparison with other approaches, mapping the different stages of the debate within learning-based theories of governance.

In part I of the book, two contributions explore the significance, for theory of governance in general, of the attempt to relate different approaches to reflexive governance to different understandings of learning and collective action. The departure point is in the new institutionalist approach, and its characteristically 'regulatory' understanding of the role of the state in taming the markets. In chapter two, Eric Brousseau and Jean-Michel Glachant explore the implications that follow from adopting a neo-institutional approach. Such an approach seeks to move beyond the dilemma between top-down regulatory approaches on the one hand, and 'pure' market mechanisms (supposedly autonomous), on the other hand. The chapter by Brousseau and Glachant examines what it would be to establish institutional frames for markets to function so as to maximise the normative expectations of all the actors involved. In chapter three, Colin Scott offers to reflect on the questions posed by these debates on regulation. His contribution is based on the idea that regulatory regimes involve three sets of functions, since they involve mechanisms for the setting of norms or rules — and monitoring by the principal of the agent in charge of implementation — feedback and behaviour modification where behaviour deviates from the norms of the system. He analyses these various functions of a regulatory regime from the perspective of the approaches to learning derived from new institutionalist conceptions of reflexive governance.

The other chapters in the book in parts II and III explore specific thematic areas, with a twofold objective. First, they seek to use the mapping of various approaches to reflexive governance recalled above in this Introduction and described in greater detail in chapter one, in order to provide a description of the evolutions at work in each of the fields under study. In this respect, the theoretical framework proposed serves, or should serve, as an analytical framework improving our understanding of the dynamics involved. It is backward-looking and explanatory. Secondly, these chapters also use this framework in a way that is forward-looking and critical. Contrasting modes of governance that are dominant in each of the fields under study, they seek to contribute to the current debates about reform, by enriching our panoply of solutions to be explored.

Part II of the book collects contributions that identify the alternatives to new institutionalism that are emerging in certain fields, which are chosen as case studies to improve our understanding of shifting approaches to governance. In chapter four, Prosser et al discuss the tensions between the neo-institutionalist and collaborative-relational (or deliberative) models of governance in the energy sector, focusing on the United Kingdom and Germany, although including certain examples from three Canadian provinces, as an example of how the management of services of general interest is undergoing transformations in contemporary societies. Their contribution examines how the liberalisation of the market of energy, ie privatisation, was accompanied by institutional innovations that, at times, presented participatory dimensions, and that also had to adapt to unexpected developments in the implementation process. The main finding is that the reforms in this sector remain largely wedded to a neo-institutionalist approach, with only very few elements of a collaborative-relational model emerging. In the United Kingdom, even where consultation takes place, this remains largely as an external check to the system, rather than as a central part of the decision-making process itself — something which the authors attribute to the important role of Parliament in representing the public interest and in the correlative distrust for alternative, and potentially competing, avenues of participation. In Germany, after attempts at self-regulation of the sector failed, there was a return to classical regulatory approaches. To a large extent, the Canadian example illustrates the same difficulty for an alternative to classical representative democracy to emerge, with a more active participation of stakeholders. In all these cases, the establishment of new, participatory processes, which should have encouraged consumers to invest in reshaping the rules, were met with distrust, as a means to circumvent traditional decision-making processes and to legitimise decisions made elsewhere, for other motives. The result is that the neo-institutionalist model — a market placed under certain ground rules — remained dominant: even where some form of consultation took place, this, the authors write, 'remained "exernalist" through the regulator passively receiving evidence from outside to incorporate into decision-making rather than attempting to organise the capacities of outside interests to contribute to a *mutual* process of learning'.

In chapter five, Simon Deakin and Aristea Koukiadaki examine the transformations of the corporate governance debate in the light of the complex and innovative governance structure set up for the construction of the Terminal 5 building ('T5') at London's Heathrow Airport. Because of the very high stakes of this project for the airport operator BAA, BAA convinced its shareholders (mainly institutional investors) to take a long-term view of their interest; it built a relationship with the sub-contractors that moved away from traditional forms of contracting and included the pooling of liabilities between the suppliers collectively, with BAA taking out insurance policies to cover certain project-wide liabilities; and it sought to manage labour relations on the site that allowed for integrated team working (cooperation between workers with different employers), that included a commitment to pay bonuses for higher productivity resulting in substantially higher wages than would otherwise have been paid, and that went through the establishment of fora for negotiation over pay and working conditions, but also for dialogue over strategic decision-making. Deakin and Koukiadaki conclude from this case study not only that 'governance structures based on deliberation and on the inclusion of multiple stakeholders can successfully emerge even in a context (...) where pressures on firms to prioritise shareholder value are strong', but also that such governance structures, in the T5 case, allowed for 'inter-systemic learning', 'that is, the possibility for learning in the sense of error correction to spill over from one systemic context to another'. Indeed, the different sub-systems at play — which the authors identify as 'corporate governance (narrowly construed to refer to company-shareholder relations), utility regulation, inter-firm contracting and industrial relations' — were forced to reconsider their routine ways of defining their values and objectives, without any one sub-system imposing its dominance above others.

Inter-systemic learning is presented as an 'alternative that focuses on the interactions within and across systems through which established roles, distinct disciplines and traditional cultures overcome in certain cases conflicting interpretations and engage in a process of social learning and development of capabilities'.

Chapter six, by Olivier De Schutter, revisits the debate between harmonisation of social laws and regulatory competition in the European Union (EU), and asks how the mapping of different theories of learning-based governance might bring new insights into this debate. Fears about 'social dumping' in the EU have been revived recently, and doubts are increasingly expressed about the optimistic view that the EU Member States would progressively converge towards higher social standards. De Schutter seeks to move beyond the usual dichotomy opposing de-regulation at domestic level to re-regulation at EU level. Instead, he shows that mechanisms allowing for an improved learning across jurisdictions could constitute a more promising avenue, provided certain institutional conditions are created. Building on the experimentalist approach to governance, he argues that instead of being conceived as a formalistic mechanism, aimed at ensuring compliance with certain values on which European integration is built, an evaluation of each Member State's successes and failures should be seen as promoting learning across jurisdictions, and as encouraging actors at the domestic level to redefine their position in the light of experiments launched elsewhere. This can strengthen accountability at the domestic level. It can accelerate the identification of innovative solutions and of swift responses to new problems. It can also lead to identify where collective action is required at EU level: in order for the range of choices at domestic level to be truly expanded, these choices should not be based on considerations of efficiency and competitiveness, in disregard of the European public interest and of the possibility for states to coordinate with one another and to make progress in one agreed direction. The chapter argues, however, that in order to achieve this, simply encouraging local experimentation is not enough. In addition, 'the pooling of lessons from local experiments, and the organisation of a deliberation about how they should be evaluated, should constitute both a disincentive for the adoption of beggar-thy-neighbour policies, and a source of enhanced accountability' ; and 'the establishment, within each EU member State, of an institution specifically dedicated to the analysis of policies conducted in other States, as well as the strengthening of transnational networks, could accelerate learning across jurisdictions, and favor policy imitation'. The question that remains open — and which, in the genetic approach to governance, is decisive — is whether this alone will be sufficient to bring about a perspective shift within the public and private actors concerned.

In part III, the authors seek to describe how our dominant understanding of governance as learning could be further improved by relying on the 'genetic' approach, the emergence of which they seek to identify. Chapters seven and eight go the furthest in assessing the specific contribution of the genetic approach to reflexive governance to current debates. In chapter seven, Peter Vincent-Jones and Caroline Mullen provide an overview of healthcare governance in England. They locate the current debates within the different versions of reflexive governance outlined above, linking the processes of privatisation and the emergence of quasi-markets to the neo-institutional model, as well as the introduction of systems of patient and public involvement to the collaborative-relational model — two parallel processes that lead the 'economic and democratic elements' to 'co-exist in uneasy tension'. However, they also show how these models remain insufficient because of their failure to ensure that the conditions they postulate, in particular conditions related to the capacities of actors, are present. Vincent-Jones and Mullen also seek to explore the promises of the genetic approach to governance by focusing on the changing role of non-governmental organisations (NGOs) in the health and social care sectors. Here, they conclude that NGOs shall have to accept a 'fundamental reconsideration of the way in which they serve the interests they represent, and how they position themselves strategically in relation to government and other actors in healthcare networks'. This, indeed, the ability and disposition of actors to rethink their position, is a key element of the genetic approach to governance: it is by ensuring such a reflexivity from those engaged in collective action that we can hope to move towards truly innovative solutions. These authors write:

> The main problem for NGOs in England is how to make the most of the opportunities presented by the new institutional and organizational environment. New Labour's enthusiasm for engaging the energies of the 'third sector' in human services has created a potential for NGOs to strengthen their position in healthcare networks, both by influencing policy making at national level, and bidding for and winning social care and health service contracts in competition with NHS and private sector bodies. However, these opportunities are accompanied by new challenges. The extension of the role of NGOs to include the quasi-market provision of (publicly funded) services directly to client groups has led to tensions with their traditionally independent public service mission (...). Furthermore, closer ties with government in the making and development of policy create dilemmas over the extent to which NGOs feel able to challenge government in promoting the interests of the particular service user groups they represent.

NGOs are thus increasingly facing conflicting loyalties, towards government or towards their constituencies, and they have to manage tensions between different roles, as spokespersons for their traditional advocacy themes and as service providers to clients, for instance. Overcoming these conflicts and tensions requires that they redefine their identity in the process: not only how they act is open to question, but also whom they are and which constituencies they are accountable to. In the genetic approach to governance, it is this redefinition that the operation of 'terceisation' should facilitate.

Finally, chapter eight, by Tom Dedeurwaerdere, explores the potential of governance networks in the field of global environmental governance. In the view of its proponents, network governance — because networks aggregate different sources of knowledge and perspectives — can be very successful in situations of uncertainty, where information is incomplete and where rationality is strongly bounded. Dedeurwaerdere revisits the debate about the promises and limitations of governance networks, by relating this debate to the genetic approach to governance and the understanding of reflexivity that this approach proposes. He does so by relying on two case studies, concerning respectively the provision of forest-related services in fragmented forest landscapes in Flanders, and the establishment of a global commons of genetic resources in the seed bank network of the Consultative Group on International Agricultural Research (CGIAR). Both cases illustrate the potential of network governance to the provision of collective goods, whether in decentralised settings as in the first case study or at global level. In particular, these examples show that network governance can ensure 'the stabilization of the cooperative outcomes resulting from the mutual adjustments of the various actor strategies', as well at 'the social learning on the content of the overall normative orientation of the interaction within the governance networks'. However, Dedeurwaerdere notes, 'missing from both is a reflection on the articulation between the strategic and normative level of the analysis'. It is this articulation that a genetic approach should favour. In such an approach, 'the stake is not so much to rely on existing reflexive abilities, whether they be capacities of self-adjustment or of cooperative learning, but to act on the conditions of emergence of reflexive abilities through the mechanism of terceisation'. Only this, and the transformation it implies in the representation the actors have of their identity and objectives, may allow overcoming 'frame conflicts' that are an obstacle (and sometimes an insuperable one) to cooperation across different perspectives. This study thus provides a particularly enlightening example of what the genetic approach to reflexive governance may contribute, in particular in the management of global commons.

IV. CONCLUSION

Taken together, these different studies illustrate the transformations in our current understandings of governance. Since the 1990s, in particular, a wide range of initiatives have emerged that seek to go beyond the public/private divide, and that seek either to rely on market-based mechanisms with some sort of regulatory control in order to ensure that the public interest is taken into account (what some have called the Regulatory State), or that experiment various private-public combinations, often in decentralised settings. These initiatives remain entrapped in what we call an 'externalist' concept of learning, in which the public interest is defined from above, outside the actors concerned, defining the boundaries which the actors are prohibited from crossing. At the same time, various forms of participatory democracy, as well as social dialogue at different levels, are making progress, illustrating the emergence of a collaborative model of shaping the public interest. While many of these innovations in participation remain closer to bargaining than to deliberation, some are deliberative in character, leading the actors involved to re-examine their preferences and to reformulate their arguments in the light of the arguments of the other side. In other terms, what we see developing in practice, is in many ways a duopoly: the neo-institutionalist and collaborative-relational models dominate the field, and few institutional solutions currently implemented truly move beyond them.

However, these studies also show the need for, and the possibility of, a leap in institutional imagination. They show that progress can be made in promoting greater reflexivity in governance processes, and that this reflexivity may be understood as the 'internalisation' of the conditions of learning. Learning, in other terms, should be conceived as an operation in which the actors themselves redefine their understanding of the problem to be addressed, and are led not simply to question the solutions that are routinely explored, but also their relationship to the problem and the way they traditionally define their interests. The different case studies collected here all move in this direction, but they do so at different levels. The studies by Prosser et al and by Deakin and Koukiadaki, based on examples respectively from the energy sector and from the governance of the BAA-led consortium for the building of Terminal 5 at Heathrow airport, note the insufficiencies of the new institutional approaches, and of the classical tool of incentives to steer decision-making by economic actors in the right direction. Both studies conclude for the need to include more deliberative elements in the governance structures set up in such areas, and they note that this could be achieved by radicalising certain participatory elements that are already present in this regard. The study by De Schutter identifies the need to operate a shift towards a more pragmatic and experimentalist approach to the fulfilment of social rights at the level of each EU Member State, in order to move beyond the current impasse, that has nothing to oppose to the spectre of deregulation than the chimera of re-regulation at EU level; and he identifies certain institutional innovations that could support such an experimentalist approach. The studies by Vincent-Jones and Mullen and by Dedeurwaerdere, finally, illustrate the promises of the genetic approach to governance, where the attempt to 'internalise' the operation of learning is pushed furthest. It is our hope to contribute, by this book, to a debate on forms of governance that should now move away from generalities, and towards specific institutional proposals.

Part I

Setting the Stage

1

Renewing the Theory of Public Interest: The Quest for a Reflexive and Learning-based Approach to Governance

Jacques Lenoble and Marc Maesschalck

I. INTRODUCTION

WHAT IS THE meaning we ascribe to the expression 'reflexive govern-ance', thereby defining the conditions a collective action must fulfil in order to ensure, to the extent possible, that satisfaction of its mem-bers' normative expectations is 'maximised'; that is, in order to ensure what is generally called 'governance in the public interest'? The expression 'reflexive governance' can only be understood if we first recall the project that has underpinned REFGOV.[1] This project emerged out of an option and an insight. The option related to how to broach the question of 'governance of a collective action'. The insight was that by reconstructing the various current investigations into the theory of governance from the angle of their theoretical assumptions about the theory of collective action, we would arrive at an important theoretical finding.

A. The Option

No one doubts that the issue designated by the term 'governance' is currently dealt with in differing ways, depending on the disciplinary approach taken (economic, legal, political-science, and so on) and the level at which a specific issue addressed is situated. Indeed, one is often struck by how difficult it is to integrate all this work into a cohesive inquiry, the issues under study being so

---

[1] The research presented in this introduction has been supported both by the 6th EC Framework Programme on Research and Development (REFGOV) and the Interuniversity Attraction Pole Programme (IAP) – Belgian State – Belgian Science Policy (BELSPO).

diverse and situated at such divergent levels. (For instance, how are we to integrate economic analyses of reform to the management of common goods with political-scientific or legal analyses about multilevel governance or with analyses of new modes of governance inspired by the theories of deliberative democracy?) Thus, under the umbrella of a single term — one that designates a common investigation into the question of governance — can be found an aggregation of studies that diverge significantly as regards the issues examined and the methodological approaches used. Besides this, however, even when the studies deal with similar issues, dialogue appears to be impossible. Often, discipline-based approaches are developed in one sphere in ignorance of studies on governance taking other disciplinary approaches in other spheres. In other words, no interdisciplinary dialogue has been organised with respect to the theoretical models being deployed within the various disciplinary approaches to the theory of governance. A salient example of this lack of interpenetration between approaches can be found in new institutional economics: this discipline deploys a particular theory of learning but remains under-informed about recent inquiry into theory of learning that relies on current pragmatist approaches developed in the field of political science, especially in the context of research on organisational theory. This situation accounts for the present state of inquiry into the subject of governance. The option that has underpinned the REFGOV project is to seek to integrate these various current investigations into governance by shifting the angle of the perspective of research. This shift consists of re-examining the theoretical backdrop to these various current investigations and engaging with the different theoretical approaches to collective action these disciplined-based studies deploy, often no more than implicitly. Let us specify here what we understand by a theory of collective action: it is a theory of the conditions that the organisation (ie governance or regulation) of a collective action must fulfil so that the action can provide for the best possible fulfilment of its members' normative expectations.

B.   The Insight

The insight is that by reconstructing the various current investigations into theory of governance from the angle of their theoretical assumptions about a theory of collective action, we will arrive at an important theoretical result. Today, our findings on this score are threefold:[2]

---

[2] See, on this reconstruction of the various theories that make up the current landscape of inquiry into theory of governance, and on these findings, Lenoble and Maesschalck 2010. It should be noted that the purpose of this reconstruction was not solely to describe the current landscape of research. In the first instance, it was intended to shed light on the theoretical reasons for the current shared commitment to exposing the weaknesses of classical approaches to governance, whether based

— An initial finding is that this reconstruction reveals that, beyond their apparent differences, the various orientations present in the current landscape of social science research into theory of governance all share a single assumption, which represents a theoretical advance. As will be seen below, it is at this level that we situate the 'reflexive' dimension that must be a feature of any way of organising a collective action if the best possible fulfilment of its members' expectations is to be ensured.

— A second finding is that this shared advance in current research in the social sciences, because it often remains opaque and is insufficiently exhibited by the various current orientations in theory of governance, is not the object of adequate 'attention' by these investigations. While, then, an adequate reconstruction of current discussion on theory of governance reveals a shared awareness of the need for the 'reflexive' organisation of governance, it also reveals a new approach to this 'reflexivity'. In other words, nowadays any advance in research into theory of governance entails an elucidation of the question of the reflexive dimension the 'success' of a collective action depends on.

— A third finding is that in reconstructing the various current approaches to theory of governance from the perspective of their conception of reflexivity, we observe that the differences among these approaches is less reflective of a deep-rooted divergence or antagonism than of a growing recognition of the need to progressively expand the conditions to be put in place to ensure the success of this reflexive operation. That is, the four theoretical currents of which the essence of recent research into theory of governance is comprised are complementary and reflect an increasingly acute understanding of the precise nature of the conditions required for the success of this operation. Our research, by drawing attention to this dimension, which is too often sidelined in current discussion on governance, has even made it possible to propose a furthering of the most recent findings about how this operation succeeds.

It is in light of this reconstruction that the meaning we assign to the term 'reflexive governance' is to be understood. This term does not in itself designate a specific and precise form of governance. Often, the expression reflexive governance is used ambiguously. This ambiguity consists of correctly defining reflexive governance through recourse to the idea of learning, while at the same time letting it be understood that, so defined, it consists of a specific, determinate form of governance. This supposed form of governance would purportedly enable us to determine precisely what forms of institutional organisation a collective action

on the traditional command-and-control regulation model or on the model advanced by neo-classical economists as an alternative to it, which in turn is based on a market theory supplemented as necessary by a theory of incentive contracts. In the second instance, the goal of the reconstruction was to account for the observable differences in ways of conceiving the institutional mechanisms that must 'monitor' (frame) the capacity for action of participants in a collective action.

should assume in order to best fulfil the 'public interest'. Thus, reflexive governance is often said by many authors who view themselves as its defenders to be a specific model of governance that 'involves the establishment of institutions and processes which facilitate the actors within a domain for learning not only about policy options, but also about their own interests and preferences'(Scott 2007). While this definition is not inaccurate, it poses the risk of generating more indeterminacy than precision. For this reason, certain observations are called for.

First, in itself this definition reduces the reflexive dimension of a system of governance to the idea of learning. To put it another way, a form of governance would qualify as reflexive if it favoured the success of the learning operation required to satisfy the normative expectations of participants in a collective action. *By limiting itself to this consideration alone,* this definition of reflexive governance covers all of the four approaches to governance (described more fully below) that comprise the bulk of current scholarly research on theory of governance. That is, not only the *collaborative-relational, pragmatist,* and the *genetic* approaches, but also the *neo-institutionalist* approach share the feature of reasoning about the conditions for 'efficient' or legitimate governance in terms of a learning operation. Thus, for instance, the approach of neo-institutionalist economics has drawn attention to the inadequacy of neo-classical economic approaches, which resided in their interpretation of economic evolution in terms of natural selection. So even if the neo-institutionalist economic approach does not explicitly call its inquiry into the theory of governance 'reflexive' and rarely deploys a theory of learning, it can indisputably be termed reflexive or referred to as an approach that aims, in contrast to approaches from neo-classical economics, to promote the learning operation of actors involved in a collective action. Clearly, the same thing applies for the three approaches we identify in part II of Lenoble and Maesschalck 2010 as working to expand the neo-institutional economic approach. These three rely explicitly on the commitment to better understand the conditions needed for the success of the learning operation.

The idea of reflexivity thus understood means simply that the transformation/ adaptation of a given context effected by a given collectivity will not satisfy, in the best possible way, the actors' expectations solely on the basis of this spontaneous display of their 'natural' competencies. A successful adaptation of this kind would require the actor to conduct a 'return' over her or his 'accustomed competencies and behaviours' with the aim of acquiring new competencies. This operation of 'reflexive return' would require specific institutional systems. Thus, if we define the idea of reflexivity through the idea of learning, all the various recent approaches developed by scholarly research (as an alternative to both command-and-control regulation and sole recourse to the market) could be termed reflexive, regardless of the significant differences among them.

This way of understanding the idea of reflexivity offers the advantage of not hiving off any one approach from the others within REFGOV. In fact, it corresponds to the strategy clearly adopted when the REFGOV network was constructed. At that time, researchers were grouped together according to their choice of one of the four approaches, without either privileging or disqualifying any of the four theoretical options.

Significant inconveniences are associated with this way of approaching the idea of reflexivity in governance, however. In particular, it prevents seeing what distinguishes these four approaches to governance from each other, once we go beyond their shared will to avoid the fallacious assumption of a process of natural selection guaranteeing the constant adjustment of our collective actions towards a 'social optimum'. What distinguishes them from each other is precisely their different ways of conceiving of the learning operation (and thus the reflexive operation that any learning operation entails). True, as has already been mentioned, many of these approaches do not undertake to develop an explicit theory of this learning operation. Indeed, this is the reason why, except when they are explicitly framed within an 'integrating' mechanism such as that organised by our REFGOV research, several of these four approaches are unaware of each other. Scholarly discussion of the question of governance is being pursued today within various disciplines, and often these various disciplinary discussions are conducted without attention to research being done in neighbouring disciplines. What this means is that the four approaches we have identified in Lenoble and Maesschalck 2010 are often unaware, not just of what they have in common (namely, that they take an approach to governance in terms of how actors' learning is facilitated), but, a fortiori, of what differentiates them from each other when it comes to their conception of the conditions for success of the learning operation. Consequently, in turning our attention to the differences in the way they conceive the conditions for success of a learning operation, we gain a further benefit.

The potential fruits of this investigation are not purely theoretical or academic. They are also practical and they relate to the construction of systems of governance. Bringing the four approaches together in order to examine them in relation to their conceptions of the learning operation reveals that they lie on a continuum. What emerges is that these four approaches reflect increasingly expansive conceptions of the conditions that must be satisfied to ensure the success of the learning operation. When they are analysed through the lens of the learning operation, things unfold as though these four approaches reflected four successive stages of a single process of inquiry, with each successive stage working to further expand the understanding of the conditions necessary for the system of governance, to enable actors to produce the best possible solution to the collective-action problem they are working to solve.

And indeed that is the reason why REFGOV's research has worked on two levels. On one hand, various theme-based studies were organised to allow for giving an account, in various concrete spheres, of the proposals for institutional design suggested by the four approaches we have differentiated and among which current studies on governance are distributed. At this level (as was observed above), none of the four approaches was privileged over the others. Each was viewed as contributing, within its thematic sphere, clarifications that were highly fruitful in addressing problems and inadequacies exhibited by present systems of governance. On the other hand, parallel to this first level, an integrative system was set up to reveal the consistency of the four approaches.[3] The issue here was to justify the idea of possible 'progressive expansion' and to show how this idea is reflected in the institutional conditions that could be set up to ensure the success of the learning operation entailed by any governance in the public interest. In order to achieve this, our theoretical research sought to: (1) present the consequences for a theory of governance of an approach that takes seriously the underlying dynamic of current research and the deepened inquiry into the learning operation that is driving it; and (2) justify at the theoretical level the validity of this dynamic of 'progressive expansion' and the search for integration.

This is why it does not seem productive to limit the definition of 'reflexive governance' (as Scott suggested) to 'the establishment of institutions and processes which facilitate [the learning of] the actors'. Any form of 'reflexive governance' is a function of the explicit or implicit conception of the learning operation that underlies it. Any inquiry into 'reflexive governance' must therefore include the question of the differences in conception of the learning operation that can today be observed in the four 'reflexive governance' approaches we have differentiated (Lenoble and Maesschalck 2010).

Accordingly, it is helpful to recall the most distinctive features of the four current approaches to governance whose perspective on governance is a 'reflexive', learning-theory-based one (see section II. below.) In so doing, we will be enabled (in section III. below) to clearly identify why it is possible to speak of the furthering and progressive 'expansion' of the conception of the conditions for success of the learning operation that a system of governance will have to take into account, if the best possible fulfilment of the expectation of actors involved in a collective action is to be ensured.

---

[3]   The method that has governed the organisation of the REFGOV research project was in no way intended to be comparative. It was intended, rather, to be integrative. What does this mean? As indicated above, our procedure has consisted of identifying and highlighting the integrating focus that allows for the reconstruction, in a progressive and expansive manner, of the kinds of institutional monitoring for the decentralised interaction advanced by the various current approaches to reflexive governance identified in Lenoble and Maesschalck 2010: pt II. Thus, for instance, the issue was not, on the basis of the study on forest management organised by the Global Public Services thematic research team, to invalidate the neo-institutionalist economic approach. Rather, the idea was, by endorsing the institutional proposals for market monitoring suggested by the economic approach to governance, to show that the 'efficiency' of institutional solutions thus appropriately highlighted by the neo-institutionalist approach is itself reinforced by, and dependent on, complementary mechanisms designed to enhance the capabilities for success of the learning operation required for fulfilment of the normative objectives identified by economists. Within this perspective, the issue is less 'comparability' than it is to give an account, based on empirical examples, of the various dimensions that each approach determines is required for a learning operation in the context of collective action to be successful. The integration of these various empirical studies was provided for by the theoretical framework we developed (see on this, Lenoble and Maesschalck 2010), which is presented hereafter.

II.   PRINCIPAL FEATURES OF THE FOUR APPROACHES TO REFLEXIVE GOVERNANCE

The first clarification, then, relates to terminology. From among the various current disciplinary approaches, we have identified four approaches within theory of governance that, implicitly or explicitly, inquire into the question of the conditions for good governance by recourse to the idea of collective learning.

The first we call the neo-institutionalist economics approach. As we explained, this term should be understood in a broad sense, because it is intended to cover both research in transaction-cost economics, as emerging out of the work of Williamson and Coase, and research conducted within the frame of reference of evolutionary theory.

The second we call the 'collaborative-relational approach through dialogue'. It could also be called deliberative, since it is distinguished by the idea that the conditions for success of the learning operation require an aggregative and deliberative shaping of the communicative competencies of the various stake-holders.

The third approach we call 'pragmatist'. As its name suggests, it is distinguished by its inquiry into the conditions for success of the learning operation on the basis of an explicit reference to pragmatist thinkers, Dewey in particular. The pragmatist approach to governance cannot however be properly understood unless we differentiate between two profoundly different trends within it. Although both these trends work to expand and further the presentation of the conditions for success of the learning operation developed by neo-institutionalist-economist and deliberative thinkers, they differ from each other in their understanding of this process of expansion and furthering. The first of these two trends is represented by the experimentalist approach (also known as 'democratic experimentalism') of Sabel et al. The second, which has concluded by identifying the insufficiency of the experimentalist approach and recommending it be expanded, was developed by Schön in collaboration with Argyris.

The fourth approach is the one we espouse. We have often referred to it as the 'reflexive' approach to governance[4] to emphasise its basis in what is intended to be the broadest conception of the conditions for reflexive return required for the success of the learning operation. However, terming this approach reflexive runs the risk of ambiguity in two ways. First, as was seen above, the idea of reflexivity seems often to be related in current work in the social sciences exclusively to the idea of learning per se, without being extended to the scope or the precise nature

---

[4] This approach is also sometimes called 'pragmatic and internalist'. While accurate, this designation may prove hard to use because it is too closely linked to certain technical philosophical assumptions. That is, this designation is based on the idea that this fourth approach, while it shares with the deliberative and pragmatist approaches the commitment to broaching the question of learning as the basis for a 'pragmatic' approach to the conditions for success of the intentionality of an action, also aims to emphasise the inadequacy of the deliberative or pragmatist conceptions associated with the pragmatic turn.

of the conditions required for the success of learning. As well, even if we wished to reserve the term 'reflexive governance' for an approach that specifies one particular conception of these conditions, the term would still court ambiguity, since it is already currently applied to several different approaches to governance. For example, Teubner's systemic theory, Sabel's experimentalist approach, and Schön's and Argyris's pragmatist theory all explicitly view themselves as theories of reflexive governance. That is, use of the word 'reflexive' is affected by the same difficulty as is the word 'procedural' in theory of law and theory of democracy. These are terms that come to be perceived at a given moment in the progress of scholarly research as reflecting a significant insight, but that are used with meanings so different that the very success of the terms risks giving rise to more ambiguity and imprecision than to theoretical or practical advances. For this reason, we suggest that the term 'reflexive governance' be limited to denoting the overall process guiding current research in theory of governance, which covers all four approaches identified here. Accordingly, to designate the specific 'reflexive' approach to governance we have developed at the Centre for the Philosophy of Law of the University of Louvain (CPDR), which is distinguished by the commitment to expanding and furthering the pragmatist trend (as expressed in both Sabel's democratic experimentalism and Schön's and Argyris's work), we suggest the term 'genetic'. The term 'genetic' is intended to take account of two factors: on one hand, the set of conditions for production (that is, *engenderment*) of actors' capacity to carry out the 'reflexive' return required for the success of the learning operation; and on the other hand, the setting up of institutional conditions likely to guarantee effective implementation of the actors' commitments.

Now we turn to a brief second clarification. It consists of a concise overview of the factors that differentiate and distinguish the four approaches to governance from each other, which have to do with those approaches' differing conceptions of the conditions for success of the learning operation required to ensure maximal fulfilment of the normative expectations of participants in a collective action.

III.   WHY SPEAK OF A 'PROGRESSIVE EXPANSION' OF THE CONDITIONS FOR
SUCCESS OF LEARNING?

The essential idea underlying this presentation of current discussion in theory of governance is twofold. First, current discussion rests on a shared conviction that any approach to the regulation of a collective action that relies on the 'natural selection' of the behaviours required to maximise fulfilment of the actors' normative expectations, leads to weaknesses in the arrangement of systems of governance. 'Selection' in fact entails a learning operation. Also, this discussion results in four approaches that form a progression with respect to the breadth of the conditions required to ensure the success of the learning operation. Each successive stage, *without invalidating* the positive advances achieved by prior approaches, deems those advances insufficient and considers that supplementary conditions must be taken into account in designing systems of governance. What essential trait characterises each of these stages? That is, what is the 'value added' that approaches two, three and four aim to bring to the prior stage? Or, to put it in other words, what is the insufficiency that each of approaches two, three and four views as having been overlooked by the approach it seeks to extend or go beyond?

We will limit ourselves to briefly presenting[5] the first stage of the progression that can be observed in current research in theory of governance (the *neo-institutionalist economic* approach — see section A. below); its ongoing expansion and furthering, first by means of the second, *deliberative* or *collaborative-relational*, approach and then by means of the third, *pragmatist*, approach in two successive forms (see section B. below); and finally the needed completion of this furthering by means of the genetic approach (see section C. below).

A.   The Externalist Expansion

The most characteristic feature of the neo-institutionalist economic approach is what we call, in Lenoble and Maesschalck 2010, its 'externalist' conception of learning and what we could consequently call its 'externalist' conception of governance. As is shown in that book, this externalist conception is observable not just in the work of both transaction-cost economists and evolutionary thinkers, but also in the writings of those who, like North and Brousseau, have worked to synthesise the advances made by those two schools of economic thought. What does an 'externalist conception of learning' mean, and what are its implications for systems of governance?

The basic idea is related precisely to the way these economists have sought to surmount the weaknesses they detected in the theory of natural selection that underlay neo-classical economic theory, and in consequence in their ascription of excessively great virtues to the market mechanism alone. The reason natural selection cannot operate in human groupings is precisely because it is a function of a datum present at the outset. As Marengo and Dosi put it:

> [A] selection mechanism can indeed, under certain conditions, select for the fittest structures, but only if the latter exist in the first place. Selection can account for the convergence of a population toward some given form, not for the emergence of such a form (Marengo and Dosi 2005: 303–26, 306).

However, the neo-institutionalists' notion is precisely that this datum present at the outset is not assumed to be subject to transformation by the learning operation itself. Any selection operation, unless 'incented from the outside', is constrained by the same limitation. This second characteristic results in what

---

[5]   See for a fuller presentation Lenoble and Maesschalck 2010: pt II.

might be called an *externalist* conception of learning. For the evolutionary thinkers and the neo-institutionalists,[6] the only way to alter the nature of the datum present at the outset consists of deploying an external factor in order to 'expand' all the initial hypotheses (or, as Simon would put it, all the routines) that are to be tested by the learning operation, in view of choosing the one that seems most powerful to solve the problem that set the collective action in motion. Innovation, ie the expansion of the existing representation by expanding the possibilities present at the outset, cannot emerge from the operation itself.

This 'externalist' approach to learning also accounts for the approach to governance, that is, the approach to the institutional systems that must accompany the learning operation in order for the latter to result in 'optimality', or at least in the form of organisation of the collective action that satisfies the normative expectations of its members to the extent possible, ie governance in the public interest. An 'expansion' of local actors' representations is needed by means of an external mechanism that 'imposes', hierarchically so to speak, a collective representation. Brousseau[7] is right to say that the evolutionary thinkers insufficiently define the form of organisation that must impose this 'expansion' of decentralised local actors' representations from outside and must ensure that learning will yield an optimum outcome overall. From this perspective, many current neo-institutionalist studies (see below, chapter two) work to make explicit the nature of these external systems that, it is argued, must increasingly take the form of hybrid, public-private partnership, systems. What is important from our perspective, however, besides the advances yielded by this identification of the nature of these systems, is the externality that they embody. The idea is present therein that only an external system could 'incent' the acquisition of the behaviours/competencies needed to allow for the most 'efficient' possible operation. This expansion of the behaviours/competencies (that is, the expansion of the representations present at the outset from among which the actors select the solutions deemed the best possible) is assumed to have the role (and to be capable) of being incented from the outside by a monitoring mechanism.

B.   The Internal Expansion

It is precisely as regards this 'externalist' approach to the conditions of learning that the second (deliberative), third (pragmatist), and fourth (genetic) approaches to governance are distinguished from the neo-institutionalist economic approach. What these three approaches have in common is a shared

---

[6]   And in fact, this is the institutional form of the solution arrived at by theorists of evolutionary games and by Cooter working in the law and economics framework. On this, see Lenoble and Maesschalck 2010: ch 3.

[7]   As Brousseau remarks, the organisation continues to be the 'black box' of evolutionist theory (Brousseau 1999: 189–215, 194).

commitment to 'internalising' the conditions for success of the learning operation. In contrast to the externalist approach, the transformation of behaviours/
desired representations is viewed as resulting from the very organisation of the
learning operation with respect to decentralised interaction. Granted, the form
that the effort at internalisation takes varies, depending on whether the approach
is collaborative-relational, pragmatist, or genetic. As has already been pointed
out, the effort at internalisation is given greater and greater breadth, in the sense
that the 'internal organisational constraints' imposed on the manner of organising
the form of cooperative action that is to be henceforward applied to decentralised
action are progressively increased. The deliberative or collaborative-relational
approach is characterised mainly by the will to organise the 'aggregate of communicative competencies'. Concretely, the issue consists, essentially, of organising
venues for cooperative deliberation by all the parties involved. It is in the increased
number of these venues for participation and the increased number of the actors
involved in deliberation that the conditions for transforming 'routines' and 'selecting' the best possible solutions for collective problems are expected to be found.
Thus, a twofold process characterises this initial effort at furthering the inquiry
conducted by neo-institutionalist economists in the broad sense.

First, there is the perception that action taken on its own by an 'external'
system of supervision will prove inadequate to yield the hoped for results. This
first idea is significant. After all, on what basis can we assume that those who will
apply this external system will do so 'in the same spirit' as that which prevailed
when the external system was set up? Is it not the case that the familiar critique of
the command-and-control approach is also relevant here? The work of Deakin
(2007)[8] makes it possible to clearly illustrate this first process, which underlies the
justification for the proposal that the approach of neo-institutionalist economics
be continued in a 'more reflexive' direction. As Deakin, working on the basis of
Teubner's systemic theory of 'reflexive law', shows, the usual law and economics
approach deals too reductively with the complexity of the processes that drive the
evolution of social behaviours. The autonomy of legal subsystems — for example, that of company law — makes it clear that a voluntarist introduction of a
'shareholding approach to corporate governance', at least into legal systems in
societies with a European orientation, will not necessarily result in the effects
claimed by those who support voluntarism in the name of economic logic. The
reason is that the 'interpretation' given to it will also depend on the traditional
cohesiveness of legal entities. These legal entities, at least in Europe, require one
to take into account the more 'integrative' dimension of the nature of the firm.
What is in question here is not just the 'cultural or ideological' dimension.
'Culture' is embedded in the legal constraints that govern the way the legal
system nowadays defines what is 'legal' and 'illegal'. Any new legal reform that
may be sought will necessarily have to take into account the inevitable effort at

---

[8]　Available at http://ssrn.com/abstractid=1002678.

the harmonisation of laws. If, then, we act on the basis of this necessary harmonisation, or congruence, would it not be more 'efficient' to improve conditions favouring such congruence by means of appropriate systems? As Deakin and Carvalho have pointed out (Deakin and Carvalho 2010), congruence might require setting up systems that favour a fuller taking into account, within companies, of all its components (the stakeholding approach) and, in so doing, a fuller account of what we nowadays call corporate social responsibility.

It is based on this first process that we can come to understand the second distinctive feature of the 'deliberative' project. Since any external system is at risk of producing effects solely as a function of the 'frameworks' specific to its addressees, it is necessary precisely to 'act' upon the way relations among these decentralised actors are organised. The 'aggregating' shaping of 'communicative competencies' among all the actors involved must be organised. It is on the basis of this deliberative involvement by all stakeholders that, thanks precisely to this communicative and deliberative system, one can look for the 'expansion' of routines that the success of a learning operation requires and, in consequence, the selection of a normative solution that will maximise fulfilment of the normative expectations of all the actors. Studies carried out as part of REFGOV by Adlard and Prosser (see below, Prosser et al in chapter 4) on the evolution of energy governance in the United Kingdom and by Vincent-Jones (see below, Vincent-Jones and Mullen's chapter 7) on the evolution of governance in the health field in England, illustrate very well the institutional initiatives taken in these two sectors towards supplementing and furthering the neo-institutionalist-economics-based reforms that accompanied the first steps towards market liberalisation during the 1980s and 1990s (that is, towards the reduction of state involvement and the increased application of free market principles in these fields). At the same time, these studies also make clear the problems and slowdowns that these 'participatory' and 'deliberative' 'reflexive' systems appear to give rise to. In fact, both studies show that the limitations of exclusive recourse to the mechanism of 'aggregating communicative competencies' to ensure the success of a learning operation are becoming increasingly clear. Undoubtedly, as is recognised in the collaborative-relational approach to governance through dialogue, it is useful to take specific action on decentralised interaction. Thus, this initial extension of the externalist approach is needed. However, it is proving in turn to be inadequate. Concerning these new institutional initiatives, Adlard and Prosser (see below, their chapter) indicate that 'the . . . most important problem is that of a lack of trust in relation to these processes . . . .. [This reform] is undermined by the serious failure of trust in relation to the new arrangements and by the failure so far to implement the types of institutional reform to re-create trust.' Similarly, Vincent-Jones and Mullen (see below their chapter) point out that the limitations of participatory procedures are becoming increasingly evident and that it is becoming clear that specific mechanisms must be set up to reinforce actors' capacitation and develop a 'capacity-building role'. However, this 'attention' to the problem of actors' 'capacity' needs to be properly understood. That is, it tends to be broached in very different ways depending on whether one takes the deliberative (collaborative-relational through dialogue), pragmatist, or genetic approach. The question of 'actors' capacities' as a condition for the success of the learning operation is not articulated in the same way by the three approaches. It is necessary here to recapitulate three points in order to clarify the issues involved in this important question.

First, we should remember that there has recently appeared, within the deliberative approach,[9] the will to break away from the belief that aggregating communicative competencies will on its own ensure respect for the conditions needed for governance capable of satisfying collective interests to the extent possible. Thus from within this approach there has emerged attention to questions of the 'empowerment' of actors as a condition that must be imposed[10] in relation to decentralised interaction and that goes beyond the sole condition of the aggregate shaping of communicative competencies. The concern here is especially to strengthen capacities for argumentation. This implies, Vincent-Jones and Mullen observe, that citizens have, or can acquire, relevant knowledge or understanding. This also implies developing methods of debate which maximise the input of relevant ideas, questions, experience, knowledge, and understanding (see below their chapter).[11] However, whatever the scope sometimes ascribed to conditions for empowerment,[12] the question of actors' capacitation is never framed in the terms that authors writing in the second pragmatist tradition (Schön and Argyris) would use, nor in the still more radical terms that would be used under the genetic approach to governance. This is because what distinguishes these latter two approaches is precisely the specific way they work to radicalise the question of the level at which actors' capacity is to be built.

Secondly, it should be noted that this question of building actors' capacity is in no way related to the expansion and furthering proposed by the first version of the third approach to governance, the one called 'pragmatist'. As has been pointed out, this third approach has taken two successive forms, with the second of these working to overcome the insufficiencies that the first (referred to by Sabel et al as democratic experimentalism) continued to be hampered by. The weakness that Schön and Argyris have revealed within democratic experimentalism is precisely that this approach obscures the question of actors' capacitation. The expansion of the deliberative approach effected by democratic experimentalism in no way

---

[9]   On this, see Lenoble and Maesschalck 2010: pt II, ch 4.

[10]   In this regard, see Burris, Drahos and Shearing 2005: 30–58, although this article conceives of capacity building, in a highly classical manner, in terms of informational asymmetry.

[11]   Contrary to what is sometimes thought, in this perspective, there is no evolution from the collaborative-relational mode of social learning towards democratic experimentalism. Rather, this kind of attention to the encouragement of social dialogue remains wholly within deliberative logic. As will be seen below, democratic experimentalism implies wholly different kinds of shift and attention.

[12]   In authors such as Innes and Booher, the emphasis goes beyond Habermas's formal approach and involves attending to the systems required to generate shared trust among actors and ensure the emergence of 'shared identities, shared meanings, new heuristics and innovation' (Innes and Booher: 33–59, 39).

relates to the question of the enhancement of actors' capacities. It relates rather to another level. The advance from which theory of governance benefits under this first version of the pragmatist trend is the insight that, besides the deliberative shaping of the communicative competencies of the actors involved, it is also necessary that the 'negotiation' be organised in an experimentalist manner. That is, it is necessary that actors be engaged in a process of joint inquiry in order to 'allow themselves' to be taught by the results of an experimental encounter between existing solutions and new problems requiring solution. In this sense, the process of 'internalising the conditions for success of the learning operation' is strengthened and a new condition is revealed, consisting of organising decentralised interaction in such a way that it is ensured that actors engage in a joint process of inquiry. This 'expansion' of the conditions for success of the learning operation is reflected, according to Sabel, in the requirement that three new conditions be fulfilled in building systems of governance: co-design (and thus collaboration among those who define policy and those responsible for implementing it), benchmarking and monitoring.

Thirdly, as was observed above, the distinctive feature of the second pragmatist trend (as expressed in the work of Schön and Argyris) and the fourth (genetic) approach to governance, drawn from democratic experimentalism, is the commitment to pursuing the inquiry already begun within the collaborative-relational approach through dialogue, ie the inquiry into the need to pay attention to enhancing actors' capacities. Certainly, democratic experimentalism, with its requirement that a joint process of inquiry be organised, has already allowed for an advance over deliberative approaches. Its error, however, is that it overlooks the 'obstacles' that may hinder the success of a learning operation when it is assumed that actors' 'spontaneous capabilities' suffice for the success of the 'joint experiment'. Indeed, no inquiry into these capabilities has been initiated within the democratic experimentalist trend. In tandem with this, the second version of the pragmatist approach and the genetic version are working to expand and radicalise the inquiries carried out by adherents of the 'deliberative' approach into the question of the conditions for actors' 'capacitation'. This expansion and furthering has been carried out by the pragmatists by means of the 'key' concept of 'defensive strategies' that actors may deploy unconsciously and that would lead actors to restrict the field of their 'representations', as compared with what is needed for the maximal fulfilment of the normative expectations held by participants in a collective action.

C.   The Genetic Expansion

The genetic approach continues to deploy this 'attention' to the question of 'defensive strategies' as it works to better think through the conditions for going beyond them. The reasoning that led to the furthering process suggested by the genetic approach can be summed up under two main headings.

i. From the Generative to the Genetic

The first point relates to the problematic aspect that continues to taint the approach of Schön and Argyris.

It is to the great credit of Schön and Argyris that they discerned the weakness of traditional approaches to governance, in particular deliberative approaches, as regards this matter of actors' capacity to form appropriate representations of the circumstances and of their own interests. They rightly saw that all the usual approaches to governance cancel out the difficulties specific to this operation. As was seen above, they revealed how often routines and defensive strategies prevent actors involved in a collective action from forming appropriate representations of new problems to be solved and from cooperatively taking part in the joint inquiry that the search for an appropriate solution entails. Such defensive strategies are clues to the existence of a 'handicap' in one's ability to suitably represent the problem to be solved — the actor remains the prisoner of what might be called a 'repetition compulsion' that obstructs the self-adjustment process needed for the operation of representation to succeed. It could be said that this repetition compulsion – or defensive strategy – points to the failure of the 'subject formation' capacity, that is, the capacity to form one's identity and be able to represent the interests at stake within a given situation. For this reason, Schön and Argyris understand very well that the operation by which one adopts an identity – that is, by which we 'represent' ourselves, we represent our 'interests' in a given context of action, and we 'present ourselves as actors' capable of interacting with other actors in order to advance our own interests – does not occur 'automatically' or 'spontaneously'. Its 'success' requires specific conditions to be present and consequently a specific form of 'attention'. This specific attention thus constitutes a condition for the possibility of success of the choice of norm. This condition reflects the need to organise reflexivity – that is, actors' return over their pre-existing frames. This 'generative attention' and the 'capabilities' that, according to Schön, it is responsible for generating, will obviously feature the priority given to the 'frames' that underlie our accustomed approaches to problems.

But at the same time, according Schön and Argyris, the mere incentive to the development of this generative attention is presented as automatically producing the attitudes and competencies required for a capacity to transform one's 'frames'. As the same authors write, it is sufficient, in a manner of speaking, to 'encourage' the actors to take such a reflexive (or, in their terminology, reflective) approach for the approach itself to develop, seemingly as the potentiation of a competency or capability that is already tacitly present in all the subjects and whose deployment merely requires that attention be paid to it. Thus the assumption is that, in some manner or another, there exist pre-given rules and capacities that are already available. This assumption is based on the belief, voiced by Schön, in the 'existence of a widespread capacity for reciprocal reflection-in-action' (Schön 1996: 353). Schön seeks to provide an accounting of this operation in terms of metaphoric learning. However, his analysis of the learning operation in the terms of metaphor reflects certain powerful assumptions. The frame each actor spontaneously deploys must be analysed as a 'generative metaphor'[13] that in a sense constitutes the actor's rule of identity. Every actor has specific interests that define her or his own identity within the social group. But a feature of this rule of identity is that it has a dual function. Its character as a 'rule' guarantees the outcome of a twofold operation.

On one hand, it allows the actor to assign to the specific context she or he is facing the 'meaning' that corresponds to her or his 'own identity' and adopt a corresponding role. On the other hand and at the same time, it guarantees its own variation, that is, its own changing adjustment to the transformations associated with differing contexts. That is why it is called *generative*. It produces a rule for the interpretation and integration of the facts. Thus it makes possible the 'representations' of specific situations and guarantees the possibility for assigning 'meaning' to them. It defines how the facts will be selected that will in turn define the meaning to assign to the situation that must be solved. This constitutes the first operation.

At the same time, and this constitutes the second operation, this rule also guarantees the success of the learning/adaptation entailed by ongoing changes in the specific contexts that have elicited the problems to be solved. This rule of identity — inscribed in actors' minds — ensures that, despite the constant newness of the problems to be solved, the actors will transpose the unaccustomed (the new) onto the known (the familiar). It is this that the idea of the generative metaphor points to: the rule guarantees social actors' capacity to re-read metaphorically, as 'analogues' of previous experiences, new situations needing solutions.

This also helps in understanding why we refer to an 'incentive' approach in connection with the theory of 'reflective' learning developed by Schön, Argyris and Rein. According to these pragmatist authors, it is in a sense 'sufficient' to pay attention to the problem of reframing for the identity rule inscribed in the frame to be automatically deployed, and for the twofold operation the rule is thought to guarantee to take place – simply because attention has been focused on the necessary 'adjustment' to the frames.

It is just this assumption of a rule stored in the minds of actors participating in a collective action, along with the incentive approach to governance associated with it that must be challenged. It is on this score that, in our view, the pragmatist project – not just in the 'Deweyan' and 'experimentalist' version of which Sabel is the exponent, but also in the more 'reflective' version developed by Argyris and

---

[13] 'The metaphor which accounts for centrally important features of the story – which makes it understandable that certain elements of the situation are included in the story while others are omitted; that certain assumptions are taken as true although there is evidence that would appear to disconfirm them; and, especially, that the normative conclusions are found to follow so obviously from the facts' (Schön 1993: 137–63, 149).

Schön – requires correcting and expanding: correcting, because the underlying assumption must be exposed; expanding because the exposure of this assumption entails, not a challenge to the organisation of governance proposed by the pragmatists, but supplementation and an indication of what it requires to reach completion.

By assuming the existence of a rule stored in the minds of each actor that guarantees each actor's spontaneous ability to adjust the representation she or he holds of her or his interests in light of changes in context, Schön and Argyris distort their initial insight in a fundamental way. This insight, it should be recalled, is indeed that the operation by which one adopts an identity – that is, by which we 'represent' ourselves, we represent our 'interests' in a given context of action, and we 'present ourselves as actors' capable of interacting with other actors in order to advance our own interests – does not occur 'automatically' or 'spontaneously'.

This is the point of the critique the 'genetic' approach to governance levels against the pragmatist theory of reflexive learning. Our critique of the pragmatist approach consists of showing that it reproduces the behaviourist assumptions made by the approaches to governance it sought to go beyond. The setting up of incentive mechanisms (joint inquiry and the provision of devices and mechanisms to induce reflective attention to the need for going beyond defensive strategies cooperatively) is expected to produce the hoped for effects of shifting and cognitive transformation. The mechanism is understood to produce on its own the behaviour looked for. The assumption is that the mechanism to some extent operates from the outside, in the manner of an incentive that activates a pre-existing rule that guarantees the hoped for behavioural transformation. There exists a pragmatic inadequacy in this way of understanding the conditions for the possibility of satisfying the intentionality that governs any action by a subject. These conditions for possibility necessitate a self-capacitating operation that no incentive mechanism can assume, in a mentalist fashion, to be taken care of by a given capability or capacity stored in every actor's mind.

ii.   *The Specific Contribution of the Genetic Expansion*

Here we will address the second component of the reasoning underlying the 'genetic' approach we have developed within REFGOV (Lenoble and Maesschalck 2010). To make up for the 'pragmatic inadequacy', then, the genetic approach proposes to expand the conditions for success of the learning operation by organising a specific 'pragmatic operation', designed to lead the actor to construct the representation she or he has formed of the new identity that the change in context requires. Since this operation of adjusting identity representation does not occur automatically, it must of course be organised. In fact, it is twofold.

The first operation concerns the actor's relationship with the 'past'. The collective actor must reconstruct the *form* its *identity* takes on through its past

actions, and this reconstruction will enable it, if needed, to adjust this form according to the changed context. We would argue that this reconstruction relates to the actor's reconstruction of its relationship with 'collective identity making'. Note the rich semantic ambiguity of the expression 'collective identity making', which implies that a collective actor experiences itself in its *organic* capacity to be organised as a collective actor 'representing and aggregating' the various members it is comprised of. However, 'collective identity making' also implies a '*modal* or *functional*' dimension, that is, a dimension related to the possibility of operating and representing itself as a collective actor in a context for action. The collective actor must experience itself through its capacity to represent itself, that is, to form an identity whose substantive representation can vary and adjust according to transformations occurring in the contexts for action. Thus, what is at issue here is the first dimension of *the installation of the capacity to be an actor* (ie, the operation of self-capacitation). This dimension works to construct this capacity to form an 'image', to be 'reflected' in an image subject to variation. For this reason, we can speak, more precisely and rigorously, of a dimension of *reflectibility*.

The second operation internal to this construction of 'self-capacitation' concerns the relationship with the future. The question governing this second process is that of 'ability-to-do'. What transformations must be carried out in the way the actor has given meaning to its identity? What means, what 'ability-to-do', must it adopt in order to ensure, in the new context that it is faced with, the realisation of this identity form 'with no fixed contents', which it defines as its own 'collective identity making'? Under what conditions can it make this form effective in the context of the new constraints on action? Thus the current situation is re-examined in the light of the identity form that underpins it (retrospective relationship associated with reflectibility), but also in the perspective of transformations necessary to ensure the fulfilment of this form in a new context for its application. This, then, is the second dimension of the *installation of the capacity to be an actor* (ie, the operation of self-capacitation). As we have just seen, it concerns the relationship with the future and works to construct the capacity to adjust one's 'image' according to what is entailed by the fulfilment of the 'identity form' one takes on as one's *destiny*. For this reason, we may speak, precisely and rigorously, of a dimension of '*destinability*'.

It is only through this twofold operation that the modification of a representation that is associated with what 'pragmatists' call 'joint inquiry' can be rescued from the 'unconscious repetition' that, through the 'defensive strategies' that are its telltale signs, limits the shifts required to solve the problem the actors are faced with. It is because they overlook the need for this twofold operation of 'self-capacitation' that Schön and Argyris's conception of the reflexivity at play in all learning is too narrow.

IV. CONCLUSION

The method of reconstruction adopted has thus allowed for two decisive advances in the conception of reflexive governance. The first consists of the revelation of the integrating focus that unites the four approaches to reflexive governance, namely the commitment, discernible in all four approaches, to expanding the conditions for success of learning operations such that, from the point of view of the expectations of the actors involved, their effectiveness as normative processes is ensured. The second advance consists of the identification of a specific issue. This issue has on one hand been obscured by the attention paid to the requirements for expanding the conditions for success in learning. But on the other hand, it could be detected only on the express condition of the exposure of this integrating focus of attention. This issue resides in the persisting indeterminacy of the nature of the role that reflexivity will be required to play within the collective action itself. Whereas the minimalist option consists of considering reflexivity as the property that makes it possible to assign features to mechanisms intended to highlight collective learning capabilities, the maximalist option consists of 'dementalising' the reflexivity approach. This approach's genetic features are thereby isolated, and a specific kind of operation on collective capabilities can be discerned therein, a kind that allows for the articulation in practice of the possible return over trajectories of action already performed, taking the necessary perspective provided by new positionings. One finding from our recapitulation also showed that all the approaches that distinguish themselves from the minimalist option have no other choice than to progress towards the maximalist option in order to take stock of their conditions for fulfilment in a fully coherent fashion.

2

'Reflexive' Market Regulation: Cognitive Cooperation in Competitive Information Fora

ERIC BROUSSEAU AND JEAN-MICHEL GLACHANT

I. INTRODUCTION: REGULATORS IN A KNOWLEDGE-BASED AND GLOBAL ECONOMY

ECONOMISTS TRADITIONALLY SEE regulation as a way to fix 'market failures', while it consists more broadly of building the infrastructure and foundations of markets (Joskow 2003; Brousseau and Nicita 2009; Glachant and Perez 2008; Brousseau and Glachant 2011). This interpretation encompasses the establishment of property rights, management of both negative and positive externalities (since complete systems of property rights are out of reach), management of long-term investments in common infrastructures and standards (especially because the lack of shared information on the future may lead to inadequate and under-investment). Upstream, to make choices in these matters, regulation implies the design of legitimate mechanisms to operationalise the notion of 'public/general' interest (Brousseau and Glachant 2010). Indeed, the simple aggregation of individual preferences in the presence of externalities and public goods, notwithstanding uncertainty, information asymmetries and bounded rationality, does not guarantee the most efficient use of resources or even the targeting of a satisfactory social outcome. Therefore, regulations imply a wide set of interrelated choices that are both highly complex and subject to strong pressures, because all individual interests have incentives to influence these essential collective choices.

A. Renewing the 'New Economics' of Regulation

The 'new' economics of regulation based on incentives, as exemplified by Laffont and Tirole 1993, consists of attempting to obtain the results of competition when competition cannot be implemented. This is a way of dealing with the many 'regulatory' failures hindering the efficiency (and even the feasibility) of public attempts to correct ex-ante market failures. The above quoted contribution and others considerably renew the practices of regulatory agencies and the 'regulation philosophy' of many governments. As perfect markets, efficient regulations are out of reach. So the challenge is to design the less imperfect regulations, and compare the benefits and costs of regulatory failures with market failures in order to decide implementation, given the cost and the actual impact of regulation (Glachant and Perez 2009). However, designing the least biased regulation — ie regulations taking into account information asymmetries and their consequences — calls for in-depth knowledge from the regulator, who should anticipate the reactions of regulated firms to the incentive schemes it designs. Moreover, assessing ex-ante the cost and benefits of feasible regulations compared to the absence of regulation, requires extensive knowledge of cost, supply, demand and customers' preferences. What is feasible, thanks to information revelation mechanisms and learning in a (relatively) stable world, becomes impossible to implement in an innovation-based economy. When the set of available products and services change, when new usage emerges, when disruptive technologies render past investments and capabilities obsolete overnight, when new entrants propose not only new services but new 'business models' too, the Government and regulator can no longer calculate the costs and benefits of alternatives. They also cannot access in time the information requested to implement incentives.

Incentive mechanisms are nothing but means of transacting information as a hidden good needed to efficiently perform a given transaction. Their implementability relies on perfect knowledge by the 'principal' of all the dimensions of the coordination problem in question when dealing with an 'agent'. As pointed out by Brousseau and Glachant 2010, when such knowledge is unavailable, a way of managing the regulatory game is to develop a pseudo and competitive market for information in which the various stakeholders are incited to disclose information and share knowledge. This is the logic of the new form of regulation, whereby the regulator in charge of completing and redrafting the 'rules of the game' in an industry organises de facto a forum accessible by all stakeholders. These later compete to influence the regulator, which leads them to disclose information. In competitive markets for goods, the level (and uncertainty) of the quality of goods traded is largely policed by competition. The same can occur in such an 'information market' if well designed. Indeed, a forum in which posts are public allows any player to challenge the information provided by any stakeholder, which is a good way to encourage truthful revelation. On the one hand, any player wants to make sure that its viewpoint is taken into account when regulation is decided. Here the reputation he or she develops by bringing useful elements to the table and participating in the implementation of efficient solutions is vital. On the other hand, any of its challengers has incentives to bring counter-evidence if possible, both in order to influence the regulation in the short run and to harm the reputation of its competitor.

B.   Sharing Information and Knowledge to Control Collective Inefficiencies and Hazards

In this chapter we build on this idea to highlight the potential of this model for learning and knowledge-building. We insist that the issue is not just asymmetric distribution of knowledge and information, according to which industry players would be informed and the regulator under-informed and ignorant. In industries characterised both by network effects and high rates of innovation, most players are ignorant. First specialisation leads to ignorance about the paths of knowledge development explored by others. Not only do actors in a given technological domain ignore what is invented in the next one, but also innovation providers often ignore how targeted users will invent around their technology. Secondly, in a competitive context, innovators have incentives to mislead other players. They therefore manipulate secrets and disclosure and spread erroneous information. It is worth noting that such strategies inhibit the credibility and quality of the entire set of available information. Thirdly, incomplete information and knowledge prevents elaboration of scenarios of possible evolutions and prediction of what is going to happen. Not only does this lead actors to make the wrong choices, but it can also lead them to brutally change their decisions when new information is revealed, resulting in unpredictable changes in the industry and the technological system. So, lack of knowledge appears to be a major issue not only for the regulator, who can hardly understand the system it regulates or foresee its evolution, but also for the players who have difficulties elaborating their strategies.[1]

Information and knowledge sharing is thus a good way of facilitating prediction and hence reducing the unpredictability of the system, which makes things easier for all stakeholders. Moreover, when multiple equilibria/paths of development are possible, information sharing is a way of building a shared vision. This guarantees neither convergence to a single equilibrium, nor the selection of the most efficient one. It facilitates, however, the compatibility of strategies and may open up space for negotiation and cooperation. The building of 'common cognitive frameworks' at least enables players to become conscious of their differences but also of the necessary consistencies in terms of strategy, technological development, marketing practices, etc. All in all, this allows better management of interdependencies.

From a theoretical perspective, this chapter lies at the frontier of three literatures. First, it draws from and participates in the development of research on the economics of regulation (Noll 1981). The related literature was totally reshaped by the development of the incentive theory in the 1980s, which had a strong influence on public policies. However, as pointed out above, the liberalisation of many industries boosted innovations in all domains, which seriously

---

[1]   As pointed out by Brousseau and Pénard 2009 in the case of digital industries, this calls for agile strategies by operators.

hampered the ability of public authorities to regulate. Moreover, the entry of many new competitors in formerly regulated industry totally overwhelmed the structure of the problem. Regulation is no longer about monitoring the behavior of a dominant incumbent to limit capture and foster entry. Regulation is increasingly about maintaining the consistency and openness of the industry. Secondly, analysis of the interplay between levels and modes of governance must also be taken into consideration. Literature on the matter has been evolving from the definition of the optimal devolution of responsibility across levels of governments (ie the efficient organisation of subsidiarity) to the management of synergies among levels of government (see Brousseau and Raynaud 2009). This later vision corresponds to the idea that levels and modes of governance have alternative properties — beyond the fitness to the scope of public goods; see Tiebout 1956, Oates 1999 and 2005 — and that this might induce complementarities. In such a spirit, the design of regulatory frameworks in terms of specialisation and the mix of public and private regulation may impact on the efficiency of regulation. Thirdly, this chapter contributes to research on reflexive governance. New Institutional Economics relies on assumptions about the 'bounded' rationality of agents and the radical uncertainty of the world we live in, making the issue of learning and innovating essential. Compared to the assumptions on which neoclassical economics is built, the issue is not only about managing information asymmetries, but about both the quality (of goods and agents) and the distribution of probability regarding future scenarios, and a way of re-combining ideas and producing new ones. This presupposes the ability to absorb ideas and so highlights the importance of shared beliefs and mental models (as stressed by Aoki 2010, for instance). In this context, governance mechanisms are not only considered as tools for solving coordination issues by designing rules and implementing them. They can also be seen as tools for generating and absorbing innovation (see Nooteboom 2000, Nooteboom et al 2007). This is illustrated, for instance, in the analysis by Brousseau, Dededeur-waerdere, and Siebenhumer 2010 on the generation of knowledge by alternative mechanisms involved in the governance of environmental issues.

We first analyse several examples of policies in which the lack of knowledge has been a central issue. Here the relationship between some specific institutional features and the lack of distribution of knowledge is highlighted. We then explore the logic of a reflexive mode of regulation for addressing the issue. This leads us to focus on the mechanisms to be implemented for favouring information and knowledge sharing. Conclusions on lessons to be drawn from the regulation of market practices and doctrines for the governance of our societies follow.

II.   THE LACK OF 'SHARED KNOWLEDGE' AS A REGULATORY AND POLICY ISSUE

A.   Three Lessons from Case Studies on Regulatory Failures

In the following, we highlight how and why the lack of 'shared knowledge' can become in itself a regulatory issue, and how, in several specific cases, it has been dealt with by the implementation of governance solutions aimed at managing knowledge (or the lack of it). The various examples we quote raise three essential points.

First, lack of transparency of information in a market or in an industry can lead to major market and industry failures because it prevents both industry participants and regulators from developing a true and shared vision of the market or industry, leading to inconsistent decisions that may result in major inefficiencies or even systemic crises. This is well illustrated by the electricity or the financial industries.

Secondly, one of the usual arguments developed to keep public intervention as light as possible is that government and public agencies are poor providers of solutions for the lack of transparency/knowledge sharing, and that if needed private solutions should emerge. The role played by rating agencies in the 2008–09 financial crisis highlights the fact that market incentives can be biased to incite private information providers to reveal the right information. Moreover, they can also fail to access the relevant source of information since they are not granted audit rights and may be unable to investigate. In addition, as shown by the case of intellectual property rights, the fragmentation of knowledge can lead to 'anti-commons' tragedies in that transaction costs for knowledge — and quite simply the complexity of identifying the relevant information holder — can prevent the efficient distribution of information, leading to market and information failures downstream.

Thirdly, the efficient provision of information and sharing of knowledge depends on adequate public-private partnership. On the one hand the relevant information is in the hands of market players. On the other, only government and public agencies have the means of inciting and forcing actors to reveal/disclose while minimising manipulation. This is well illustrated by the solutions currently in place to deal with the financial crisis. It is also highlighted in the way regulation for product safety was achieved in the European Union (EU). The latter illustrates the power of multilevel (and multimode) principles of governance. The involvement of multiple players and combination of local with generic (and of private with public) regulatory capabilities is a good way to manage learning and adjustment processes; the challenge being, of course, to successfully design mechanisms that allow synergies among levels of governance.

B.   Defaults in Knowledge Distribution

The lack of integration in the regulatory framework in the European energy industry (Hogan 2002; Dubois 2009; Glachant and Lévêque 2009) has resulted in major fragmentation of knowledge that prevents both efficient management of the current network structure at union level and consistent planning of future investments, and so hinders better integration of the industry (European Regulators' Group for Electricity and Gas (ERGEG) 2009). Due to the will of Member States to keep control of their energy policy, which is considered essential to sovereignty, the EU has failed to unify the regulatory details of energy networks. Here the so-called 'comitology' principle applies due to the extensive reliance on the 'subsidiarity' principle, combined with the absence of strong enough normative capability at union level. In practice, therefore, the EU regulation is decided by Member States with parliaments voting on the details of regulation 'transposed' from EU directives negotiated and decided upon by all kind of committees. Actual regulations are then implemented by national regulatory authorities in function of national agendas and national regulatory frameworks. This results, in particular, in non-harmonised and non-transparent methodologies for managing congestion in each national space (Glachant, Lévêque and Ranci 2008). The management of congestion, and therefore network and production capacities, then lies in the hands of each national regulatory system. There are no comprehensive common procedures and process for monitoring the operation and the development of European networks.[2] The so-called 'European network plan' is merely a listing of the facilities considered as of 'European interest' by each national authority (sub-national in Germany and Denmark). Fragmentation of knowledge is, among other factors, a way of protecting established interests thanks to cognitive lock-ins that prevent the recognition of obvious enhancement opportunities. Indeed, short and long-term management of capacity could be 'Europeanised' if regulators and transporters invested in common tools enabling them to pool information and knowledge.

The current financial crisis is also a significant illustration of the impact of insufficient knowledge sharing and production (Bhatia 2007, Eichengreen 2008). The financial instruments that have been developed since the early 1980s allow for the pooling of risk and re-scheduling of piles of debts, in particular by transforming debts contracts and futures into securities. As highlighted by the bankruptcy of major banks and by the current attempt to reorganise the assets of the banking system, information on the individual risks carried out by initial titles and contracts was lost in the aggregation process of these contracts into

---

[2]   The largest black-out experienced in Europe in November 2006 (15 million customers disconnected), for instance, revealed that national grid operators interpreted the same generic rules in very different ways. Even within some countries, like Germany, two interdependent levels of grids (like transport and distribution) can be managed independently from each other, preventing any easy recovery from incidents.

sophisticated financial title deeds, so that neither individual nor systemic risks could be identified by operators and regulators. The regulatory framework that resulted from deregulation of the financial industry thus failed to identify the major threat of defaults in conveying information on real risks, resulting in blindness and the collective impossibility of understanding the logic of the dynamics of the system, especially its propensity for catastrophic systemic failure. This led both actors and the regulatory authorities to combine wrong decisions. As pointed out by Aglietta and Scialom 2011, several of the necessary dimensions of financial reforms are therefore oriented toward explaining the knowledge needed to monitor the industry. In particular, standardised methods of risk reporting and of measuring the quality of assets should be developed and generalised as an enabling condition for the regulator to assess risks and control them by implementing the relevant and verifiable set of thresholds needed to perform both micro- and macro-prudential regulations. Also, an interesting dimension of the new regulatory policy is the way it forces major players to provide the regulatory authority with the necessary information to divest them in the case of failure. The logic is to mitigate the moral hazard due to the 'too big to fail' principle, according to which regulators cannot credibly threaten large banks because of the potential impact of sanctions on the stability of the financial system. By forcing them to provide receipts on the way to unbundle their assets and activities in the case of failure, the regulator reinforces the credibility of his or her enforcement means.

C. The Limits of Private Ordering in Ensuring Knowledge Sharing

Fragmentation of knowledge is sometimes considered a second rate issue, since agents can always create 'private' solutions for accessing knowledge. Either they do it on a contract basis — relying on the principle of the incentives theory that multiplies the analysis of truth-revealing mechanisms, on the basis of the so-called mechanism design (see Nobel Committee 2007)[3] — or by creating self-governed communities. However, this supposes the absence of market failures on the information market as well illustrated by the EU wholesale electricity market. The case of intellectual property (and internet regulation) shows how the rush toward community-type self regulation, while providing a pragmatic response to attempts to privatise the public domain and essential facilities, leads to a fragmentation of information and information spaces. This latter is misunderstood by many players. A (skilled and benevolent) knowledge aggregator would assess the costs/benefits of self-regulations versus public regulations; and might discover the possible institutional patches to be implemented to control

---

[3] Nobel Committee 2007, available at www.nobelprize.org/ nobel_prizes /economics/laureates/ 2007/ecoadv07.pdf.

for an over-fragmentation of the information and knowledge space. As high-lighted below, because it concerns the 'market' for knowledge, the case of intellectual property is also interesting because it is a direct illustration of the inefficiencies raised by a too high fragmentation of the governance of knowledge exchanges, which is the point made in this chapter.

It is well known that the lack of market transparency is a condition for exercising market power. At least, it allows manipulation of the market by those who are informed, resulting in all kinds of misallocations and inefficiencies (Borenstein 2002; Borenstein and Bushnell 1999; Bushnell 2007; Newbery 1998; Newbery et al 2003). Private provision of information, especially in the absence of regulation, does not systematically allow for the efficient provision of the requested information to clear markets efficiently. This is well illustrated by the EU electricity market. Up to the present day this market has yet to be organised as a transparent 'power exchange'. So over-the-counter (OTC) transactions domi-nate the wholesale trade. This 'OTC market' is, however, relied upon to generate 'prices' that serve as references for many actors, notably buyers willing to compare their deals with the market price. For a period of time these 'prices' were produced by specialised service firms (like Platts). However, the production of this information was not regulated and proved to be subject to market manipu-lation. Basically, Platts was collecting information by surveying the largest players on this OTC market. The latter were releasing information on a voluntary basis by communicating 'relevant OTC prices' (for different periods of time and horizons). The release of these 'relevant prices' was used by dominant players to influence potential buyers. The absence of regulation or monitoring of the provision of information shared by actors on a market typically prevented the players and the regulator from making 'informed' choices.

Elkin-Koren 2010 on her side, shows how the open-source and creative commons types of solutions for dealing with the increasing privatisation and decentralisation of the governance of the information space are far from equiva-lent to public and generic solutions. In a nutshell, both the evolution of digital industries — in which it is becoming easier and more efficient to establish property rights and enforce contracts on a decentralised basis (see Hadfield 2000 and Brousseau 2004) — and of property rights policies — pushed by US industry lobbies, the US Government and many governments worldwide, have been considerably reinforcing the rights of holders of intellectual title deeds since the early 1980s, see Lessig 2004; Jaffe and Lerner 2004 — considerably reduced the scope of the 'public domain', this space in which knowledge and ideas are freely available to all. This increasing privatisation and fragmentation of knowledge results in a 'tragedy of the anti-commons'; with the costs and complexity of access to knowledge deterring it from being shared as well as recombined in innovation (Heller and Eisenberg 1998, Heller 1998). In response, communities of software developers, artists, or scientists have been developing, especially since the 1990s, models of licensing conditions aimed at mimicking the properties of the public space. 'Open licenses' (eg 'open source' in software, 'creative commons' in works of authorship) allow users, inventors and creators to freely access and to invent around the creations of those who decide to release their innovation on the basis of such licenses. As nicely demonstrated by Elkin-Koren 2010, the use of private ordering to govern works of authorship and creation may not necessarily promote access to works. In a many-to-many licensing environment, where every user can design its own license, licenses might create barriers to access. The need to study the scope of restriction of each piece of circulated knowledge/creation to avoid infringement generates uncertainty and may give rise to a problem very similar to the tragedy of the anti-commons. To guarantee access, terms of access must be standardised. So, externalities and public good characteristics call for central intervention to mitigate the impact of private ordering on access and use of information goods. This example also highlights the benefits of homogeneity and publicness of access to information, and the fact that fragmented knowledge — and in this case the lack of understanding by creators and inventors of the logic of the law, notwithstanding the policy-makers' lack of knowledge of the complex relationship between the strength of property rights and innovation (Jaffe and Lerner 2004) — can result in regulations underperforming.

D.   Articulating Public and Private, Central and Decentralised Ordering

These elements lead to consideration of the interplay between public (and more centralised) and private (and more decentralised) governance solutions as a way of dealing with the interplaying issues of governing knowledge exchanges and sharing. In the early days of building the integrated EU market in the 1990s, one of the major challenges faced by Europe was the 'quality of product' regulation. Indeed the production and marketing of most consumer goods was regulated on the basis of long-standing regional or national traditions, resulting in a highly fragmented market with non-tariff barriers that were frequently much higher than tariffs. Indeed they often concerned the processes by which the goods were to be produced, which in practice prevented a supplier from serving several markets simultaneously when contrasting regulations were involved. Beyond conflicts of interest, harmonisation of product regulation would have represented a huge cognitive challenge since it would have required understanding of alternative technical solutions, and discussions on the respective benefits and costs of alternative technologies, so as to decide the best regulation or to agree on the implementation of parallel regulations. To a certain extent this is what happened since one, or the pillar, of the internal market construction was the principle of mutual recognition, by which a product regulation accepted in country A is also accepted in country B and vice versa. However, it was not sufficient for two reasons. First, when regulations are grounded on different logics — eg one focusing on the characteristics of products, the other on the features of the related production processes — compliance is not easy to manage both for market players and the enforcers. Secondly, in the specific case of product safety, it raised the issue of minimal levels of safety and/or the 'readability' of the system for consumers; another cognitive issue. To manage this puzzle the solution finally adopted was to switch from regulations focusing on the characteristics of products and processes to a regulation focused on objectives, and to combine this principle with self-regulation. The basic idea behind the first principle was that it would be almost impossible to harmonise standards focusing on products and processes, which would in any case distort competition in the short run, and hamper innovation in the long run. On the other hand, focusing on targets and minimum thresholds of security was a way of addressing the policy issue, without forcing civil servants and diplomats to understand and negotiate the technology in each industry. To efficiently define the targets in each industry, negotiations involving businesses, consumer associations and relevant branches of the civil services enabled the targets to be established. It was left in the hands of the industry to fix on a voluntary/self-regulation basis the best individual and collective way to reach these targets. Businesses are indeed fully responsible for complying with the targets; while of course they can cooperate to develop technical solutions and self-regulated labels aimed at meeting these targets and even reaching higher levels of performance (see Kessous 2000). Thus in the case of product safety regulation, the decentralisation of the regulatory capability — in exchange for extended liability — was a way of addressing the knowledge gap encountered by regulators.

III.   THE LOGIC OF REFLEXIVE REGULATIONS

As often claimed, our economies are characterised by two major trends: an accelerating pace of innovation and increasing global integration. The combination of the rise of the knowledge-based economy and the globalisation of markets and industries results in a permanent re-engineering of the framework for collective action. In the specific case of markets this results in continuous innovation in the Schumpeter meaning (new products, processes and forms of organisation, etc) combining with the permanent co-invention of new usage between suppliers and users of new technologies (in whatever sense: technical, but also business methods and organisation), and the permanent evolution of market structures (due to the entry of new players and the integration of markets). It results in a high level of uncertainty due to the unexpected and unpredicted recombination of existing components and an increase in new and unexpected changes in the structure of central issues. Traditional regulations and regulatory frameworks are designed to cope with stable environments. Whether we are speaking of the traditional command and control approach or more contemporary incentives, the theory and practice aims to optimise the institutional responses to market failures. Regulators rely on the accumulation of experience to design regulations that allow markets to perform or a dominant firm to deliver a satisfactory quality/price mix. In the context of permanent reframing of the issues at stake, these traditional practices always propose workable solutions too late. Once learning is put into practice, compromises negotiated and new rules enacted, solutions are no longer relevant since innovation in all domains has transformed the structure of the problem. At the same time there is a strong need for collective regulations to manage 'externalities' and allow a smooth and fair competitive process, in particular by avoiding the endless capture of dominant positions in fixed cost industries.

Reflexive governance, in this context, is an option and the solution to most regulatory issues because it is based on permanent learning and adaptation to new conditions. Thus, it seems to be a set of principles enabling, if not optimal, at least workable management of the dialectic between coordination needs (externalities) and competition requests (innovation and challenges of existing rents).

A.   Why Public Regulators Might be Useful Agents for Knowledge Sharing

As pointed out in Brousseau and Glachant 2010, the logic of reflexive regulation is to establish regulators as arbiters among knowledge (and interest) holders. Regulation bodies should be considered as an arena where stakeholders have interest in revealing private information/knowledge, because they are involved in a process of calling for new 'rights' that matter for competition (rights of access to resources, rights to supply, rights to prices, etc), or at least of reshaping and revising the delimitation of the respective rights of industry participants and market players. By publicly settling disputes (creating precedents), by organising hearings and public consultations (green books and white papers) to discuss the future of the industry and its regulation, by organising more informal conferences aiming at establishing consensus and shared vision, the regulator acquires information. As both arbitrator and rule-setter, the regulator is in a position to organise truth-revealing mechanisms based on competition among stakeholders. Indeed, it is in the interest of the latter to reveal credible information aimed at convincing the regulator to rule in their favour. Regulators benefit from credible, while biased, information from the other stakeholders, who are all encouraged to challenge the information and knowledge provided by any player in order to confine its 'rights' as much as possible. Lobbying and suiting should not (only) be considered sources of costs and biases; they are also vital channels for conveying the necessary information and relevant knowledge to the regulator (Broscheid and Coen 2007). While this is essential in a moving environment, this point was already made by Stigler who claimed that regulatory bodies tend to be stupid when not dependent on lobbying (Joskow 2005).

In the context of globalisation of the economy, and at least of strong regional integration, especially in Europe, the sharing of knowledge should not be limited by national boundaries. In addition to the fact that it allows the alignment of regulatory policies and practices within the scope of the current competition arena, as illustrated by several examples discussed in the previous section, it allows greater efficiency in managing knowledge for regulatory purposes. Indeed, knowledge is of general purpose and many of its uses are unpredictable because knowledge creation draws on replication, recombination and insights based on previous knowledge (Foray 2004). Thus what is invented here can be useful elsewhere, even if not directly. Moreover, knowledge is non-rival in its use. It is therefore optimal to share it at the widest possible scale among regulators and stakeholders. Moreover, strong strategic asymmetries could result from unequal access to the specific knowledge that enables understanding of the way the industry and market performs, of the potential of innovation and of the dynamics at play in the industry. Also, if sharing knowledge is not performed among regulators on a transparent basis, private firms will attempt to maximise the exploitation of differential of knowledge development across jurisdictions to generate and exploit their dominant position. Sharing knowledge is thus an antitrust measure per se too

B.   Is International Cooperation Among Regulators Relevant?

In such a context, what should be the role of public regulators and how should they deal with this issue of gathering and redistributing knowledge, or at least favouring its sharing? It is not obvious, indeed, that national regulators should be implied in such an activity. First, there is the traditional criticism of wrong incentives of public regulators. Secondly, there is the criticism of coordination among regulators. The principle of subsidiarity suggests not overloading the other levels of governance with 'irrelevant' information and knowledge. Moreover, it might play again the logic of independence of the various authorities, which is associated with a well-designed federalist system. Lastly, if knowledge is non-rival, its wide scale diffusion comes at a cost because learning efforts must be performed. Knowledge is difficult and costly to absorb, so can be suboptimal to systematically share it.

Thus, on the one hand, it might be advocated that private pools and private regulators could favour the adequate exchange of information among industry players, since it is not the role of the national regulator to exchange information and develop coordinated regulatory efforts (that, in addition, is not always feasible because national regulators might have conflicting interests if they are required to privilege their domestic 'national champion'). There is, however, a risk of collusion among the powerful industry players that could attempt to rely upon their ability to play simultaneously in several national arenas (especially by 'logrolling markets' among dominant competitors),[4] both to hide some information from national regulators (and other small competitors and stakeholders),

---

[4] Logrolling is the trading of favours or quid pro quo, such as vote trading by legislative members to get public action in the interest of each legislative member. In the Public Choice approach it is associated with exchanges of votes among politicians. However, it must be interpreted as a more general notion that describes the barter of reciprocal behaviour and attitudes.

and to mitigate the informational competition imposed by regulators in each of these arenas. Secondly, there is a risk of 'tragedy of the commons' on revelation, since providing relevant and exhaustive information to the private informational intermediary is no longer a dominant strategy. Even in clubs, strategic games among competitors can lead to a war of attrition in revelation.

On the other hand, not only can public regulators play a positive role in revelation, but they can also favour the diffusion and absorption of information. Since they are directly interested in enhancing the level of the informational competition by multiplying checks, national regulators have an interest not only in creating an arena favouring contradictory debates, but also in codifying knowledge to favour absorption (see Foray 2004, on codification). The incentives exist within national boundaries, but they also play beyond them. Once codified, knowledge becomes more easily transmissible. The low cost of transfers, to other national regulators and the potential number of checks and potential for amendment that they represent, result in a high level of possible social benefits.

It is also worth noting that beyond competition among stakeholders to influence the design of the rules of the game, competition among regulators might also exist. On the one hand, regulators have a mutual interest in sharing information and knowledge to better monitor players in their jurisdiction. On the other hand, there is also competition to establish precedents and innovative practices among regulators. In common law countries, the careers of judges strongly depend on their ability to establish precedents that are not ruled out by later decisions (Choi and Gulati 2004, Posner 2005). This induces competition very similar to that which takes place among scientists. Leading scientists are those who have successfully proposed theories that are relied upon by other scientists to explain actual phenomena or make progress in theories, without reversing the theory. To a large extent, the careers of regulators, and the international prestige of regulatory authorities, is highly dependent upon their ability to establish principles and practices recognised as 'right' by others, and de facto endorsed as precedents. Thus, two competitive processes interact to stimulate revealing of information and knowledge: one between stakeholders to influence the rules of the game; one between regulators to influence the doctrine of regulation.

Polycentrism in matters of regulation also play a secondary role. It results in de-facto checks and balances among regulators. When new stakes arise because of innovation or crisis in the performance of the industry, opacity and uncertainty may prevent the regulator from making any appropriate decisions, while the regulator must act in an emergency situation. This could allow some players to benefit from capturing the regulator, since the latter has no time to organise the open fora requested to guarantee truthful revelation. In a multilevel and decentralised context, however, it is highly unlikely that large players succeed in capturing all (national and regional) regulators at the same time. Thus, polycentric and multilevel governance, while generating costs and delays due to redundant efforts, discrepancies in implemented solutions and efforts to harmonise them, result in democratic checks and balances since full capture is impossible.

C. The Regulator's Weapons

Beyond the organisation of open fora, the regulators benefit from three other sets of tools for revealing information.

First, regulators are agenda setters. They decide to open new fora and to reach a conclusion when they consider a debate is over. This ability allows them to control capture of the process by industry players, especially by playing on the timing of information revelation (ERGEG 2007-b and 2007-c). This importance of agenda setting can be illustrated by the 'open season' process used by investors in infrastructures to calibrate their investments. In the gas industry, for instance, transporters open their investment projects to pre-booking by users. This allows information revelation by users before deciding the actual capacity to be built. While 'open season' can be spontaneously offered by the essential facility investor, it is frequently pushed by regulators to strategically 'open' the investment process at a certain time and in a certain manner. Such a process forces users to reveal their actual needs before the end of the season, and is aimed at limiting strategic games between suppliers, especially the creation of bottlenecks resulting in market power and the possibilities of collusion. It must be pointed out, in addition, that when it is relied upon in a regulated industry, the 'open season' procedure is a way for the regulator to decentralise the revelation of information and anticipate potential sources of exercising market power (ERGEG 2007-a, Hauteclocque and Rious 2009).

Secondly, beyond the establishment of general principles, regulators often have to design rules to implement these principles in practice. This results in the setting up of technical committees no longer comprising lawyers and the chief executive officer, but engineers and most often those with an in-depth knowledge of the field. These technical committees are strong tools of information revelation, since actual implementation constraints are revealing. Moreover, engineers are often driven by the logics of technical efficiency and performance of the service, which leave aside strategic considerations.

Thirdly, there is another forum that can help regulators: financial markets. Indeed industry players have an interest in revealing information to financial analysts because they are also competing on financial markets to raise funds (or at least to benefit from good evaluation to avoid strong pressure from stakeholders and even hostile takeovers). Financial analysts are often fully aware of the details of competition and strategic moves in industries and they have incentives — since this is their added value and one essential component of their essential commercial asset — to disclose information (Toledano, 2010).

IV.   ORGANISING INFORMATION AND KNOWLEDGE SHARING

A.   The Social Benefits of Making Knowledge Public

Beyond the traditional role devolved to regulators — namely enabling the market to perform despite its failures; and framing the behaviour of dominant firms when competition cannot be implemented — regulators play an essential informational role in the context of a knowledge-based and highly competitive economy.

First, it is essential to avoid long-lasting dominance of the market by 'innovative incumbents' capable of remaining at the frontier of knowledge both because they capture the flows of revenue needed to invest in research and development (R&D), and because their expertise and informational advantage allows them to control the development or the technology. Indeed, due to the combination of network effects, the constraints of standardisation of interfaces, switching costs of users, critical mass threshold at the implementation stage, privilege access to clients and established quality labels, the presence of dominant players can often result in the development of the technology on which their strategic advantage is built, and hindering of the chances of development of alternative and disruptive technologies. In such a context, the role of regulator is to place as much knowledge as possible in the public domain so that citizens and users can pressure incumbent firms to effectively provide them with the services and the prices made possible by advances in technology; and potential competitors may access technical and economic information to enable them to better target their innovation, development and marketing efforts.

Secondly, most industries today are organised on a modular basis and their organisation may evolve along very different and contrasting paths. Indeed, new principles of coordination among changing components of a complex system are implemented on a decentralised basis. Given initial endowment and the process of transmission, very different paths of systemic evolution can be followed, resulting in contrasting structures on the supply side and in marketing practices and technologies. The resulting uncertainty matters because when it is too high, investment and innovation efforts may be hindered. On the other hand, sharing information and knowledge on the evolution of the industry, its technologies and markets, as well as its business models, enable the framing of strategies to secure long-term decisions. Two mechanisms are at play. First, common discoveries of mutually beneficial solutions might result from collaboration in solving issues. This might result in the building of common interests when developing specific solutions. Secondly, the exchange of 'evolving and clarifying forecasts' — that is expectations becoming increasingly specific with the development of knowledge and the shortening delay to the deadline — about needs, capacities and technologies can result in the progressive building of a shared vision of the future, which is partly self-fulfilling since it is implemented by coordinated development and investments.

A third factor making it worthwhile to share information and knowledge is the need to prevent systemic crises that might result in the collapse of the regulated system (Glachant, Lévêque and Ranci 2008). Information sharing plays a role in 'mutual insurance'. In the case of energy networks, for instance, and especially electricity networks, knowing the level and evolution of the aggregated available capacity of reservoirs and storage capabilities, of pipes and grids at different time scales, decreases the risks of wrong decision-making by network operators. Catastrophic changes can even be better prevented if, in addition, knowledge on the micro-structure of the system is permanently updated by exchanging of information on the daily, or even hourly, decisions for injecting/withdrawing and balancing flow. The same holds true for avoiding crises and disruptions in financial markets, transportation networks and information infrastructures. In every case, transparency that can be ex-ante organised by the regulator allow more decentralised management ex-post of the resources that can flow more freely and on a more voluntarily basis across actors on the basis of short-term markets and spot transactions, instead of being frozen by wary, blind and risk-adverse actors.

B.   Regulating and Promoting the Exchange of Information

Regulators therefore appear to be market intermediaries (or platforms in the logic of two-sided markets) that provide (among other things) a common information space for the sharing of knowledge and of 'perspectives' to players, but also to other stakeholders in the industry. Their role in standardising, publicising, and controlling the agenda of information revelation and knowledge sharing at industry level is therefore essential. In concrete terms, their role of 'information platforms' between competitors, between the supply and demand, between the industry, consumers and citizens, calls for the opening of information seasons (like 'gas open season' or 'electricity rolling seven years statement') that define the communication rules (eg setting appropriate rules for the disclosure of identified commercially sensitive and non-sensitive data, establishing codes of conduct for the information sharing for 'market consequential events' such as plant failures, grid repairs, reservoir closures, etc), formats of data exchange, principles of data release and access to data, formatting of information systems (eg smart metering for retail billing and settlement).

In a context of multilevel governance linked to globalisation of the economy and the processes of regional integration, two types of additional tools appear vital for enhancing the quality of information sharing: the sharing of knowledge and the development of common doctrines. Regulation is indeed no longer managed on a national (or infra-national) basis. The increasing interdependencies among industries and markets and the actual scale of operation of industry players, call for the emergence of international (at least regional) entities and for cooperation among national regulators.

As is true at the national level, information sharing can be internationally improved by transparent and harmonised 'editing rules' that enable the systemic storage and cost-free retrieval of information. The internet provides an infrastructure for the building of smart, easily updatable and ubiquitously accessible information repositories. The Wikipedia model, in particular, can be relied upon to develop a knowledge-sharing platform that can be shared by all industry stakeholders under the supervision of regulators. The latter are indeed in a position to initiate the emergence of such platforms because they need them to enhance their regulatory capabilities — first by 'mapping' of the existing situation; secondly, on the basis of benchmarking and the revelation of best practices — and because their central and neutral position on each national market ensures they detain part of the relevant information and knowledge. Such platforms would be open to (controlled) contributions by the various stakeholders (ie the regulators themselves, state regional authorities like the European Commission, industry, consumer and citizen associations, etc) and evolve according to their needs. Such 'value adding' registrars of knowledge (and information) would allow the accumulation of knowledge, systematically challenging the information posted and all kinds of assessment and benchmarking exercises. Hence they can become tools for maximising spillovers in the progress of knowledge on the complex social technology needed to build and regulate complex markets, with probable strong cross-industry and cross-jurisdiction mutual enrichment.

The second mechanism by which information sharing and knowledge building can be sustained is the organisation of 'fora of regulatory fora' in which stakeholders and national regulatory authorities voluntarily contribute to produce, shared vision, harmonisation of practices, and (non-binding) common rules and principles (see Eberlein 2005; Eberlein and Grande 2005; Eberlein and Newman 2008;[5] Coen and Thatcher 2008-a and 2008-b). This is clearly one of the processes by which the European Commission can influence regulatory practices. In domains in which the Commission does not have explicit regulatory powers, these fora can be quite informal, such as the Florence Forum for electricity or the Madrid Forum for gas. Also, national competition authorities are sharing knowledge among themselves, and also with the European Commission competition authority (Directorate General for Competition (DG COMP) through an established European network. Intergovernmental entities are more formal when national governments devolve authority to organisations like EU regulatory agencies. Since 1975, such agencies (eg the European Railway Agency, the Agency for the Cooperation of Energy Regulators) have been set up in successive waves in order to meet specific needs on a case-by-case basis. These are independent bodies with their own legal status, and are funded by the EU budget (and in some cases directly benefit from specific fees or payments). They have been proving

---

[5] Available at: www18.georgetown.edu/data/people/aln24/publication-25787.pdf.

their relevance in the field of shared competences when strong cooperation between the EU and Member States is needed (whereas pooling authority on the issue within the Commission would have been resisted). These agencies may be responsible for implementing community standards, or providing direct assistance to the Commission and Member States, in the form of technical or scientific opinions and/or inspection reports, or creating networks of national competent authorities and organising cooperation between them, with a view to gathering, exchanging and comparing information and good practices, or even for market monitoring (when specified in the basic statutes). However, these bodies benefit from limited delegation of authority because of the need to comply with the EU institutional balance of powers; in a context where both Member States and the European Commission are frequently combating to keep their established domains of authority. This is why the essential power of EU agencies is based on their ability to organise information revelation, and from the fairness of their procedures for reaching consensus on best practices.

V.   CONCLUSION: REGULATORY PRACTICES AND REFLEXIVE GOVERNANCE

As pointed out in this chapter, a reflexive approach to regulation is the only way to elaborate market regulations for accompanying the permanent innovations of our knowledge-based and open access society. Reflexive principles allow taking into consideration the actual interests of all stakeholders in the light of the progresses in the understanding of issues and their technical/organisational/behavioural solutions. The resulting 'evolving-consensus-based soft-regulation' relies on the permanent renegotiation of compromises in the light of an evolving understanding of the issues at stake, partly due to the evolving nature of these issues due to the impact of knowledge of the technology, strategies and the mindsets of actors. This results in markets that are more 'resistant' to failure thanks to better-designed regulations, to governance mechanisms aimed at dealing with them and to the improved capabilities of actors in managing them. A common understanding of the nature of the problems and the state of the system allows us to benefit from the speed of decentralised adaptation, while avoiding catastrophic evolutions resulting from myopic and non-cooperative strategies. Moreover, in a permanently evolving environment, the ongoing assessment and challenge of existing regulatory principles allow them to evolve and be renegotiated (which increases both their efficiency and legitimacy).

Our understanding of the theory of reflexive governance identifies four degrees of reflexiveness. First, there is the idea that contractual compromises can be a means of taking into consideration the preference needs and know-how of other parties involved in a process of coordination/cooperation. Then comes understanding of the preferences, capabilities and beliefs of all the parties interrelated by explicit or implicit relationships (externalities) in an identified system. Thirdly, agents involved in an interactive system might share their experience and develop a common vision as a result of collective action. This shared experience results from jointly-organised efforts in testing, assessing and elaborating. Lastly, some processes oriented towards the cooperative management of problem setting and solving may result in the development of a common cognitive framework, which is then 'internalised' by all involved parties.

Our New Institutional contribution to the analysis of reflexive governance applies to mechanisms that are primarily concerned by the three first levels, particularly the third. Indeed, New Institutional Economics per se at its current stage of development has little to say about individual cognitive frameworks (see Introduction). At the same time, our approach is compatible with the fourth level of 'reflexive governance', as analysed by the editors of this book. In post-modern societies, society is so fragmented that the development of 'common cognitive frameworks' may prove less feasible than the (partial) sharing of information to maintain awareness of the parallel evolution of problems (and their vision) encountered by various communities. Soft and evolving regulations, coupled with mechanisms of information sharing and cooperative knowledge building that characterise today's regulatory arena, appear to prefigure the ruling methodology that will prevail in post modern societies.

3

Reflexive Governance, Regulation and Meta-Regulation: Control or Learning?

COLIN SCOTT[1]

I. INTRODUCTION

A CENTRAL ACHIEVEMENT of regulation scholarship in recent years has been to problematise the idea of control. If the idea and practice of control is problematic, then one possible solution is to find better ways of achieving the desired level of control. However, literatures which emphasise the role of institutions in shaping policy activities have placed particular emphasis on problems of knowledge and communication which underpin weaknesses in regulatory regimes. I argue in this chapter that an emphasis on knowledge shifts the central concerns of regulation away from control to learning. The central question which I address in the chapter concerns how we understand the ways that participants in regulatory regimes learn about their environment and the problems they face and the appropriate measures to take to address the problems. Following the themes of this book I seek to evaluate contrasting ideas about the mechanisms of and potential for learning within regulatory regimes presented by perspectives on reflexive governance that are found within the literature on regulation.

The application of ideas of reflexive governance to regulation provides part of the response to disenchantment with traditional forms of government regulation on grounds of both expense and ineffectiveness. The ineffectiveness critique has been particularly vigorous, noting the fragmentation of power associated both with processes of globalisation and the growth importance of both corporate and non-governmental organisation (NGO) capacities (Black 2000: 600–01). An

---

[1] I have had considerable assistance in writing this chapter from engagement with participants in the Reflexive Governance in the Public Interest Project, notably Jacques Lenoble and, in particular, members of the Sub-Group on Services of General Interest, Tony Prosser and Peter Vincent-Jones. I wish to thank Peer Zumbansen for very valuable comments on an earlier draft of this chapter.

important question is to what extent reflexive forms of regulation may be identified which address these perceived problems. A central concern within the field is to seek to bridge the gap between conceptions of regulation that continue to place the promulgation of rules and the exercise of hierarchical control by government and agencies at the centre of the model and those ideas which see the capacities of public bodies for direct control to be limited and consequently seek to harness the governing capacity of businesses and NGOs. Whilst much of the literature has been concerned with governmental regulation, practices of self-organisation and self-regulation have achieved increasing prominence. This is intriguing because there is necessarily a high degree of reflexivity about self-organising practices, but challenging because of concerns about legitimacy and effectiveness of self-regulatory regimes.

I address the dual challenges associated with the disenchantment with public regulation, on the one hand, and the concerns around the legitimacy of self-regulation on the other. Part of the answer lies in showing how the two may be effectively linked. Ayres and Braithwaite subtitled their seminal contribution to regulatory theory, *Responsive Regulation*, with the phrase 'transcending the deregulation debate' (Ayres and Braithwaite 1992). What they sought to capture in that idea was that the quest for more effective and legitimate regulation should increasingly be concerned with working more effectively with the capacities for self-governance of regulated entities. This ambition has both an enforcement dimension — seeking to promote compliance by firms without formal enforcement, and a techniques dimension, promoting effective self-regulation through the threat of more intrusive regulation.

From the responsive regulation approach have emerged further ideas about linking of governmental capacity to self-governance, including 'nodal governance' (Burris, Drahos et al 2005), 'steering-at-a-distance' (Kickert 1995), 'smart regulation' (Gunningham and Grabosky 1998), 'really responsive regulation' (Baldwin and Black 2008) and 'meta-regulation' (Parker and Braithwaite 2003). The strength of these approaches is that they recognise that the capacity to deliver on regulatory objectives lies primarily with those who are regulated, rather than those who regulate. Parker envisages a role for law in helping 'to connect the internal capacities for corporate self-regulation with internal commitment to self-regulate' (Parker 2002: 246). Within Parker's conceptualisation of meta-regulation, reflexive learning has an important role in contributing towards self-regulatory capacity (Parker 2002).

I have suggested previously that law, and the hierarchical ambition that it represents, may provide only one of the possible mechanisms through which self-regulatory capacity might be affected by external steering (Scott 2008). In this chapter, I further develop the idea that organisations with self-regulatory capacity may, under certain conditions, also be stimulated by their participation in communities and/or the discipline of competition in markets and other institutional settings. Just as community and competition provide alternatives to hierarchy as modes of control (Hood 1998, Murray and Scott 2002, Lessig 2006) so too they may provide alternatives to law in stimulating learning processes. Community, in this context, refers to participation in the making of and subjection to social norms and their application through mutual observation and application of social sanctions such as withdrawal of approval and ostracisation. Learning in communities may be stimulated through the seeking of approval, a desire for belonging, and an altruistic concern to contribute to the development of community. Where such activities involve an engagement with other community members, an openness to changing views of interests in, and objectives of, outcomes, then they may have reflexive characteristics.

Similarly, subjection to competitive disciplines may also stimulate learning not only about what buyers may want, but also about an organisation's own role and capacity for action within that market. Such community and competitive stimulants to learning may, I suggest, be characterised as meta-regulatory effect whether in combination with each other and/or hierarchy or on their own. Though the boundaries of meta-regulation are not yet fully worked out, its core idea is that the self-regulatory capacities of individuals and organisations may be subjected to steering.

A reflexive conception of meta-regulation acknowledges that the capacities of individuals and organisations for self-regulation extends beyond implementation and compliance to include the setting of objectives, but suggests that the legitimacy of such activities is liable to be premised upon the inclusiveness and character of such self-regulatory processes. A primary focus on learning offers a means to understand the potential and limits of such ideas. Although the literature on reflexive governance has chiefly addressed policy-making and related processes for making regulatory norms, it is arguably in the area of implementation that the greatest payoffs might be found from governing more reflexively. This is because successful reflexive processes may underpin greater understanding and commitment by those affected.

I start this chapter with an elaboration of concepts of reflexive governance in the context of regulation. I proceed then to suggest that much of the economic analysis of regulatory institutions, though it may involve learning, is essentially non-reflexive in character. I suggest that the challenges of engaging non-state and supranational capacity in addressing contemporary problems of regulation have been a key factor in opening up more reflexive ideas of learning within regulatory governance, first at the level of policy-making and the setting of regulatory norms. The emphasis is on understanding the conditions under which thicker conceptions of proceduralisation may contribute to more reflexive learning processes and how this thicker conceptualisation of process may be extended to the implementation stages of feedback and behavioural modification in regulatory governance. I conclude by suggesting that an enriched conception of meta-regulation provides an effective way to conceptualise the linkage between the state and the widely diffused capacities which are capable of making regulation legitimate and effective.

II.   REGULATION AND REFLEXIVE GOVERNANCE

A shift in the emphasis of governance mechanisms away from direct provision of services and welfare towards arms-length oversight of service providers has been characterised as the 'rise of the regulatory state' (Majone 1994, Levi-Faur 2005). Whilst there is no consensus on exactly what is connoted by the term regulation (Black 2002), a primary focus of the literature on regulation has been on the activities of agencies in monitoring and enforcing rules which attempt to control aspects of social and economic behaviour (Selznick 1985). This conception of regulation provides a starting point for analyses which significantly extend both the cast of actors involved in regulating, and the range of mechanisms which are deployed, seen by some as the logical extension of the modes of the regulatory state (Knill and Lenschow 2004), and by others as evidencing the emergence of a 'post-regulatory state' (Scott 2004, Zumbansen 2008). Such analysis focuses on the limited capacity of government and its agencies to direct actors in social and economic fields as to what they should do. This critique offers a sustained attack on the idea of 'command and control' informed variously by concerns that governmental decisions will crowd out market activity, that governmental agencies have too limited knowledge and capacity to control directly the behaviour of others by reference to rules or that the communicative capacity of legal and political sub-systems limits the capacity for direct intervention in economic and social life.

Underpinning this last form of the critique is an anxiety that the law, once conceived of in terms of general principles of universal application, has become materialised such that legal rules take on a high degree of detail and also specificity as to whom they apply. Such a materialisation of law, associated both with welfare state and regulatory growth, creates a variety of risks — that the integrity of the legal sub-system may be damaged, that the regulatory activity may be so juridified as to undermine its capacities, or that failures of communication mean that regulation has no effect — the 'regulatory trilemma' (Teubner 1998 (originally published in 1987), see also Nonet and Selznick 2001 (originally published in 1978): 100).

There is increasing recognition of the regulatory capacity not only of other parts of government, such as departments and courts (Department of Commerce and Treasury 1995), but also for non-state actors such as businesses and NGOs (Abbott and Snidal 2009). The acknowledgement of the diffusion of regulatory capacity has tended to undermine classical conceptions of bilateral regulatory relationships as the intentional exercise of hierarchical power by agencies over others (Prosser 1999: 200). In its place has emerged a more complex institutional conception of regulatory spaces populated by a variety of actors with preferences and attributes which shape their behaviour within the broader environmental constraints and relationships characterised by 'interdependence of powerful organizations which share major public characteristics' (Hancher and Moran 1989). Equally, the modalities of regulation are increasingly conceived of as extending beyond the hierarchical application of rules to include mechanisms which depend also or alternatively on competition, participation in communities and/or architecture (Lessig 1999; Murray and Scott 2002; Lessig 2006: 340–46). Such an approach suggests the emergence of 'regulatory pluralism' (Gunningham and Sinclair 1999).

If regulation is a process occurring within spaces which involve interdependent rather than hierarchical relationships, then arguably effective action is likely to involve learning about the capacities and preferences both of oneself and others. Accordingly, in this chapter, I address the variety of ways in which institutionalist perspectives conceive of the modes of learning within regulatory regimes and the ways in which they have supplemented or displaced a traditional focus of regulatory scholarship on control with learning.

The displacement of control with a model of interdependence has two sets of implications. The more obvious implication is that regulation is no longer conceived of as simply something imposed on one by another. A more radical implication, not recognised within all institutionalist theories, is that it is not only the implementation of a regime that is shaped by learning processes, but also the objectives and overall orientation of the regime (Bratspies 2009: 605). Such an analysis gives recognition to the capacities of actors to shape regimes within interdependent relationships. It is consistent with a characterisation of governance more generally as multi-polar in the sense that power is located with governmental and non-state actors with a degree of interdependence between them (Perez 2007).

The interdependence analysis is troubling for some because it deviates from the tenets of democratic theory which suggest that regime objectives should be determined by elected politicians rather than by actors within a regime (Freeman 1997). Accordingly these observations require a degree or reconceptualising as to how the public interest is represented within public policy processes. In chapter one of this volume, Lenoble and Maesschalck define reflexive governance in the public interest as involving processes of collective action in which the 'members' normative expectations are "maximised". In other words there is an outcome from the process that is not pre-determined but which is accepted by the participants because of the learning process within which they have engaged. Such a conception of public interest carries with it a requirement that all affected by a regime are able to participate in the applicable processes. Though we may be able to identify examples where this occurs, it provides a challenging general requirement (Calliess and Zumbansen 2010: chapter 2). Paradoxically, the 'the enlargement of participation makes the definition and protection of the public interest precarious and problematic', as participatory processes are liable to reflect imbalances of power in society and risk excluding the larger polity (Nonet and Selznick 2001 (originally published in 1978): 102).

The problem of learning is exemplified by responses to the global financial crisis of 2008 which has left both governments and banks scratching their heads over what went wrong in market and regulatory regimes in which, as they see it, regulators had broadly appropriate powers and market actors were subject to broadly appropriate controls. It appears that neither governments nor market actors sufficiently understood the interdependence between market actors and between national regulatory regimes and, in particular, the nature and extent of the systemic risk created by the way the global financial markets had evolved (HM Treasury 2009: 35–45). On this analysis it is developing a better capacity for learning, rather than for control, that has potential to prevent the re-emergence of a crisis of this kind. Put another way, and contrary to a dominant view of the issue found in the press and popular literature, is it possible that the crisis was a product of too little engagement with the self-regulatory and learning capacity of businesses, rather than too much (Zumbansen 2009)? The issue of how the conditions for appropriate learning may be developed is primarily a question about institutions.

The focus on institutions provides a corrective to understandings of regulatory processes which are primarily linked to the attributes, motivations and behaviour of the individuals involved in such processes. With an institutional approach we understand the behaviour of actors as constrained by what can be done and imagined with institutional structures that are typically unresponsive to immediate functional demands. The concept of institutions is understood somewhat differently in each of the branches of the social sciences for which 'institutions matter' in shaping how things happen (Black 1997: 54). Nevertheless, it is possible to conceive of new institutionalist approaches as engaging with the idea that formal and informal institutions (including social and cultural norms exhibiting a degree of regularity) shape the way that regulation operates, determining to some degree what is knowable and doable both by regulators and by other actors within the regulatory space.

In chapter one, Lenoble and Maesschalck distinguish the external perspective on learning and governance from internal perspectives. The dominant theoretical form of such external perspectives (in which the conditions of social learning are located outside the learning operation) is that of neo-institutional economics with its emphasis on markets and quasi-markets, and evaluation through performance management and competition as alternatives to more traditional bureaucratic governance (Williamson 1996). The participants in such processes come to them fully formed, expressing preferences through market decisions and sometimes also through consultation or the pursuit of grievances. It might be argued that learning within the latter form is not truly reflexive since 'theoretical and practical validity claims are naively taken for granted and accepted or rejected without discursive considerations' (Habermas 1988 (originally published in English in 1976): 15).

The widespread adoption of forms of marketised governance of energy markets provides a central example of the external perspective (discussed extensively in chapter four of this volume), as do attempts to stimulate quasi-markets in health care through competition amongst providers to provide services to healthcare providers, even within fully public provision of healthcare (chapter seven of this volume). The Australian Government directly links the objectives of its programme of regulatory reform to a set of regulatory performance indicators (RPI) (Francesco and Radaelli 2007: 41–44), permitting both a whole of government assessment of performance against the indicators, but also enabling laggard agencies and departments to be more readily identified. League tables are, of course, not without critics who point to weaknesses associated with the use of performance indicators in terms of both risks of gaming and of downgrading of important objectives which are difficult to capture within such indicators (Bevan and Hood 2006). In each instance consumers of services are expected to learn about quality and price of provision and to exert market pressures on suppliers through the choices they make. Their preferences, however, are not targeted by this approach, but are assumed to be stable.

Turning to the internal perspectives, Lenoble and Maesschalck distinguish three strands, each of which is progressively more reflexive — the deliberative, pragmatic and genetic. The deliberative strand emphasises dialogue between the key actors, emphasising their communicative capacities as a key resource for developing a regime. Accordingly, the deliberative model seeks to promote participation of key actors in decision-making. Lenoble and Maesschalck suggest that important strands of thinking which seek to deepen this communication in a pragmatic way may be identified in the 'democratic experimentalism' literature associated with Charles Sabel and others (Dorf and Sabel 1998), and distinctly, in the work of Donald Schön and Chris Argyris (Argyris and Schön 1978). The experimentalist strand is chiefly concerned with the manner in which decision-making processes promote experimentation through co-design of processes, benchmarking and monitoring. It lacks a focus on developing the capacities of the actors themselves (Lenoble and Maesschalck 2010). Schön's work adds this emphasis on enhancing the capacities of the actors. The ambition is to tackle 'the actors stereotyped behaviours or routines' (Lenoble and Maesschalck 2010: chapter 6 section 2). This literature has informed concerns within legal scholarship to develop a reflexive and proceduralised form of law, discussed below (Black 2000, Black 2001).

Their own 'genetic' approach, they suggest, constitutes a further deepening of this pragmatist trend. This last approach involves both the effective conditions to engage the reflexive capacity of the actors as required for the learning operation and, once that actors' commitments are established, 'the setting up of the institutional conditions likely to guarantee effective implementation of the actors' commitments' (Lenoble and Maesschalck 2010: chapter 6 section 1 § 1.). This characterisation is open to the criticism that it is contradictory to describe commitments within such reflexive processes as fixed where, in principle, such commitments should be open to re-negotiation even during the process of implementation as further discovery occurs through such processes.

Within the context of an examination of regulatory governance I have found the distinction between external and internal forms of reflexive governance helpful. Indeed, I would question whether the external forms are truly reflexive forms of learning. If reflexive governance is to meet some of the challenges of contemporary regulation, it is important to identify examples of the internal forms of reflexive governance, but also to understand the conditions under which they might emerge and be valuable in supporting the development of regulatory capacity. Two distinct properties of policy issues for decision have been linked to the emergence of more dialogic forms of decision-making within regulatory governance. The first concerns policies over which there are very marked divergences of world view, and the second where a decision-maker understands there to be a high degree of uncertainty surrounding the issue for decision (Bratspies 2009). In some instances these two sets of properties overlap. In the case of energy regulation in Canada the more reflexive forms of governance, involving elements of deliberation and experimentation were found in issues concerning effects of plant construction on first nations land rights and in the development of policies on renewable energy (Armstrong, Eberlein et al 2007: 51–52). More reflexive governance forms offer mechanisms for addressing problems characterised by fairly profound conflict through seeking to engage the ideas, preferences and world views of those actors. The literature on decision-making suggests that another area of potential application of more reflexive governance forms is where uncertainty exists to an extent that more conventional Weberian rational decision-making might lack legitimacy. In their study of telecommunications regulation, Hall, Scott and Hood contrasted the Cartesian-bureaucratic decision-making style deployed where knowledge was available and objectives commanded a reasonable consensus with an adhocratic-chaotic decision style used in conditions where neither agreed objectives nor appropriate knowledge were fully available (Hall, Scott et al 2000: chapter 8).

A critical element of this internal reflexive governance approach is the element of cognitive reframing which it supports, as the interests, ideas, and preferences of actors may be re-cast, underpinning change in their capacities and appetites (Vincent-Jones and Mullen: chapter seven of this volume). This provides a link to the sociological literature which is concerned to investigate the cognitive limits to action arising from relatively fixed world views and preferences and seeks ways to exploit the potential for stimulating re-framing of what is thinkable and doable in terms of preferences and capacities of key actors (Goffman 1974). Thus, the operation of the process is not only or chiefly acting on the relevant policy or decisions, but rather on the participating actors themselves, with consequences for policies, decisions and, critically, implementation. A radically reflexive process in this sense may affect outcomes not only in terms of policy solutions and instruments, but also the way in which the problem is conceived.

If it is accepted that regulation is characterised by relationships of interdependence amongst many different kinds of actors, then it is helpful to conceive of regulation as occurring in regimes (Scott 2006). Regulatory regimes are conventionally thought of as systems of control which involve setting of norms or rules, feedback and behaviour modification mechanisms (Hood, Rothstein et al 2001). Classical approaches to regulation tend to treat the institutional features of regulatory regimes as unproblematic, and focus on the regulatory rules and their enforcement by agencies. New institutional economic approaches to regulatory governance substantially focus on organisational choices and mechanisms of monitoring and control, working with an external conception of regulatory governance, and retaining a quite hierarchical conception of the regulatory capacity of the state. The application of an internal conception characterises reflexive regulation as

> procedure oriented rather than directly focused on a prescribed goal, and seeks to design self-regulating social systems by establishing norms of organisation and procedure. At its core are participatory procedures for securing regulatory objectives and mechanisms that facilitate and encourage deliberation and mutual learning between organizations (Gunningham 2009).

Reflexive governance, in this sense, is involved with fostering learning that goes beyond simply learning about variety in governance instruments and extends to learning about the preferences and commitments of the actors themselves. Necessarily such processes require decisions about which organisational mixes to deploy as part of deciding what processes may be appropriate.

III.   NON-REFLEXIVE GOVERNANCE AND THE ECONOMICS OF STATE INSTITUTIONS

A central implication of the claim that institutions matter within the new institutionalist literature generally is that choices over appropriate organisations for regulating significantly affect the operation of regulatory regimes. The new institutional economics makes organisational choices central to its analysis of regulatory capacity. Choice of organisational structures is accompanied by the introduction of mechanisms to limit the downsides associated with any institutional choices. Such choices are not restricted to the decision as to whether to regulate through a government department (Department of Commerce and Treasury 1995), an agency or a court, but also include questions concerning the use of public enterprise or regulated private enterprise (Trebilcock and Prichard 1983) and the balance between public and self-regulation (Horn 1995) and public or private enforcement (Shavell 1993). Within the economic literature, reflexivity generally has a limited role since the preferences and capacities of actors are assumed rather than problematised. This may be explained partly by the opposition created in the literature between hierarchies and markets. Markets are spaces in which actors learn about the preferences of others through interaction, and law and regulation are external to that, correcting failures sporadically through exerting corrective control. Law is accorded a narrow, controlling role. A richer and alternative conceptualisation perceives law as being constitutive of markets with a potentially wider role in facilitating a variety of social interactions, of which market transactions is one (Shearing 1993). Arguably, the strands of literature addressing the problem of appropriate organisational choices for regulation which consider supranational and self-regulatory governance problematise the role of law and hierarchy in creating governance conditions in a more challenging way.

Within new institutional economic theory, regulation presents the problem of delegation and, associated with it, significant asymmetries of information as between both government and regulatory agencies and between regulatory agencies and regulated organisations. In the face of such high costs we may wonder why we should delegate at all. Part of the reason for delegating is that government and legislature may not know enough to be able to specify exactly what is to be done. Agencies are established to develop expertise and to learn about the regulated sector as to use the discretion delegated to them to pursue the objectives of the legislature. Delegation also provides a degree of insulation from government, enabling countries to make credible commitments to stable policies in particular sectors (Levy and Spiller 1996). As is noted elsewhere in this book, within some parliamentary systems of government delegation to agencies is problematic, a feature which not only has the capacity to undermine the objectives of neo-institutional economics in supporting delegation to agencies, but also wider objectives for transferring governing and reflexive learning capacity to new actors and sites (Prosser, Adlard et al: chapter four).

Due to the focus on delegation, a chief concern of the economic literature is the problem of control over agencies (Horn 1995). Insofar as the approach is about learning, it is about learning what others are doing and how it may be controlled. In the case of regulatory agencies the risks are that they develop their own policies, deviating from those of the legislature (Shepsle 1992). In the case of firms it is assumed that they will seek to maximise profits and seek to avoid regulatory drags on their profits to the extent that they can. Cast in terms of learning, each of the actors in regulatory regimes needs to learn both about the actions of others and about what it should itself be doing.

A key approach to the learning about what others are doing include instituting of systems of monitoring over agents. Such systems include regular reporting requirements, but might also extend to exchanging staff, for example between agencies and government departments. The long-observed practices of agencies and regulated businesses recruiting from each other's ranks, the revolving door (Makkai and Braithwaite 1992), also establish a degree of monitoring. Considered in principal-agent terms classical regulatory theory, which conceives of private interests shaping regimes to suit their purposes (Kolko 1965, Peltzman 1976), can be recast with the regulated businesses as principals seeking to monitor and control regulatory agencies. Recruiting experienced regulatory officials is one of the mechanisms for doing this.

Institutional economics also assigns a role for markets in learning about regulatory performance and exerting a form of control over regulators. On one view the main form of such scrutiny emerges from the labour market for staff in agencies. Whilst such market oversight may be beneficial, it may also encourage a variety of forms of rent-seeking behaviour. One example is the incentive on regulators to make regimes more complex through use of detailed rules rather than general principles, as such complexity increases the market value for former agency officials as employees in regulated firms (Horn 1995: 59–60). External labour markets are not the only form of control which deploys competition over reputational issues. It is increasingly common for both governmental and non-state bodies to pit regulators against each other in performance league tables. One example is the use of scoreboards for implementing legislation administered by the European Commission over the Member States (Mendrinou 1996). National officials and politicians are encouraged to jockey for position as the best implementers of EC measures, as indicated by formal transposition of EC directives.

Markets also feature in the mechanisms under which regulatory regimes are set in competition with one another to attract business activity to their jurisdiction. The origins of the theory of regulatory competition lie in Tiebout's observations about the potential for using competition as a mechanism for learning about appropriate levels of expenditure on public goods funded through local taxation (Tiebout 1956). The problem Tiebout was addressing is that it is difficult to ascertain from voters how much expenditure they are prepared to pay from taxation. Tiebout noted that consumer voters may relocate to areas where taxes are lower or public services better (Tiebout 1956: 418). There are some fairly stringent assumptions as to when Tiebout's theory might operate, relating to the mobility and knowledge of voters that are rarely likely to be met. However, there are perhaps rather more instances of regulated firms which may deploy their knowledge and mobility to engage in regulatory arbitrage, though there is limited empirical evidence that firms do move in search of less stringent regulation or that governments 'race to the bottom' as might be expected (Radaelli 2004). Insofar as the theory of regulatory competition is about learning (Zumbansen 2006: 550), it is concerned with the potential for regulatory regimes to innovate and find better and more proportionate ways to meet their public objectives without scaring away those regulatees who have the capacity to relocate to more favourable jurisdictions. Competition within a single jurisdiction is also possible, as where self-regulatory regimes compete with each other, facing the upward pull of the reputation of the regime and the downward pull of potential and actual members seeking to minimise regulatory burdens (Ogus 1995).

Learning processes which depend on the variations in institutions and approaches in different jurisdictions have been the subject of diffusion studies which are only loosely concerned with competition. Puzzling over the growth in independent regulatory agencies in most European countries, Gilardi, applying the insights of new institutional approaches to political science, suggests that this trend can be understood in part as a top-down process, as where EU legislation requires the setting up of independent agencies to regulate network industries (Gilardi 2005: 89–90). Bottom-up explanations look to political or other local factors in shaping change, notably the need for creating credibility in policies through isolating them to a degree through the creation of independent agencies (although this requirement has limited application in many sectors and is of greatest significance in network industries which require a high degree of capital investment) (Gilardi 2005: 87–88). Gilardi's third category, horizontal explanations are most explicitly linked to learning processes. Here the interdependences between countries are reflected in processes of emulation. He suggests that certain institutional structures have become 'taken-for-granted' and where they are not there may still be symbolic benefits to be gained by copying from others (Gilardi 2005: 90). The learning process here is about reshaping what is taken for granted, as independent agencies have progressively become a and perhaps **the** normal form for state regulation in Western Europe. The process here engages states partly in competition for innovation within regulatory regimes that deliver more effectively but with fewer burdens on business, but partly also in community processes within which they learn about how others have solved problems.

IV.   REFLEXIVE GOVERNANCE BEYOND THE STATE

The challenges presented by supranational and non-state regulation have stimulated considerable innovation in both practice and thinking about the development of deeper learning processes within regulatory policy-making. As such thinking must inevitably address the role of the state, it is frequently required to address also the relative role of community and market in stimulating not only control but also learning. The theory of regulatory competition has been largely concerned with understanding the behaviour of competing jurisdictions, it also bears on the choices to be made by federal or proto-federal governments as to whether to coordinate through harmonised regulation, or to permit competition between regimes. Mechanisms of coordination can be organised through hierarchical or community-based mechanisms. The European Union, for example, permits competition on levels of corporate and personal taxation (though with some scrutiny of overall fiscal policies through the Stability and Growth Pact), but has substantially sought to harmonise employment protection measures through law. In this context the development of the Open Method of Coordination (OMC) is of considerable importance as it has created more community-based mechanisms for coordinating policies among EU Member States whilst seeking to take advantage of innovations at Member State level through processes of surveillance, benchmarking and mutual learning (Hodson and Maher 2001, Trubek and Trubek 2005). In this respect the OMC is similar to many of the processes coordinated by the Organisation for Economic Co-operation and Development (OECD) which use mechanisms of learning and soft coordination rather than top-down controls over Member States' community of governments as an alternative to hierarchy (Schäfer 2006).

Sabel and Zeitlin have hailed the development of the OMC as a key example of an experimentalist form of deliberative democracy involving:

(a) the setting of 'framework goals';
(b) 'measures of gauging their achievement';
(c) regular reporting on performance; and
(d) periodic revision of both framework goals and reporting procedures (Sabel and Zeitlin 2008: 273–74).

Consistent with ideas about fragmented governance, they do not suggest that these functions have to be located within a single organisational structure, and find that some version of the experimentalist mode extends beyond the use of the OMC within the EU to include many other policy areas, having become central to contemporary EU governance (Sabel and Zeitlin 2008: 274). The partial displacement of the community method of law-making by more deliberative mechanisms is of considerable significance because of its engagement of competitive and community-based processes as part of the regime both for developing and implementing regulatory policy in the EU. It offers a pluralised vision of policy-making in which no one is in charge, but the learning of each of the participants is brought to the table both in assessing performance and revising goals.

If the move to supranational governance represents one central challenge for contemporary regulatory theory, then the acknowledgement of non-governmental power is another. Just as the EU recognises that the main capacity for both learning and implementation lies in the Member States, so there is increasing recognition at national level that non-state actors have important capacities not only for implementing but also initiating and revising regulatory regimes (Black 2003). Perhaps the strongest examples of this phenomenon are found in the area of environmental protection where there are strong examples both of community and market governance emerging as alternatives to state regulation.

Problems associated with environmental damage take a variety of forms. Classical economics defines one set of problems as arising from externalities — harms such as pollution where the cost is not borne those taking the benefits of production. A second set of problems is associated with common-pool resources where individuals have incentives to exploit the resources excessively, even thought the degradation of the resources will adversely affect all users. To both these sets of problems there has been an increasing recognition of the potential for reflexive solutions which to varying degrees engages the self-organising capacity of those who might otherwise damage the environment and of other key stakeholders within the regulatory space (Orts 1995, Richardson 2002: chapter 3). A central challenge identified within the literature concerns the linkage of state capacity to self-organising capacity to create effective regimes. From the perspective of reflexive governance this is about harnessing the learning capacity associated with non-state actors. The regimes which we might consider range between those developed by individual companies through those of trade associations, other private organisations (such as standards bodies) and those developed collaboratively with non-governmental organisations (NGOs) and or governments. Recent research at the transnational level suggests that regimes which engage businesses, NGOs and governments are becoming increasingly common as the logic of interdependence asserts itself (Abbott and Snidal 2009).

At the level both of individual firms and trade associations, the motivation for developing or engaging with non-state norms include concerns with protecting their reputations to reduce the stringency of externally imposed regulation (Gunningham and Sinclair 2002: 134). The concern with reputation creates a hybrid set of pressures which involve aspects of competition and community, which may be characterised as the 'social license to operate'. The social licence comprises the implicit permission required of society, without which no business can legitimately operate and may be experienced more or less intensively depending on the degree of engagement an industry has both with its geographic and broader communities. Examining the environmental performance of the pulp-mill industry Gunningham, Kagan and Thornton concluded that the pressures associated with the social licence have the potential to affect the content and implementation of the legal regime for regulatees, but also constitute 'the primary source of beyond-compliance measures of the good citizenship variety' (Gunningham and Sinclair 2002: 51).

Key instruments for firms to address these concerns and deliver on their capacity for action are the development of codes of practice and standards. From the perspective of reflexive governance a central question is how these codes are developed. Whereas the processes for developing technical standards have been reasonably well documented (Hallström 2004), we know rather less about the development of industry codes. In some cases governments take an interest in what would otherwise be purely non-state activity with a view to enhancing the non-industry participation (Baggott and Harrison 1986).

The relatively opaque character and limited participation of interested parties both tend to limit the reflexive claims of industry codes as compared with technical standards. There could be a significant role for governments here in facilitating more open and participatory processes. This could be done through the incentive of reduced external regulation for businesses participating in and complying with such codes and through seeking alignment between participation in such processes and the advancing of the reputational interests of affected firms. An example of such a facilitative role for regulators is found in the Victorian scheme for developing Environmental Improvement Plans (EIPs) in what are effectively local environmental standards, together with processes for monitoring and securing compliance, which are set through engagement between businesses and affected stakeholders, facilitated by the Environmental Protection Agency (Gunningham and Sinclair 2002: 159–62). The EIPs are characterised by a strong degree of engagement between industry and stakeholders in defining both the nature of the problems and the solutions and by a significant degree of innovation in resolving environmental problems. Gunningham and Sinclair's evaluation suggests that they command the broad support both of industry and community stakeholders (Gunningham and Sinclair 2002: 168–69). They note also, that in the case of laggards, regulatory inspection is an ever-present threat to promote compliance (Gunningham and Sinclair 2002: 170–71).

In the case of common-pool resources, the potential for self-regulation is somewhat different since the participants in the regime are simultaneously regulatees and beneficiaries. A further important strand of new institutional economics addresses the regulation of 'common pool resources', such as fisheries and irrigation systems, where narrow self-interest would encourage those with access to the resource to deplete it excessively ('the tragedy of the commons' (Hardin 1968)). Elinor Ostrom has tracked the emergence of cooperative solutions amongst the resource-users to developing self-governance norms and mechanisms (Ostrom 1990). The regimes which she observed are characterised by a high degree of commitment amongst participants in making the norms work. What Ostrom defines, in essence, is the emergence of effective regimes of self-regulation in which the resource-users deploy their capacity to participate in making the rules, monitoring for non-compliance and enforcement and dispute resolution through the application of graduated sanctions. An essential aspect of such regimes are the learning processes within which users learn about the resource they depend on and their own use of it and the use made by the community as a whole, and about how incentives and rules affect the sustainability of the resource for all (Ostrom 1990: 55–56). Ostrom's analysis deploys an external perspective on learning, since it does not look to or expect such regimes to exert changes in preferences of the members of the community. Arguably, contemporary debates about climate change go further in their implicit or explicit advocacy of reflexive processes for the community as a whole in dealing with a global issue with similar characteristics to the problem of common- pool resources. An explicitly reflexive approach to climate change is of particular interest where it includes both interactive goal-formulation and interactive implementation amongst its key processes (Voss, Bauknecht et al 2006: 435).

Whilst questions of organisational choice for regulation are of considerable importance (and of central interest to new institutional economics), regulation scholarship within political science and socio-legal studies tends to focus on the distinct processes of regulatory regimes — the setting of norms, feedback and monitoring and behavioural modification. The following sections of the chapter consider the role of learning within these processes and, in particular, evidence of the potential for the more reflexive governance processes evidenced both in policy processes and the scholarly literature.

V.   REFLEXIVE POLICY-MAKING IN REGULATION

It is arguable that the focus on formal and informal mechanisms of oversight which characterises the economic approach to organisational choices risks embedding ideas of distance and limited engagement between regulators and their constituencies. Such a focus may overstate the capacity of regulators to achieve their objectives. A central problem in regulatory policy-making, captured in the idea of information asymmetries, is that much of the knowledge of how regulated activities operate, and where costs and benefits fall, lie with regulated actors and other stakeholders. This problem is partially addressed by policy-making mechanisms which engage actors within regulatory regimes in a degree of learning and give recognition to the diffusion not only of interests but also of knowledge about the regime.

Whilst proceduralisation of regulation has been an important theme in the European literature on regulatory governance, it is arguably in the United States that the most proceduralised examples of regulation have emerged. However, the form of proceduralisation is legalised and arguably has few reflexive characteristics. The 1946 Administrative Procedure Act gives to interested parties a right to participate in rulemaking proceedings and the potential for judicial review of adverse decisions. For new institutional economics proceduralisation is perhaps more about control than learning, permitting participants to engage in '"fire alarm" oversight' (Horn 1995: 49). The strength of such an approach from a learning perspective is that it enables regulators to collect knowledge and, to some extent, test it with other participants within the process. Such an adversarial approach is never likely to get beyond external modes of learning, since it invites participants only to present their own position, frequently entrenched, rather than to engage in any significant form of dialogue over their positions (Freeman 1997). Where judicial review is available, but linked to less procedualised decision-making, it is possible that the threat of litigation may do more to encourage some degree of bargaining between interested parties and regulators, but still on a bilateral basis, thus inhibiting engagement with a wider range of actors (Hall, Scott et al 2000: 178).

Elsewhere, better regulation programmes within both the OECD and developing countries prioritise the development of more extensive consultative procedures over the making of regulatory policies (Kirkpatrick and Parker 2004). Such consultations are typically geared to getting better information about costs and benefits of proposed regulation, including the impacts on third parties, rather than engaging in a more extensive engagement over the nature of problems to be addressed and potential solutions (Brown and Scott 2009). Conceived of in terms of the broader literature on proceduralisation, such consultation mechanisms are a 'thin' form of proceduralisation. Thin proceduralisation accords with a liberal model of democracy under which the objective is to aggregate preferences and within which preferences are exogenous to the process and remain unchanged (Black 2000: 606–07). The learning envisaged is of the external rather than the reflexive kind.

A 'thick' concept of proceduralisation entails a deliberative model such as that associated with the work of Habermas (Weithölter 1985, Habermas 1996, Black 2000: 607–08, Prosser 1999: 209–13) and is more demanding in terms of a requirement to establish conditions for 'equal and uncoerced participation of all in a deliberation in which each recognises the other and puts forward arguments that the other is likely to accept' (Black 2000: 609). Applied to regulatory practice, the thick version of proceduralisation involves a variety of roles for regulators in mediating between participants in deliberative processes. These roles include translation between participants with different ways of expressing themselves (for example as between technical and lay understanding) and the mapping of discussions and seeking to resolve areas of difference (Black 2001:47–57).

As noted, a rationale for recasting regulation to support proceduralisation and learning arises from a recognition of the limited capacity of governments and regulatory agencies to regulate because of the fragmented character of power within regulatory regimes. A radical implication of this insight is to conceive of non-state actors as having a central role in regulating with the possibility of state organisations engaging in processes of monitoring and indirect steering. Cast as a question of institutional choice, such an approach recognises that much of the capacity both to set and meet objectives lies with non-state actors.

If we give recognition to the central regulatory role of non-state actors then how are we to think of the ways they learn about what they should do? One approach is to suggest that if such actors have quasi-public power then they should be subjected to similar procedural requirements as those applying to public bodies (Kingsbury, Krisch et al 2005). An alternative approach is to recognise the embeddedness of non-state actors, variously, in markets and communities, and to the extent possible rely on market and community mechanisms to promote appropriate solutions (Scott 2006). More likely it is not hierarchy, market or community, but each, together or separately which provides the reasons for non-state actors to develop their self-organising capacities in ways which seek to include others in their learning process in search of some version of the public interest which may align to their private interests. It is important to better understand the conditions under which such processes are stimulated and, where they are not, how processes of rebalancing or collibration through applying more law, more community pressure or more market discipline might correct this (Dunsire 1993).

VI   MONITORING AND FEEDBACK

A central function of an effective regulatory regime involves feedback mechanisms to detect deviations from the applicable norms. The effect of positive and negative feedback is a key insight of systems theory (Kooiman 2003: 200–02). Feedback has both thin and thick versions. Cast in conventional hierarchical terms, feedback mechanisms typically involve public agencies gathering information through requiring reporting or the making of inspections and visits to those they oversee and, in some cases, receiving complaints. This is the thin version of feedback. Market mechanisms also provide a thin form of feedback, where consumers give voice to problems they have with products, and where league tables show how a regulator or a business is performing. Other examples include educational reforms which seek to regulate schools through empowering parents by giving the right to choose schools and information about the performance of schools on which to make their choices. Such mechanisms encourage learning both among the consumer group and the supplier group as each becomes more sophisticated in their appreciation of appropriate levels of quality in educational provision. Such feedback does not typically involve a wider engagement over the appropriateness of the regime and its objectives.

Within a thicker and more reflexive conception of regulatory governance, a primary role for feedback has less significance for day-to-day regulatory compliance and a greater role supporting the development of a regime through considering how effective it has been and whether its parameters require revision (Nonet and Selznick 2001 (originally published in 1978): 109). As noted above it is a key feature of the experimental governance model of Sabel and Zeitlin that such feedback on performance should be linked to the revision of the regime. Such processes relate also to Argyris and Schon's conception of double-loop learning — with the potential to revise not only the regulatory settings, but also the 'underlying norms, policies and objectives' (Argyris and Schön 1978: 2–3).

The thicker conception of feedback, based on a central role for learning, is strongly articulated in Parker's model of meta-regulation, and in particular the concept of 'triple-loop learning' as an ideal both for self-regulatory governance and for the role of law within meta-regulatory regimes (Parker 2002: 298). For self-regulatory governance, she envisages processes of evaluation and revision first within particular self-regulatory programmes, secondly within the broader corporate management and thirdly through reporting to external regulators and stakeholders (Parker 2002: 278). Adopting a similar perspective in the context of nursing home inspection, Braithwaite et al observed that the self-taught individual inspector model in England inhibited learning when compared with the vibrant team exchanges that were observed between Australian and US inspection teams. Elaborating on triple-loop learning they suggest that the first loop is the feedback from an inspector to the nursing home, the mechanism through which

> the innovation is diffused to all wings of the facility, all facilities in a nursing home chain or all provisions across one trust. The third loop is that the regulatory system diffuses the innovation to all nursing homes across the nation (Braithwaite 2008: 168–69).

Although modelled for a public regulatory regime, the logic could equally apply to substantially self-regulatory regimes.

Some aspects of contemporary better regulation doctrine provide mechanisms which support a thicker role for feedback. So, for example, it has become routine to require reviews of new regulatory policies after their implementation and to link these to sunset clauses which bring about the end of a regime after a period of years unless it is renewed through a further process and positive decisions. Radaelli suggests that sunset clauses are a paradigmatic example of meta-regulation, in that they provide structural controls over the regulatory process (Radaelli 2007: 196). They also have a strong reflexive dimension. Official guidance in the United Kingdom on sunset clauses suggest they are not appropriate where a measure implements EU law (and cannot be revised significantly or withdrawn) or where the measure is likely to have a long-term role, but may be appropriate where measures involve fast moving technologies or uncertain effects because of technological change, where they respond to particular crises or where there is a significant degree of opposition to a measure (Department for Business Industry and Skills nd). Broadly these are the conditions which would favour reflexive governance processes in regulation more generally, discussed above. Inevitably, where such renewals do occur they are likely to involve revisions. It is an open question how reflexive the processes of review and revision will be in practice.

VII.   CHANGING BEHAVIOUR

A third central element to regulatory regimes is the mechanism for modifying behaviour that deviates from the norms of the system. Orthodox conceptions of this function focus on formal enforcement of regulatory rules. However, significant quantities of empirical research in a number of jurisdictions suggest that much regulatory enforcement has a more responsive quality to it, involving regulatory and regulatee in discussions over compliance and a gradation of sanctions, formal and informal, available for application (Cranston 1979, Bardach and Kagan 1982, Grabosky and Braithwaite 1986, Hawkins 2002). From this research, Ayres and Braithwaite combined theories of responsive law (Nonet and Selznick 2001 (originally published in 1978)) and game theory to construct an enforcement pyramid with informal sanctions of education and advice at the base, and more stringent sanction from warnings through to civil and criminal penalties and licence revocation at the top (Ayres and Braithwaite 1992, Braithwaite 2008: 89). This widely observed and implemented model of enforcement permits agencies to engage businesses in learning as to how they may comply, but offers a reciprocal opportunity for agencies to learn why compliance may be problematic and, where enforcement officials have sufficient discretion, to allow some adaptation of the regime on the ground. The centrality of this pyramidal approach to enforcement to the model of 'responsive regulation' demonstrates the significance of implementation processes to contemporary regulatory theory.

How reflexive are such enforcement processes? Within the responsive regulation model the view of learning is essentially an external one, within which regulator and regulatee have positions on what they do and how they do it shaped by exogenous factors (Ayres and Braithwaite 1992). However, the theory of responsive regulation has spawned a wider literature which uncovers examples of internal forms of reflexive governance. The literature on tax compliance provides examples of cognitive reframing, addressing the problem of tax evasions such that tax compliance becomes 'the right thing to do' (Braithwaite 2009: 148). The central problem in such research is how to shift non-compliant taxpayers into categories where they perceive themselves to be members of a tax-paying community, frown on evasion, with a willingness to report on the cheating of others (Braithwaite 2009: 148–49).

Tax enforcement may appropriately be a bilateral affair between tax authorities and citizens. In other instances actors other than agencies may have enforcement capacities of an informal or formal kind. The pyramidal approach to enforcement has been adapted to engage not only state agencies, but also businesses and NGOs in processes of enforcement (Gunningham and Grabosky 1998: 397–404). Whilst the three-sided pyramid has the virtue of engaging this wider group of actors within the regulatory space, if the enforcement capacity of others is not coordinated, of course it risks disrupting relationships between regulator and regulatee, for example where an NGO uses enforcement capacities more stringently than the regulator, and in ways which may restrict learning by either enforcer or enforcee (Scott 2004: 159). A key challenge of reflexive regulation is to exploit the interdependence of key actors within regulated sectors so as to shift emphasis on the enforcement pyramid from control to learning. Arguably, Braithwaite's reconceptualisation of the three-sided pyramid as 'networked escalation' (Braithwaite 2008: 94–96), which incorporates the idea of capacity-building — the strong helping the weak — offers the beginnings of a more reflexive approach to securing compliance.

VIII.   CONCLUSION: META-REGULATION AND REFLEXIVE GOVERNANCE

The recognition of the limited power of state regulatory authorities, and relatedly of the interdependence of the variety of actors who populate regulatory spaces presents profound challenges both to the theory and practice of regulation. Attempts to address asymmetries of information and rigid approaches to enforcement yield some progress in enhancing regulatory capacities. Whilst official programmes of better regulation give considerable emphasis to alternatives to classical regulation, and to the development of stronger processes of consultation and review, it has proved difficult to shift official regulatory practices away from a fixation with rules and control.

The more radical implications of interdependence are recognised within theoretical strands which attempt to make more of the capacity of businesses and NGOs both for self-regulation and regulation of others, alongside governments and agencies. Such an approach gives to government a role both in observing and facilitating more reflexive processes in the development and implementation of regimes. There are documented examples which correspond fairly well to deeper reflexive processes which might be expected both to advance and perhaps change the understanding of both problems and solutions for participants and, because of this, command greater support. Such a role for government and agencies is well captured by the concept of meta-regulation — the steering of self-regulatory capacity — only if we conceive of meta-regulation as requiring an engagement between some approximation of all affected participants.

The implications for regulation are radical if governments are no longer to determine objectives but to delegate them to decision-making within participatory regimes which they oversee. Regulation '[is] a paradigmatic function of responsive law' (Nonet and Selznick 2001 (originally published in 1978): 108) and such responsive law 'may require a relaxation of central authority in the interest of more effective cooperative action' (Nonet and Selznick 2001 (originally published in 1978): 100). The adoption of a more responsive form of regulation is a high risk strategy, since the necessary openness creates a degree of political contestation around the purposes of law 'generating forces that help correct and change legal institutions but threaten to undermine institutional integrity' (Nonet and Selznick 2001 (originally published in 1978): 78).

Furthermore, government oversight need not be the only steering mechanism with meta-regulatory effects. Many examples of broadly based private regulation appear to have been stimulated either by market mechanisms or concerns about participation in communities, or both (as with Fair Trade and forestry regimes (Taylor 2005, Cashore 2002)), with limited or no participation of government. Indeed, the 'social licence to operate' discussed above not only constitutes a social source of steering over the behaviour of firms, but also over the behaviour of governments in setting and enforcing regulatory norms (Gunningham and Sinclair 2002: 51). If meta-regulation is a primary concept for giving legitimacy to such diffused regulation then it must admit the possibility of market or community-based steering and not just regulation of self-regulation by government (Scott 2008: 175–78). There is considerable promise in the capacity of meta-regulation effectively to link self-regulatory capacity in a way that moves us beyond a preoccupation with control so as to observe and support the development of learning processes in the shadow of state, market and community.

Part II

Beyond Neo-Institutionalism

4

Neo-Institutionalist and Collaborative-Relational Approaches to Governance in Services of General Interest: The Case of Energy in the UK and Germany

TONY PROSSER, HELEN ADLARD,* BURKARD EBERLEIN,
GABRIELE BRITZ AND KARSTEN HERZMANN

I. INTRODUCTION

T HIS CHAPTER WILL examine some of the hypotheses of the REFGOV project through empirical studies of experience in the United Kingdom and in Germany.[1] Both studies will examine liberalisation; that of energy markets and their regulation in the United Kingdom and energy network access in Germany. The UK study also examines changes to participative arrangements

---

* This chapter reflects Helen Adlard's own views and was written before she joined the Infrastructure Planning Commission.

[1] The theoretical structure for this chapter was derived from the theoretical framework developed by Jacques Lenoble and Marc Maesschalck (Lenoble and Maesschalck 2010: pt 2) on the basis of the 2006 Synthesis Report 'Beyond Neo-Institutionalist and Pragmatist Approaches to Governance' and Synthesis Report 2 'Reflexive Governance: Some Clarifications and an Extension and Deepening of the Fourth (Genetic) Approach' in 2007 and in chapter one of this publication. This theoretical frame developed four theoretical models of reflexive governance; that of institutional economics, the collaborative and relational approach, democratic experimentalism and the internal and pragmatic, or 'genetic' approach. In addition, chapter one makes an important distinction between an essentially 'externalist' approach to learning, associated with the neo-institutionalist approach, and one which successfully internalises the conditions for successful learning through arrangements for the transformation of behaviour and desired outcomes. This framework was applied to arrangements for network access in Germany, and in the UK to energy regulation and to the arrangements for participation in planning decisions relating to the energy mix, with further reference to Canadian experience. It became evident very early on that the dominant model was that of neo-institutionalism and 'externalist' regulation, with only limited developments beyond this. The

in land use planning directly shaped by problems of security of supply in the energy sector. Some brief elements from the Canadian study of electricity market liberalisation in three provinces will be provided as well. No attempt will be made to provide a comprehensive account of the findings of these studies, which are available separately.[2] Rather they will focus on key findings relevant to the general themes of the study; those of the ways in which energy liberalisation was associated with means for incorporating the general interest through opportunities for social learning, and the way in which these procedures were able to address unanticipated outcomes.

This chapter will be concerned mainly with the first of the approaches to reflexive governance identified in Lenoble and Maesschalck's work (Lenoble and Maesschalck 2010: part 2); that of the 'neo-institutionalist economics' approach. There will be some reference to the 'collaborative-relational approach through dialogue' but not to the 'pragmatist' and 'experimentalist' or the 'genetic' approaches. The reason for this is simple; the energy policy studies did not reveal any evidence of the latter approaches, and relatively few of developments from the 'neo-institutionalist' approach to the 'collaborative-relational' one. A key concern will be the extent to which an essentially external conception of learning, as identified in chapter one of this book, can be broadened out into one which internalises the conditions for success of the learning operation where '[i]n contrast to the externalist approach, the transformation of behaviours/desired representations is viewed as resulting from the very organisation of the learning operation with respect to decentralised interaction'. The collaborative-relational approach, which is also referred to in chapter one, thus consists 'of organising venues for cooperative deliberation by all the parties involved'. As we shall see, such limited attempts to develop this approach as are apparent in the case studies do not go so far as to threaten the overall predominance of the 'neo-institutionalist economics' approach. This chapter will conclude with suggestions for how these developments could be strengthened and taken further.

II.   DOMINANT AND EMERGING APPROACHES TO ENERGY GOVERNANCE IN THE UK

A.   The Development of Energy Liberalisation and its Limits

In the United Kingdom the dominant theoretical model in the institutional framework in the energy field is that of institutional economics. This reflects that fact that the process of 'marketisation' of the UK energy sector commenced

---

chapter thus concentrates on the necessary conditions for establishing such a model and for developing means by which it can be transcended and a more collaborative and relational approach adopted.

  [2]   See the reports available at http://refgov.cpdr.ucl.ac.be/?go=publications.

earlier than in other comparable countries and proved to be more far-reaching. Thus, the former state monopoly of British Gas was privatised by the Gas Act 1986, and later full competition for both industrial and household users was introduced; the sector is now highly competitive. Similarly, almost all the electricity sector was privatised under the Electricity Act 1989 (and the remainder, the nuclear stations, have since been sold) and this included splitting generation into competing enterprises, separate from transmission, distribution and supply. Full competition was introduced in generation and later in supply. Both gas and electricity markets are now closely intertwined, with companies offering 'dual fuel' deals, although there has been considerable market consolidation since the early days of liberalisation, with now only six major players in the household energy supply market. The model for both energy sources is thus competition-based, with coordination taking place primarily through bilateral contracting between different enterprises and with consumers.

Reflecting the institutional economics approach, however, the process of marketisation was supplemented by extensive regulation. Most obviously, this took the form of the new regulators for gas and electricity, now combined as the Office of Gas and Electricity Markets (Ofgem). In brief, this regulator has a variety of functions which include consumer protection, policing competition, and some social goals. The regulator is also responsible for setting periodic price controls for the remaining monopoly areas of transmission and distribution. A further important intersection of contractual governance and regulation has occurred on the highly technical question of how the purchase of electricity from suppliers can be coordinated (this is particularly complex given that electricity cannot be stored). The initial approach was to use the pool, a form of spot market supplemented by contractual hedging against fluctuations in price. This proved highly unsatisfactory, especially because it enabled dominant generators effectively to fix the market in their favour; lower input energy costs and reductions in the capital costs of generators were not passed on to consumers. The pool system was replaced in 2001 by the New Electricity Trading Arrangements (NETA), a complex mixture of self-regulation through an industry code and regulatory oversight; this was extended to the whole of Great Britain in 2005 as the British Electricity Trading and Transmission Arrangement (BETTA). This combination of self-regulation and a degree of regulatory oversight is precisely what one would expect from the institutional economics approach; its aim is coordination for efficiency, not generalised social learning. Despite the reforms, problems of undue exploitation of market power in the wholesale electricity sector still remain (Ofgem 2009).

What has been the role of the regulator in organising social learning? In one sense the role of the regulator has been to encourage private coordination through the contracting process between private parties; in this sense its work can be seen as overseeing self-regulation by participants in the markets themselves, again something we would expect to see from an approach based on neo-institutional economics. An increasingly strong procedural emphasis of the regulator has been on encouraging participation through consultation before key decisions are reached, normally in the form of issuing detailed consultation documents and through the giving of reasons for decisions. These form a central part of Ofgem's approach. However, they are firmly rooted once more in the neo-institutionalist economics approach and provide a good example of the 'externalist' approach identified in chapter one. Thus, the regulator asks for evidence and then waits for it to be given by outside interests in a form which can be used to contribute to decision-making; the regulator does not directly organise the relevant social interests, but instead adopts the role of a passive recipient of information from other actors in the process. The nearest thing to the organisation of such interests was the work of Energywatch, the statutory consumer protection body established alongside the regulator; however, Energywatch was abolished in 2008 with its responsibilities passing to a general consumer representation body covering all sectors. This 'external' approach to participation and consultation is a characteristic of the UK utility regulators, to be contrasted with a more internal approach adopted by more 'social' regulators such as the Health and Safety Executive and the Food Standards Agency with direct representation of interests on the regulator's own board and its own meetings being held in public.

To what extent was this approach successful in incorporating broader aspects of the public interest? A crucial issue became that of security of supply, where the orientation towards open markets and efficiency characteristic of the model adopted on privatisation was to cause difficulties. After privatisation, there was a rapid move from reliance primarily on large coal-fired generating stations as the major source for electricity to the use of small gas-powered stations. These could be developed quickly, and had a particular appeal to supply companies that wished to branch out into generation, as was permitted by the rules adopted at privatisation. The result was that the United Kingdom became heavily dependent on gas as a source of electric power generation; by 2006 gas was used for 40 per cent of electricity generation, and by 2010 the United Kingdom is likely to be dependent on imports for 40 per cent of gas, rising to 80–90 per cent by 2020. The UK Government attempted to influence the market through a moratorium on new gas-powered stations from 1997–2000; the Energy White Paper of 2003, whilst developing a framework for dealing with climate change, envisaged continued reliance on the market framework with some further support for renewable sources of energy. The paper was unenthusiastic about the development of new nuclear generation (Department of Trade and Industry 2003: para 1.24).

At this stage, then, broader matters of the public interest were seen as primarily a matter for limited government intervention; the market with regulation by Ofcom to ensure that it worked effectively was seen as the major means of organising the energy sector. However, things looked rather different by the time of the next energy review of 2006 (Department of Trade and Industry 2006). This made more radical proposals for ensuring security of supply, including the development of new strategic gas storage facilities, but most notably through developing new generating capacity as older stations came off-stream; by 2025 new capacity equivalent to 30 per cent of current capacity would be required. Very controversially, nuclear generation would have a role to play in the future UK generation mix. New nuclear stations would be proposed, developed, constructed and operated by the private sector which would also meet decommissioning costs and its share of long-term waste management costs. Planning procedures would be changed so that national strategic issues would be discussed elsewhere than in the public inquiry into individual generating stations.

The process, however, met with an unexpected setback when Greenpeace successfully challenged the decision to support the development of nuclear stations in the High Court.[3] The basis for the challenge was that the consultation undertaken by the Government had been inadequate, both because it had ignored a legitimate expectation created by a Government promise in the 2003 White Paper of 'the fullest public consultation' before policy on nuclear generation was decided, and because the consultation actually undertaken was inadequate to comply with the Government's obligations under the Aarhus Convention, notably that to 'provide opportunities for public participation in the preparation of policies relating to the environment' (article 7). This was despite the fact that a consultation paper had been issued and responses invited; there had also been seminars (including a 'stakeholder seminar' specifically on the nuclear power issue), conferences, receptions and other meetings. The Court held that the consultation exercise was 'very seriously flawed' because the consultation paper was merely an 'issues paper' seeking comments on which issues were important; it contained no proposals as such, and the information given to consultees was wholly insufficient to enable them to make an intelligent response. The information was particular inadequate on the economics of nuclear power and the disposal of nuclear waste.[4] As a result the Government had to repeat the consultation process; the White Paper which eventually emerged in 2007 had little new to say, and reiterated the Government's preliminary view that was in the public interest to give the private sector the option of investing in new nuclear power stations (Department of Trade and Industry 2007).

The process described so far raises two important issues related to the 'neo-institutionalist economics approach' to reflexive governance. This approach appears to have worked reasonably well in deciding the more economics-based issues, such as setting price controls for the network infrastructure and policing fair competition between the different participants in the energy sector. However, broader questions of the public interest were handled much less well, notably those relating to security of supply. This approach tends to dismiss these as externalities to be handled by the political process; however, the political process

---

[3] *R (on the application of Greenpeace) v Secretary of State for Trade and Industry* [2007] EWHC 311 (Admin).

[4] For a summary of the successful grounds for review, see [116]–[117] of Sullivan J's opinion.

itself did not handle them effectively and, in particular, its approach to public participation on a key policy issue was found to be wanting by the High Court. This might suggest that there was scope for broadening the process to a more deliberative, 'collaborative-relational' approach. However, this was not something required by the Court; its decision was that the 'externalist' conception of governance needed to work better, not be replaced by a different model. Thus, had the Government supplied adequate information to consultees on the major questions, its approach would have been acceptable to the Court. Nothing in these events suggests any move beyond the 'neo-institutionalist economics approach'. However, the question of security of supply was a major influence on other reforms which will now be considered, and it might have had further potential for 'progressive broadening' of the conditions for success of learning.

B.   Security of Supply and Planning Procedures

A key element in the 2006 energy review was that land-use planning procedures would be changed so that national strategic issues would be decided in a forum elsewhere than in individual public inquiries; this was relevant to developments such as gas storage facilities, but most particularly to the development of new nuclear generating stations. In land-use planning there has long been a concern with public participation as a central element in the process (for origins see Report of the Committee on Public Participation in Planning (the Skeffington Report) 1969). The most important means of such participation was historically the public inquiry, and this remains the major source for public participation in major decisions. However, other, more flexible means of participation have been used for the determination of general planning policy, notably the examination in public, and informal consultation has grown enormously, in part due to the impact of the Aarhus Convention. However, in the view of the Government, the public inquiry is an inappropriate tool for determining policy issues, in particular the need for a major development such as a new generating station. Experience has not been good with recent inquiries, such as that in 1985 into the last nuclear station to be built (Sizewell B) and into Terminal 5 at Heathrow Airport; the latter sat for 524 days and the approval process took a total of eight years.

In 2007 the Government published a Planning White Paper proposing a radically different system for the approval of major infrastructure projects, including new electricity generating stations and gas storage facilities (Department for Communities and Local Government et al 2007). The proposals are now implemented in the Planning Act 2008. In brief, the Act provides for the minister to issue a National Policy Statement setting out national policy in relation to a specified description of development. In doing so, the minister must engage in consultation and have regard to the responses received in deciding whether or not to go ahead with the proposal.[5] The minister must also respond to any resolution of Parliament or recommendation of a Parliamentary committee on the matter. Where an application is made for development consent for a 'nationally significant infrastructure project' (including electricity generating stations and gas storage facilities), this will be determined by a new Infrastucture Planning Commission, appointed by the minister. The Commission will be bound in most circumstances by the National Policy Statement, although it may diverge from it on limited grounds, including where it is satisfied that 'the adverse impact of the proposed development would outweigh its benefits'.[6] In making its decisions, account must be taken of the results of consultation, which must be undertaken by the applicant for permission before the application is made; local authorities are also to be invited by the Commission to submit 'local impact reports' on the likely impact of the proposed development.[7] The Commission itself has power to determine its procedure; in particular, its examination should take the form of consideration of written representations; oral hearings should only be held where necessary to ensure adequate examination of the issue or to give an interested party a fair chance to put its case.[8] Public open-floor hearings must also be held on request, though the aim of the procedure is to avoid the lengthy cross-examination characteristic of the public inquiry. Much of the procedure is to be determined by regulations which have not yet been published.

The general aim of the new legislation is thus to separate out the general question of the need for a development from the more detailed and local issues relating to the individual project; the latter will be for the Commission, and will be subject to a more flexible procedure than that of a full public inquiry. Considerable scepticism has been expressed by campaigners as to the likely effects; the procedure is seen as pre-judging the most important issues, whilst leaving participation arrangements only for the details, and these will be without the rights to effective cross-examination characteristic of the public inquiry. It may be, however, that this is to dismiss the new regime too quickly. There is a good case for differentiating the general policy proposals, for determination nationally, from the more detailed questions relating to individual projects. Much will depend on how effective the new consultation arrangements will be.

Two points need to be made in relation to the general REFGOV themes at this point. First, on the basis of what has occurred so far, the new proposals do seem to be very much still in the 'externalist' mode. Thus, consultation is a means of gathering information and views which can be considered by the minister in determining the national policy statement and put before the Commission in its decision on an individual project. There are no attempts, at least so far, to create

---

[5]   Planning Act 2008 s 7.
[6]   Planning Act 2008 s 104(7).
[7]   Ibid ss 42, 47, 50.
[8]   Ibid ss 90–1.

new venues for cooperative deliberation by all the parties which would characterise a move to the next level of a 'collaborative relational approach through
dialogue'. It may be that this could arise through the arrangements adopted for
consultation by the minister and by the Commission as part of considering the
application. However, the second point is that trust is seriously lacking in this
area, something to which the inadequate consultation on the energy policy issues
contributed. We shall return to both these points later; first, however, something
needs to be said about the German experience of liberalisation and, in particular,
the question of network access.

III.   DOMINANT AND EMERGING APPROACHES TO ENERGY GOVERNANCE IN GERMANY[9]

A.   Energy Liberalisation and Network Access; the First Model and Associations' Agreements

Liberalisation came later in Germany, and the industry structure was very
different from that of the United Kingdom and other European countries. Thus,
energy supply was already provided by private enterprises, and was highly
fragmented, involving over 1,500 network operators. In 1998 the German Energy
Industry Act (EnWG) was reformed for the first time because of the need to
implement the first EU gas and electricity directives.[10] Germany adopted an
approach to liberalisation based on negotiated access, and this took the form of
associations' agreements negotiated by the stakeholders in the sector (*Verbände-
vereinbarung*). Thus, cooperation took the form of voluntary agreements
between the private actors. The agreements built a framework for the terms on
which system use was granted on a contractual basis; they were not legally
binding norms but rather recommendations or guidelines; they did however
codify the conditions of network access and laid down access charges and tariffs
between system operators and users, as well as the methods for their calculation.
The agreements also set out the terms for technical and organisational cooperation for network.

This appears to be very much in line with what we would expect from a
neo-institutional economics approach to market governance. Thus, initiative is
left to private parties through the use of contract. What is remarkable, however,
was the very limited role for public regulation in the process, unlike the case of
the United Kingdom and other European countries. Britz and Herzmann (2008:
20) attribute this to the fact that 'the spirit of deregulation was rather strong
within the German government and the public debate at that time'; it also reflects

---

[9]   This section draws heavily on the REFGOV report by Britz and Herzmann (2008).
[10]   Council Directive (EC) 96/92 concerning common rules for the internal market in electricity
[1997] OJ L27/20 and Council Directive (EC) 98/30 concerning common rules for the internal
market in natural gas [1998] OJ L204/2.

the need to coordinate an already decentralised industry rather than to keep in check a formerly publicly owned dominant player in the markets. Reflecting this orientation, the negotiated network access approach was labelled a 'market solution' or 'deregulation by self-regulation' by the Government, while regulation was deemed as an antagonist to competition rather than a necessary precondition for competition in a market with natural monopolies. However, the implementation of associations' agreements led to a corporatist approach to regulation (Britz and Herzmann 2008: 20).

Thus, rather than having an independent regulatory authority, the regulation necessary to establish and protect new markets was delegated to associations.

This approach raised serious problems for the protection of broader public interests, which were in some cases completely excluded from the institutional arrangements. Thus, the associations of industrial consumers played a prominent role in energy politics, and indeed were signatories to the first associations' agreements. As a third player an association representing the interests of municipal public utilities joined the negotiations from quite an early stage. However, domestic (household) energy consumers were completely excluded from the negotiations, as were other stakeholders such as environmentalists, agricultural consumers, foreign companies, public utilities and energy traders (Britz and Herzmann 2008: 21). At a later stage with the negotiation of the third electricity agreement in 2001, the German Association of Consumer Advice Centres and Consumer Councils did take part in the final round of negotiations, but refused to sign it as a protest at its shortcomings in protecting consumer interests (Britz and Herzmann 2008: 22). Moreover, the Federal Government as the 'trustee of consumer interests' was not directly involved in the negotiations. It did have (although it did not use) powers to enact general terms of network access in default of agreement between the associations, but had only indirect influence on the negotiations themselves. Other supervision of individual cases by the courts and the European Commission was possible but hardly took place. Furthermore, a rather general market survey was carried out by the German Monopolies Commission, a committee acting as an independent board of experts in questions of competition policy, which had initially agreed with the method of using associations' agreements as they expected it to lead to faster market opening (Britz and Herzmann 2008: 24).

However, when the associations in the gas sector could not agree, the public authorities stepped in to take further action. The European Commission threatened to initiate infringement proceedings and the German Government used the threat to the industry that it would establish a regulatory authority for the gas sector. Agreement was then quickly reached, but this was found to be inadequate by the German Monopolies Commission, which now was also highly critical of arrangements in electricity as threatening liberalisation and risking a return to the pre-liberalisation position of secure but very expensive supply (Britz and Herzmann 2008: 25).

Further reform of the Energy Law took place in 2003; however it did not amount to fundamental change in the regulatory approach. It implemented the gas directive and created a legal framework for the associations' agreements. This was needed because in the absence of a legal commitment individual network operators could diverge from particular aspects of the agreements and negotiate contractual conditions on their own (Britz and Herzmann 2008: 26). The agreements still lacked a directly binding legal effect, but the amended law stated that conditions for network access had to comply with 'good professional practice'. Such practice was to be assumed so long as the clauses of individual contracts were in compliance with the standards defined in the associations' agreements, which were themselves published in the Federal Bulletin as were provisions of state law. This reform thus strengthened the legal status of the associations' agreements by awarding a degree of state recognition (Britz and Herzmann 2008: 26). It was only a temporary provision, but even after its expiry the 'good professional practice' approach continued to be applied by the courts.

Thus, the first stage of liberalisation was based around the negotiation of contracts by private parties rather than regulatory decisions taken by a public authority; it was closed to interests and viewpoints outside the industry and large industrial consumers. This represented a fundamental weakness in the process as it limited any opportunities for broader social learning. Moreover, it should be noted that it was the industry associations which were responsible for determining the content of the agreements, not individual enterprises. This meant that the arrangements were also strongly corporatist in character (Britz and Herzmann 2008: 20). This form of corporatism once more excluded important interests, including domestic consumers and, to a considerable degree, the Federal Government itself. Thus both the model of governance adopted and the corporatist nature of the institutional arrangements had the effect of seriously limiting the extent to which any learning could take place through the incorporation of outside viewpoints. In the absence of any supervisory authority, even 'external' arrangements for an 'externalist' conception of learning were lacking. This was supposed to take place through decentralised market transactions, but the corporatist nature of the agreements looked very different from any fully decentralised process. As a result, according to Britz and Herzmann (2008: 38) in the case of network access the legal framework did not provide for such sufficient mending of the market mechanism in order to be called an institutional economics approach. Furthermore, the *centralised* approach of the associations' agreements, which set general conditions for all contracts between network operators and their clients, can neither be described as a pure market approach nor can it be classified as an institutional economics approach.

B.   Energy Liberalisation and Network Access; the Second Model and Creation of the Regulator

Impetus for reform came from the second EU electricity and gas directives.[11] These effectively prevented Germany from continuing with the approach based on associations' agreements and instead meant that henceforth network access had to be regulated by a national regulatory authority (Britz and Herzmann 2008: 28). After considerable and difficult regulatory debate, a new Energy Industry Act came into force on 13 July 2005; this was a much longer and more detailed statute than its predecessors; it established a national regulatory authority as well as introducing new regulatory instruments.

The new federal authority took the form of the Federal Network Agency (*Bundesnetzagentur*), a successor to that previously existing for telecommunications and postal services, and had new regulatory responsibilities for the energy sector. These were stated as follows: '[r]egulation of energy and gas grids shall provide a basis for an effective and genuine competition for energy supply as well as safeguard a highly productive and reliable grid operation in the long-run'. In addition to this federal regulator, complementary authorities were established at the level of the 16 German states (*Laender*) with responsibility for regulating local energy system operators providing energy for fewer than 100,000 clients or whose grids do not cross the borders of German states. A common committee was created to facilitate communication between the different authorities.

A major responsibility of the Federal Network Agency is to ensure non-discriminatory third-party access to networks. The legal framework thus sets out model requirements corresponding to the access scheme in the former associations' agreements for electricity, and establishing similar provisions for establishing non-discriminatory gas network access. To some extent it continues to rely on cooperation between private actors and stipulates duties of cooperation between them, but with important new elements. These include non-discriminatory access to the network guaranteed and regulated in more detail by statute; further unbundling of grid operations in vertically integrated energy supply companies, as well as ex-ante and ex-post price regulation. The former includes a duty to apply for approval of network charges and the introduction of incentive regulation; the latter the supervision of market abuse.

To consider these in more detail, the statute provides a general right to network connection for all potential buyers and sellers under adequate, non-discriminatory and transparent conditions, which must not differ from those network operators which apply within their own business or to associated companies. Claims for

---

[11]   Council Directive (EC) 2003/54 concerning common rules for the internal market in electricity [2003] OJ L176/57; Council Directive (EC) 2003/55concerning common rules for the internal market in natural gas [2003] OJ L176/57.

network connection and network access can be enforced by court order or by an order by the regulatory authority. According to Britz and Herzmann, however (2008: 31),

> [t]he crucial point of the change in the regulation of network access in Germany has been that prices and conditions are no longer subject to private actors' negotiations and association agreements, but are stipulated by law to a larger extent and are controlled by a powerful regulatory authority.

There is also a detailed framework for price regulation; the basic model is cost-based, but in emerging markets a more market-oriented approach may be adopted. Furthermore, there is the possibility of adopting an incentive-based approach to price regulation, as is characteristic of the British utility regulators and which has recently become the standard approach of the German energy regulator.

As Britz and Herzmann have emphasised, this appears at first sight to represent a move 'from deliberation to hierarchy' with initial approaches to market access based on negotiation between private associations being replaced by direct regulatory intervention, similar to 'command and control' regulation. However, as they also stress, this would be to misread the recent history. The drawing-up of the associations' agreements did not in fact provide effective deliberation as 'the process of developing associations' agreements was not oriented on facilitating communication, deliberation and participation, but rather on bargaining and haggling' (Britz and Herzmann 2008: 38). The process was in fact inflexible and characterised by an imbalance of power; interests of those other than the energy industry and of large industrial consumers could only be introduced into the process by state actors, which did not take part.

If the first stage of network access does not resemble anything truly deliberative, the second stage is also not a simple example of 'command and control' regulation. This raises the important issue of the degree to which the regulator itself is able to act as a focus for participatory procedures, something already discussed in relation to the United Kingdom. The duties applying to the regulator do include duties to monitor aspects of energy markets, to evaluate the regulatory structures, and to report on a number of other aspects of its work and use of regulatory instruments. It is also required in some circumstances to set up committees, hold hearings and to engage in consultation and facilitation. In these respects it does resemble the operation of Ofgem in the United Kingdom, though, as with the UK regulator, nothing in the statutory requirements goes beyond the 'neo-institutionalist economic' model of an externalist conception of learning. The extent to which there is potential to move beyond this will be considered in the next section of this chapter, after discussion of similar potential in the UK institutions.

IV. LESSONS TO BE DRAWN FROM RELIANCE ON THE 'NEO-INSTITUTIONALIST ECONOMIC' APPROACH IN THE UK

It will be recalled that the approach adopted in the United Kingdom involved breaking up previously unified dominant enterprises through privatisation and a combination of liberalisation and regulation. Unlike Germany, an independent regulator in the form of Ofgem and its predecessors was set up immediately; however, it took some time for it to adopt effective participatory techniques through consultation and reason-giving (Prosser 1997: chapters 4, 6). When this was done it was through the adoption of highly 'externalist' techniques involving requesting the submission of evidence from interested parties which is then evaluated by the regulator and forms the basis for its decisions, for which reasoned justifications are given. In relation to major decisions, successive rounds of such consultation may be carried out, each building on the previous one. To a considerable degree this process has been successful within its own terms; the House of Lords Select Committee on Regulators, in a recent report, noted that '[s]everal representatives of regulated industries have told us that communication channels are working well and they feel fully consulted and in the loop'. Moreover, '[r]egulators seem to have put a lot of effort into developing their consultative procedures. Witnesses from regulated industries frequently commended the regulators for developing consultation procedures that are thorough, open and continually improving' (Select Committee on Regulators 2006–07: paras 5.6, 5.24). Indeed, one of the few criticisms of the process was that too many consultation papers were published; in 2005–06 Ofgem published no fewer than 218 consultations and other documents.

It appears, however, that this 'externalist' model of governance has difficulty in coping with two types of issues. The first is that of effective consumer representation, even within a predominantly market-based model. The institutional form for such representation has been subject to constant change. Thus, for gas, a separate Gas Consumers' Council was established at privatisation to perform a representative function and to advise the regulator; for electricity the regulator appointed regional committees with a coordinating national council. After the unification of the two regulators, a new independent consumer council was established to cover both fuels, and it adopted the title of Energywatch; similar arrangements were adopted for other regulated utilities. Energywatch achieved a relatively high public profile; however its performance was criticised as unimpressive in relation to its costs by a Parliamentary committee, and various studies found evidence of serious tensions and adversarial relations between consumer councils and regulators (Committee of Public Accounts 2005–06). The Government then issued two consultation papers culminating in reform by the Consumers, Estate Agents and Redress Act 2007. This legislation abolished Energywatch, passing its responsibilities to a new National Consumer Council representing the interests of consumers in all sectors, which has now taken the title Consumer Focus. The Act also required that the regulators prescribe service standards and the Secretary of State may require that providers of services are to be members of approved redress schemes.

These difficulties in establishing effective consumer representation may show an inherent weakness in the 'neo-institutionalist economics' approach. Under this model, consumers express their preferences through the marketplace. They do so as individuals, and so to set up collective means of representation is both unnecessary and difficult to make compatible with other aspects of the model. In particular, it does not sit easily with an 'externalist' conception of governance, in which learning is based on the regulator responding to external stimuli (in a way analogous to market transactions) rather than taking steps to organise learning processes which may transform input through collective deliberations.

The second problem that the system has faced has been difficulty in coping with a number of public policy objectives which cannot easily be internalised by the regulatory body. One example has been discussed earlier; that of security of supply. A second is that of climate change policy. As we saw earlier, the model adopted at privatisation led to the 'rush to gas' seen as potentially raising major security of supply issues, whilst the meeting of climate change goals has been a major theme in governmental energy policy, especially since the 2003 Energy White Paper. The main point is that both security of supply and climate change policy are matters for government rather than independent regulators, and there has been some doubt as to how they can be fitted into regulatory decision-making. A further such issue is that of fuel poverty, which has been aggravated by recent major fuel price increases; the Government has a policy and objectives on this area, and has increasingly also expected the regulator to play a role.

One effect of the growing salience of these issues is that the role of the regulator has been changed; it no longer makes sense to think of Ofgem as a *wholly* independent body (although it remains independent from the Government in its day-to-day decision-making). Thus, the Utilities Act 2000, which set up the reformed system of unified energy regulation, included a power for the minister to issue guidance to Ofgem on social and economic matters and Ofgem must have regard to this in its decision-making.[12] Such guidance was issued after consultation in 2002; it was amended in 2004 after the Energy White Paper, and a further draft was put out for consultation in 2008, setting out the Government's policies and expectations as to the regulator's contribution. On the issue of sustainable development, Ofgem's statutory duties were amended to require it to have regard to this issue in its decision-making; the Energy Act 2008 upgraded the importance of this duty and changed the reference to consumers whose interests Ofgem is to protect to 'existing and future' consumers. Thus there have been statutory attempts to broaden the range of matters relevant to Ofgem decisions; the Government has now committed itself to further broadening by

---

[12]   ss 10 (inserting a new s 4AA(3) into the Gas Act 1986) and s 13 (inserting a new s 3B into the Electricity Act 1989).

amending Ofgem's duties to include security of supply and reducing carbon emissions. What is lacking, however, is any structured set of institutional procedures for the joint development of principles through deliberation. Policy remains a matter for government using its standard processes, not a joint matter for government and regulator through a form of deliberative collaboration.

As was described above, the security of supply issue has moved public participation issues to a new set of fora; those in land-use planning which will be used for the decisions to be taken on new generating stations and extensions of existing ones, and also on gas storage facilities. It should be noted first of all that the initial consultation on the policy change to acceptance of the need for new nuclear capacity was deeply flawed, as the High Court established. This was largely due to its extremely 'externalist' nature; the Government simply issued a paper setting out the key issues with limited information to be submitted from outside for it to use in decision-making; there was no attempt to engage even in a minimum of reflexive debate to create opportunities for mutual learning. Although the High Court forced the Government to repeat the consultation exercise with the provision of fuller information, even at this stage the approach was very much the 'externalist' one, and indeed was criticised heavily once again for failing to meet the minimum requirements of this model; for example public statements by ministers suggested that the outcome had been pre-judged before the consultation had been completed.

Decisions on the developments of facilities will now be taken under the new procedures under the Planning Act 2008. It should first be noted that planning procedures have in the past been characterised by a tension between the 'externalist' approach for participation and one which is closer to the 'collaborative or relational' approach. This in turn reflects a fundamental set of tensions within this area of law between a 'private property' approach to protect the interests of landowners, a 'public interest' approach designed to implement public policy goals, and a more effectively participative approach in which a range of different interests can be represented in decision-making (McAuslan 1980). Thus, the traditional mode of the public inquiry represents a mix of both approaches; its adversarial nature does permit the participation of interests, including interest groups, through a form of deliberation, whilst leaving the ultimate decision to the minister. Thus it accepts that there are competing public and private interests, but assumes that a consensus solution can be possible through participation and compromise on each decision. However, it does not actively organise social interests to facilitate participation, but merely provides a means for inputs by outside interests, in particular by property owners. This has given rise to serious problems through the lack of resources of those attempting to participate, and through restrictions on the ability of inquiries to debate fully underlying issues of government policy.[13]

---

[13]   See *Bushell v Secretary of State for the Environment* [1981] AC 75.

As the traditional adversary public inquiry has been unsuitable for examining policy issues, it was replaced in some areas of planning by less adversary procedures, for example the examination in public used for the development of regional spatial strategies, which is an informal way of considering only selected issues with no right for parties to be heard. Alongside this there have also been attempts to enhance the collaborative capacities of those participating; these form part of the process of consensus-based collaborative planning of the 1980s and 1990s. Thus, the Planning and Compulsory Purchase Act 2004 and the accompanying 2004 Planning Policy Statement 12 provide new guidance for stakeholder engagement, emphasising that this should be early, use methods of involvement relevant to the communities concerned, provide continuing involvement rather than simply a one-off event, and build involvement into the process for the preparation and revision of statutory Local Development Documents; a published Statement of Community Involvement is also required. The Local Government Act 2000 also placed a duty on local authorities to prepare local community strategies, often setting up a Local Strategic Partnership bringing together the public, private, voluntary and community sectors to do so. Thus, in these areas of planning there are distinct elements of a more collaborative or relational approach, without, however, any developed form of monitoring or benchmarking which could develop a more general process of social learning through the experience gained in these different approaches.

It is also striking that these developments are not concerned with major infrastructure projects; indeed, one procedure which could have contributed to such an approach in relation to them was never used. This was that of the Planning Inquiry Commission, power to establish these being included in the Town and Country Planning Act 1990.[14] This would have been a two-stage process, with the first being a roving, unrestricted investigation followed by a local inquiry. The process would have been highly unpredictable and would have directly impinged on government policy itself, which explains why it was never employed.

Can the reforms under the Planning Act 2008 provide an opportunity for the development of a more collaborative or relational approach to major infrastructure project developments? A cynical view, shared for example by campaigning organisations, is that it is designed to do precisely the reverse by pre-empting local decisions through the making of national policy statements by government without the need for any formal process of inquiry into them, and by weakening the opportunities offered previously by the adversary public inquiry, which, whatever its weaknesses, did at least offer the possibility of detailed examination of proposals through legal techniques of cross-examination. On this view the new proposals not only fail to develop anything beyond an 'externalist' approach but restrict further this minimal approach to social learning. A contrary view is that

---

[14] Town and Country Planning Act 1990 s 101.

the inquiry system was unworkable in relation to major infrastructural projects, and that the sheer length of procedures was itself a deterrent to any form of public participation; moreover, individual inquiries were unsuitable for considering developments closely related to national policies. The new procedures can be seen as providing greater accountability for national policy through requiring it to be made public in advance after a process of consultation; the further safeguards through requiring developers to consult and through the processes before the Infrastructure Planning Commission will provide opportunities for scrutiny other than by adversarial cross-examination. Thus, this could provide a basis for developing something closer to a more 'collaborative-relational' approach.

Which of these views is more appropriate will only become clearer after the details of the requirements for consultation and participation appear when regulations are issued under the Act, and when we have some practical experience of the process. However, it is possible to point to three potential problems which may constitute obstacles to progression toward a more 'collaborative-relational' form of social learning. The first is that the reforms were explicitly based on a concern to minimise the administrative cost and delays imposed by earlier participative arrangements; one of the themes has been to increase central control over the participation process at the individual decision-making stage to minimise such cost and delays. This hardly provides a promising basis for a more reflexive and thus unpredictable approach. The second problem is that of the uncertain relationship between the use of more decentralised techniques for learning and the development of national policy on the framework for electricity generation; again, decentralisation is likely to threaten what government still regards as its prerogative of national policy-making, which can mean that the scope for decisions on more local implementation can be seriously constrained, and indeed pre-empted.

The final, and most important problem, is that of a lack of trust in relation to these processes. The importance of trust in public administration and in economic life has been increasingly recognised (see for example Fukuyama 1995, Hollis 1998, O'Neill 2002). Absence of trust is indeed one manifestation of deeper tensions; for example, markets both require trust for their operation and create essentially low-trust environments through the associated model of man as a self-interested utility maximiser (Hollis 1998: chapters 6 and 8). Similarly, if policy is decided centrally, participation in local decisions may increase mistrust as these decisions are seen as shams unable to influence *faits accomplis*. Possible means of overcoming problems of trust will be identified near the end of this chapter.

V.   LESSONS TO BE DRAWN FROM RELIANCE ON THE 'NEO-INSTITUTIONALIST ECONOMIC' APPROACH IN GERMANY

It will be recalled from the discussion of Germany above that attempts at self- and co-regulation of network access failed, and produced what appeared to be a 'return to hierarchy' through the creation of an independent regulatory agency with legal powers of intervention. The first lesson to be drawn is a simple one; that there are major limits to the participative opportunities offered by self-regulation. As was described earlier, major interests were excluded from the process, notably household consumers and even government itself. This contributed to a highly unstable process that did not even comply with the requirements of even the most basic form of 'externalist' participation. The failure to reach agreement on an associations' agreement for the gas sector also meant that the process of self-regulation failed in its own terms of creating a basis for agreeing basic rules to facilitate network access.

Secondly, there is an important distinction to be made between deliberation and bargaining (Britz and Herzmann 2008: 38–39). The development of the associations' agreements did not involve a process of mutual learning; it 'was not oriented on facilitating communication, deliberation and participation, but rather on bargaining and haggling' (Britz and Herzmann 2008: 38). The very weak role of central government, and the absence of a supervising regulatory authority, meant that participants were not forced to reassess their own positions and to reach consensus, but rather to try to maximise their own interests through a bargaining process, one profoundly influenced by imbalances of power between participants. This points to a weakness in the 'neo-institutional economics' approach to governance; as chapter one of this book suggested, it is highly 'externalist' in nature and sees the process of reaching agreement as a series of trade-offs between preferences and interests, not as a means of mutual learning. Indeed, as noted above, the initial German approach failed even to meet the basic requirements of this governance approach.

If the German experience points to the limits of self-regulation, it also suggests that the reformed arrangements introduced in 2005 are not simply a 'return to hierarchy', not simply an example of 'command and control' regulation. Thus, Britz and Herzmann point to three ways of improving social learning within this new form of sectoral regulation; these are enhancing the process of self-regulation, 'mending' the market's ability to act as a learning method by improving the conditions for its functioning or simulating the effect of market forces, and enhancing the learning capacities of the regulatory authority itself (Britz and Herzmann 2008: 39–59).

Thus, self-regulation can be enhanced by the development of rules to give guidance as to the most appropriate means of coordination; apart from those directly provided by the law itself, the latter can also require cooperation by market actors whilst limiting the scope for the outcomes which can be reached, and providing that, should there be a failure to reach agreement, the public authority can substitute its own. Thus

> the agency tries to take part actively in some of the processes in a non-hierarchical way, and secondly, it now tries to integrate all interests concerned. Within these processes the agency does not see its prior task in executing the law, but in a 'Moderation' of the self-regulated processes of quasi-rulemaking of private actors. (Britz and Herzmann 2008: 41).

Stimulation and simulation of market forces can take place in ways which enhance its ability to develop a 'discovery process' through transparency obligations, and through the development of incentive regulation which aims to establish the same sets of incentives as an operating market where natural monopoly problems make the latter unfeasible. The normal form of the latter is through price controls set to encourage efficiency savings, which can be retained by network operators should they exceed those assumed when the price control is set; which have been the basis for price control in UK public utilities since 1984, although Ofgem is currently reviewing the appropriateness of this approach for the future.

Turning to the regulatory agency itself, the agency has a number of duties which have a reflexive character. Thus, for example, it is required to monitor the development of specified aspects of the energy markets, including the degree of competition and transparency in them, and the development of competition in networks from the domestic consumers' point of view. Monitoring is defined as 'a systematic, reflexive, periodical or permanent view on and analysis of the actual state and the changes of complex alterable systems by an agency, which is not mandatorily linked with some further legal consequences' (Britz and Herzmann 2008: 48). The agency also has evaluation duties, reporting on the experience and results of the regulatory arrangements after two years. It also has to issue an annual report covering all the sectors regulated, and every second year the Monopolies Commission must report on the development of market-making and competition in the energy sector and on the use of regulatory instruments.

The agency must also coordinate its activities with the regulatory authorities of the *Laender*, with the regulators of other EU Member States and with the European Commission. It must engage in consultation of interests and maintain a dialogue with market actors in developing legally-binding market rules. These consultations take the form both of exchanges with representative associations and broader procedures after the publication of concepts or questions and then seeking responses. The procedures also aim to involve associations representing household consumers, who may take part in hearings and may open an abuse proceeding against a network operator; this is a major advance on the previous arrangements where such associations were excluded from the process. The regulator can also appoint a scientific advisory committee. Importantly, and in contrast to much German constitutional tradition, the agency also has important quasi-rule-making powers of its own to fill normative gaps, although it does not have the power to issue full ordinances, which is only available when special constitutional conditions are met.

Important as all these examples of more 'reflexive regulation' may be, a note of caution should be sounded here. All of them (except those resulting from the federal structure) have long been familiar in UK regulatory practice, and have been increasingly incorporated into UK legislation. What the German reforms have achieved is certainly not a move from the 'externalist' model to a more collaborative or relational one; instead it has secured the conditions for a properly operating 'externalist' or 'neo-institutionalist economics' approach to governance.

One final lesson can be drawn from the developments discussed here; this is the importance of national constitutional traditions in determining the scope for different forms of reflexive governance. Thus, the United Kingdom is a strongly Parliamentary-based democracy, and accountability for policy is seen as a matter for Parliament questioning the minister. There is a considerable mistrust of other institutions at the level of policy-making (though not of its implementation) and this explains some of the difficulties in developing participative institutions outside Parliament at this level. It also explains the continuing role of Parliament in scrutinising national policy statements under the Planning Act 2008.[15] In Germany, also a strongly Parliamentary-based democracy, a constitutionally-influenced distrust of regulatory agencies with substantial policy-making or rule-making powers also contributed to an early preference for forms of self-regulation which proved inadequate to incorporate the whole gamut of different interests in this field or to incorporate any general public interest (Britz and Herzmann 2008: 13–16).

VI.   TRANSATLANTIC COMPARATIVE LESSONS AND INSIGHTS FROM THE CANADIAN CASE

The three provincial case studies of electricity market reform (Alberta, Ontario, Quebec) in the multi-level context of Canadian federalism and North American regional integration under the North American Free Trade Agreement (NAFTA)[16] support but also complement the lessons apparent in the UK and Germany cases.

First, the Canadian case provides confirmation and evidence for the dominance of liberalisation and market reform as the paradigm of recent energy policy. The advent of US energy market liberalisation exerted strong pressures on Canadian counterparts to follow suit, in the context of an asymmetrical trading

---

[15]   See, in particular, the Planning Act 2008 s 9.

[16]   The detailed report on the Canadian case ('Electricity Market Reforms and Governance Models – Canada Energy Case Study', Toronto, September 2008) is available at: http://refgov.cpdr.ucl.ac.be/. For a comparative analysis of energy policy in Canada and Germany see Eberlein and Doern (2008).

relationship that leaves Canadians concerned about access to US markets. At the same time, liberalisation was promoted by provincial politicians who embraced neo-liberal ideology[17] as a way to enhance efficiency that had arguably suffered under the traditional 'Hydro' model of public monopoly. These two factors combined strongly to favour the dominance of the 'neo-institutionalist economics' approach — at least in terms of the political agenda.

Secondly, however, and not dissimilar to the transition problems noted in the German case, the *implementation* of a proper 'institutional economics approach' proved quite complicated and remains in many respects incomplete. The history of electricity market restructuring in Canada is indeed as much one of policy reversals and re-regulation as it is one of 'marketisation' (Trebilcock and Hrab 2006). Next to the contingencies of botched reform attempts, the legacy effects of the traditional Hydro model (and its continuing legitimacy with citizens) and the constraints of the traditional Westminster model of executive control play important roles in accounting for the incomplete transition to the 'externalist' model.

The institutional economics model requires the establishment of regulators that monitor (self-regulatory) market developments to ensure market efficiency, and that may also address, to some degree, negative external effects. There has been a significant growth of new bodies and authorities in the sector, reflecting functional differentiation along the value chain and the separation of a regulatory function post-liberalisation. However, in all three provinces, elected officials have generally been reluctant to delegate effective regulatory powers to newly created agencies, and have preferred to keep tight political control of the liberalisation process. This even included direct and ad-hoc political intervention, more typical of the previous, hierarchical public monopoly model, as in the case of the Government of Ontario that intervened to reverse the deregulation of residential electricity tariffs, after consumer protests over price spikes.

This incidence also points to a larger interesting issue emerging from the Canadian case studies, namely a certain resistance by the general electorate to see its role transformed from recipients of a (subsidised) public service to consumers in a much more volatile, liberalised electricity market. However, this has not translated into demands for more progressive forms of participation and deliberation about the public interest goals involved in energy supply. Citizens focused on traditional channels of communication in an electorally-driven political process in order to defend their vested interests and often (especially in Ontario) elected officials obliged by reneging their political commitment to market reforms in the face of political backlash.

Therefore, thirdly, regulators (or other bodies or venues) could not emerge as an independent institution available to organise or host new participatory and

---

[17] With the exception of Quebec elites who took a pragmatic, liberal approach driven by trading interests, ie the prospects of lucrative electricity exports to the United States.

social learning processes, however imperfect these consultative mechanisms may be in practice (as demonstrated by the UK case). While new bodies such as the Ontario Power Authority have organised broad consultation exercises (about the future supply mix in Ontario), the primacy of executive decision-making under the traditional Westminster model of representative democracy has not been challenged. Alternative venues for effective stakeholder participation and social learning processes beyond the electoral link between citizens and elected officials have not been created (although, in fairness, this seems to have happened in other policy areas such as healthcare).

At one level, one might argue that this high degree of centralisation of decision-making in the provincial government alleviates concerns about integration of competing public policy goals when there is a division of roles and powers between regulators (and/or other bodies of decision-making) and the political executive, as seen in the United Kingdom. The definition of the 'public interest' in the Canadian provinces seems to rest firmly lodged in the traditional political process with the provincial executive at its helm. New issues such as security of supply and climate change are fed into the regular political process. To be sure, there is intense interest group activity surrounding these issues, but this occurs in a logic of lobbying (with clear asymmetries of influence between industry versus other groups), not in an approach of cooperative deliberation. While this constellation may deliver certain benefits associated with a clear allocation of decision-making powers, it has significant costs as well — it clearly impoverishes the deliberative quality of the process.

In sum, the resilience of national constitutional traditions, as noted above for the UK and Germany case, thus seems to act as an important constraint on the development of more advanced models of social learning and participation.

VII.   FUTURE DIRECTIONS AND PROPOSALS FOR DEVELOPING GREATER REFLEXIVITY OF GOVERNANCE IN ENERGY

A.   Likely Future Directions within the 'Externalist' Model

In considering future directions for reflexivity in the governance of energy, there are two different issues for consideration. The first is the way in which development is likely to take place within the 'externalist' model of governance; this is the model which is likely to be maintained should current approaches be perpetuated. The second is the question of what action can be taken through institutional reform to permit a broadening of the conditions for success in learning to take governance closer to a more deliberative, 'collaborative-relational' approach.

Turning to the first issue, in the United Kingdom the first problem will be how to incorporate successfully into regulatory decision-making broader issues of climate change and security of energy supply. The system of regulation was established well before these concerns arose, and was designed primary to police competitive markets and act as surrogate for markets in areas of natural monopoly. The key objective was that of regulatory independence from government, primarily to encourage private investment in the industry through avoiding unpredictable government intervention. However, these new concerns are also the responsibility of government as well as being highly relevant to regulatory decision-making itself. It is possible that the key concept of regulatory independence will change to one of regulatory partnership between regulator and government. This does not, however, imply any broadening beyond the 'externalist' model of governance. Such partnership already exists in other areas of UK regulation, for example in the regulation of food standards and of health and safety. We can see some moves towards it in reforms undertaken to the system of utility regulation over the last 10 years, such as the power for ministers to issue social and environmental guidance to regulators and the re-drafting of their duties to include having regard to sustainable development. What is most likely is that relatively minor reforms of this type will continue without fundamental change to the regulatory system.

In relation to the planning issues relating to security of supply, what is most likely here is also a continuation of the 'externalist' model of governance. The reforms in the Planning Act 2008 will most probably result in a streamlining of the procedures, with a greater separation between the levels of determining national policy and local implementation, but without major innovation in the techniques for public involvement. What may be lost is the role of the traditional adversary public inquiry with use of cross-examination to probe government proposals in detail. However, a possible result of this may be that the use of the courts increases as an alternative means of securing outside scrutiny of proposals, and as an attempt to increase the effectiveness of consultation requirements and commitments to consult by government. As we have already seen, challenge in the courts has already been used successfully in relation to the inadequate consultation on security of supply issues and the move towards the building of fresh nuclear capacity. A particularly important question will be the extent to which both procedural and substantive rights under the European Convention on Human Rights apply in this area following their incorporation into domestic law by the Human Rights Act 1998. So far the approach of the courts has been cautious, but there is no guarantee that future decisions will not be more interventionist.[18] Whatever the role of the courts, however, it is not likely to result in the imposition of requirements which go beyond that of the 'externalist' approach.

Turning to Germany, what seems likely is a continuation of the existing trends resulting from the 2005 reforms. Given the relative novelty of the model of the independent regulatory agency in Germany, there will be learning from other

---

[18] See *R v (on the application of Alconbury Developments Ltd) v Secretary of State for the Environment, Transport and the Regions* [2001] UKHL 23; *cf Tsfayo v UK* [2007] LGR 1, ECtHR.

nations which have a well-established tradition of such agencies, notably the United Kingdom. Indeed, such learning from national experience will be facilitated by European Union developments, notably the issuing by the Commission of annual reviews of energy liberalisation and regulations, continuing a well-established practice in the liberalised electronic communications sector (see eg European Commission 2009). It is also likely that there will be further developments in the more reflexive regulatory approaches identified above; notably monitoring, consultation and facilitation, and the development of more effective agency rule-making powers. Once more, all these developments can be placed firmly within the 'externalist' or 'neo-institutionalist economics' approaches to governance; indeed, as was noted above, the importance of the 2005 reforms was to establish the conditions for the successful working of this model, not for any broadening beyond it.

In the Canadian case, finally, the primary challenge for the immediate future seems to be to fully implement a coherent 'externalist' approach to electricity market governance, before attention can turn to 'broadening' or 'internalisation'. There are signs in the province of Ontario, for example, that a new balance between political control of major policy directions (investments, fuel mix) on the one hand, and giving room to market mechanisms in an arm's-length regulatory process of 'controlled liberalisation' might be emerging. It remains to be seen, however, to which extent this will be accompanied by the establishment (and empowerment) of alternatives sites (such as independent bodies) or venues and mechanisms that would allow for a broader, and more cooperative deliberation of public interest goals in energy supply.

B.   Conditions for the Broadening of the Externalist Model

In this section discussion will turn to the ways in which the model described above could be 'broadened', resulting in transformation into a more deliberative approach closer to the 'collaborative-relational approach through dialogue' identified in chapter one of this book. It will include both the basic principles necessary for such a broadening and some of the institutional reforms to achieve it.

The most fundamental obstacle to such broadening is that of absence of trust. This has meant that it has been impossible for new procedures to be introduced without them being regarded as merely symbolic means to justify publicly decisions already taken privately. Any proposals for new public participation have been regarded as shams. Thus, any proposals for broadening reflexive governance must primarily be a means of restoring trust in the participatory process. It is particularly important where there is a move to a more ambitious and deliberative (or even experimentalist) approach to participation, where by definition the ground-rules are weaker than in the 'economic-institutionalist' approach. The absence of trust, particularly where decisions appear pre-empted, has been the major problem in the UK experience described here. As in the *R (on the application of Greenpeace) v Secretary of State for Trade and Industry* case,[19] absence of trust is likely to make recourse to the courts more likely, yet this compounds the problem because adversarial litigation is itself a low-trust form of monitoring government. Problems of trust exist at both national and at local level, and are seriously exacerbated by confusions between each level of decision-making.

The UK experience has a number of other implications for the establishment of a more deliberative approach. The first is that the *level* at which decisions are made is central to effective institutional design (a point already evident from research on multi-level governance). Clarity is crucial on the relationship between procedures for participation in national policy-making on the one hand, and local sub-policies and local implementation on the other. It is essential that procedures are adopted that are sensitive to the level of decision in question, and in particular that that decision taken at one level do not pre-empt those at others, making any form of participation in the latter meaningless. In the past in the United Kingdom, national policy has (at least in theory) been subject to Parliamentary accountability, but it has been possible for decisions included in it to be reopened at the local level. The reforms under the Planning Act 2008 can be seen positively as a recognition of the distinction between national policy and local implementation; however, the predominant role of the national policy statements and resulting fears that they will pre-empt later stages of participation have led to a crucial lack of trust in the procedures.

The second principle which can be drawn from the UK experience is that the timing of participatory arrangements is of great importance. This might appear obvious but the past practice suggests that it is not; the late use of participatory procedures after decisions have been assumed to have been finalised, and the rushing through of proposals with only limited time for participatory arrangements have contributed substantially to the absence of trust. Against this, of course, has to be balanced what may be important reasons for avoiding serious delays in the taking of major decisions, especially in the context of energy supply where problems have to be anticipated many years in advance. Moreover, the formal means of participation through lengthy public inquiries may both exhaust the resources of campaigning groups and delay necessary developments. What is needed is a set of procedures which are both flexible and well-planned to make participation effective.

Finally, in attempting to combat the low level of trust in relation to current participatory procedures, an effective system for monitoring and benchmarking is essential. In the UK experience, there have been only very limited arrangements for the monitoring of the effectiveness of participatory arrangements and for

---

[19] *R (on the application of Greenpeace) v Secretary of State for Trade and Industry* [2007] EWHC 311 (Admin).

benchmarking them to establish best practice. This is in marked contrast to the now highly developed procedures to monitor policy-making to achieve 'better regulation' (see the discussion by Colin Scott in this volume). Yet, more effective forms of independent monitoring are essential to develop both reflexivity (through learning from experience) and trust.

These principles derivable from the UK experience lead to suggestions for possible institutional reforms to contribute to a 'broadening' of the process of decision-making so as to contribute to greater reflexivity. The first is simple in principle but difficult to achieve in practice; it is for a clear hierarchy of decision-making with policy determination at the top. The arrangements under the Planning Act 2008 go some way towards this through the system of national policy statements; however, what is necessary is that policy be made publicly and that there are arrangements for participation in its formulation. It has yet to be seen how these will be established; their success will be made more difficult by the problems of lack of trust described above. What is essential is that the Government retains responsibility for making policy, but does so in a more reflexive way. At the level of individual decisions on major infrastructure projects, the major change is that these will be taken by the Infrastructure Planning Commission rather than by ministers, but within the framework established by the policy statements. This division of responsibilities is acceptable so long as the Commission is open and participative in its procedures; much will depend on how it determines the balance between a more inquisitorial approach and one similar to the conventional public inquiry. The final level, which is that of local implementation, is where there is scope for greater experimentation. One useful example to learn from may be that of the UK Committee on Radioactive Waste Management (CoRWN) which adopted a consultation process on waste disposal involving a range of different techniques, coupled with a 'voluntarist' approach passing initiatives to local communities (Defra 2006).

This identification of a hierarchy of reflexive arrangements should permit a considerable degree of difference and experimentation between the different levels. Once more, however, the problem of trust is raised; if discretion in the design of participatory arrangements is left to public authorities, how can we be sure that it will not be based simply on administrative self-interest? This leads to two further institutional recommendations. The first is for the establishment of a Council for Participatory Governance. This would be a body independent of the administrative authorities which organise participation with the specific task of monitoring the arrangements in practice for participation at each level and analysing their capacities for facilitating social learning. An important role of the new body would be that of benchmarking and publicising examples of best practice. Similar bodies have existed previously to supervise some areas of administrative justice, for example the (now defunct but likely to be resurrected) Administrative Conference of the United States and, in the United Kingdom, the recently established Administrative Justice and Tribunals Council. The emphasis of the proposed body would, however, be somewhat different; it would have the task of facilitating public participation in official decisions, reporting on the use of different institutional forms for such participation and collecting and distributing examples of best practice. This monitoring might seem to represent an additional burden for hard-pressed public bodies; however, by taking a more coherent approach to participation it could prevent much duplication of effort and perhaps avoid the serious burden of legal challenges where such participation has proved inadequate. Perhaps the nearest current practice is to be found in the role of the healthcare regulators in monitoring the performance of healthcare organisations in involving service users and the public, discussed by Vincent-Jones later in this volume.

A further role for such a Council could be to assist in the organisation of groups within civil society to enable them to undertake more effective participation in administrative decision-making, taking over the functions of some existing bodies and with a general remit of providing advice and support for groups otherwise unlikely to be properly represented in decision-making at both local and national levels. This would have to be conducted with some sensitivity, given the importance of autonomy for such groups and fears of state interference in them. However, it would be possible to build on experience of developing independent bodies for consumer representation such as Energywatch and the National Consumer Council, both of which were publicly funded but achieved a strong reputation for effective independence.

Finally, as a further means of developing trust, institutions taking major decisions could be required to undertake a form of participation impact analysis which would be signed off by the new Council before participatory arrangements were put into place. A report to the Council would also be required after the process had been completed. As chapter three by Colin Scott explains, we already have a commitment to the use of Regulatory Impact Assessments as part of the process of reducing administrative burdens; we are also seeing the beginnings of more systematic monitoring of public bodies to ensure compliance with human rights obligations. Participation impact analysis would provide a further means of monitoring to ensure that participatory requirements are not ignored, and would be a major source of information for the Council in developing models of good practice.

Turning to Germany, there is limited scope for development beyond the 'neo-institutionalist economics' approach. However, some key themes may still be identified which can offer guidance for future development. Thus, the researchers concluded that more reflexive approaches might only be applicable under certain conditions which were not met in the case of energy network access regulation in Germany. In relation to the development of further reflexivity, '[a] crucial precondition seems to be that the actors involved have an abstract reason or incentive to contribute to any general interest'. (Britz and Herzmann 2008: 61). There was no such orientation to the general interest amongst network operators in Germany, and so attempts to move beyond the 'neo-institutionalist economics' approach were doomed to failure. There is, however, some scope for institutional reform to improve reflexivity through changes to the regulatory framework; these involve the development of more comprehensive self-monitoring and external monitoring systems providing for an effective search for alternative options for decisions and decision-taking. More developed consultation and facilitation arrangements and more effective rule-making powers for the regulator would also provide an important contribution to greater reflexivity.

In the Canadian case, a key condition for moving any closer to reflexivity is to convince actors to think beyond the confines of the traditional political process. This is also an issue of trust — trust in the value of broader inclusion of stakeholders and of mechanisms of collaborative deliberation; trust that these venues and mechanisms will not be empty shells for ritual consultation about issues that have already been decided by the Government, or that will ultimately be subjected to the reductionist logic of party-political competition. There are some isolated practices in the Canadian cases from which more progressive approaches to collaborative deliberation might develop — the corporatist pact between the Quebec Government and civil society in an attempt to forge a consensus on the future shape of the energy system; or (maybe the most advanced case) the participation of aboriginal communities in hydro-dam development in Quebec. However, a more generalised movement towards reflexivity requires deep changes in the political culture, changes that we are not likely to see in the immediate future.

VIII.   CONCLUSIONS

In one sense it is hardly surprising that the 'neo-institutionalist economics' approach has been the dominant one in the field of energy policy. In both the United Kingdom and Germany (as well as, to a more limited extent, in Canada), this sector has been subject to extensive liberalisation, for reasons of national policy and because of general EU liberalisation. In both nations the development even of such an 'externalist' conception of learning has been gradual (or even incomplete in Canada); in the United Kingdom the assumption was initially that most learning would take place through market mechanisms, leading to the eventual 'withering-away' of the regulator or its incorporation into the general competition authorities (Littlechild 1984). As the impracticability of this became evident, the regulator had to take an approach which was less technicist and more based on learning through consultation; however this remained 'exernalist' through the regulator passively receiving evidence from outside to incorporate into decision-making rather than attempting to organise the capacities of outside interests to contribute to a *mutual* process of learning. In Germany, the attempts to rely on a form of corporatist self-regulation were doomed to failure both through their inherent instability and their exclusion of major interests, including the general interest represented by the Government. They were replaced, after EU pressure for reform, by a form of regulator which may be susceptible to the adoption of procedures for reflexivity, but again only on an externalist basis. One point is clear; the adoption of this form of regulatory body is not an alternative to the operation of the market, far less a restriction on its operation, but an essential prerequisite for market operation.

In the UK arrangements, one major weakness can be attributed to constitutional factors. This is the separation between policy-making, seen as the prerogative of government and to be held accountable through Parliament, and the operation of the market and its regulation. It is clear that major aspects of the regulatory process are dependent on policy decisions by government on issues of climate change and security of supply, and these need to be incorporated into regulatory decision-making. It is in relation to these decisions, notably those relating to the future energy-mix best designed to ensure security of supply, that the problems of reflexive social learning have been most acute. The changes made in this area by the Planning Act 2008 do have some potential to clarify the relationship between policy-making and discrete decisions which can be taken locally, and so to provide a framework in which a more experimentalist approach could be taken to participative arrangements. However, this is undermined by the serious failure of trust in relation to the new arrangements and by the failure so far to implement the types of institutional reform to recreate trust. The new arrangements will incorporate mechanisms for consultation and participation, but on current plans seem unlikely to provide opportunities for the development of a more collaborative-relational approach, let alone of any of the approaches which go beyond this.

In a way similar to the constitutional factors in the United Kingdom, the major weakness of the Canadian approach lies in the dominance of the traditional Westminster-style political process, both in constitutional and cultural terms. This has severely limited, if not prevented, the emergence and empowerment of alternative sites and venues for more collaborative deliberation on public interest goals, beyond political lobbying and interest group politics. Even the transition to a proper 'neo-institutionalist economics model', under which independent regulatory institutions could serve as site for nascent participatory processes, has proved difficult. Any movement towards more reflexive governance models requires, first of all, the establishment of trust in the (democratic and policy) value of collaborative governance techniques, so that isolated examples of more advanced practices can gain momentum.

More broadly, the limited progress towards reflexive governance models noted in the different case studies seems to indicate that established power relations and vested interests in the status-quo of governance regimes constitute a formidable obstacle to the emergence of more advanced models of social learning and collaborative deliberation. The comparison with the healthcare sector suggests that policy-specific factors may also play a role: institutional arrangements in the energy sector seem to be more politicised and less fluid, and may thus be less amenable to the introduction of more collaborative governance techniques.

5

Reflexive Approaches to Corporate Governance: The Case of Heathrow Terminal 5

SIMON DEAKIN AND ARISTEA KOUKIADAKI

I. INTRODUCTION

THE 'CORPORATION' CAN be understood as a multi-functional institution which performs a variety of tasks in a market economy. Foremost among these is the coordination of the inputs of different corporate 'stakeholders' or 'constituencies' in such a way as to generate a net surplus. The corporate form is a composite of the many rules and conventions which shape the behaviour of agents with a view to making this possible. Arguments about the 'public interest' are very much at the heart of the corporate governance debate. It is rare to see the case for shareholder value, for example, expressed solely in terms of the rights of investors. Rather, the interests of shareholders are seen as standing in for those of society as a whole. This is true, above all, for principal-agent theory, whose leading exponents argue that the shareholder value norm is a means to an end, the end being, in this context, the efficiency gains which will flow from more effective monitoring of management and the reduction of agency costs (Jensen 2000). Adherents of shareholder activism also invoke the public interest when they claim that shareholders are capable of speaking for a wider set of social interests when they seek to put pressure on companies to adhere to social and environmental standards (Monks and Sykes 2002). Stakeholder theorists see the corporation as a focus for 'team production' between a range of groups, not confined to shareholders, each of which has an active role to play in governance (Blair and Stout 1999); their view too is based on a particular view of which institutional arrangements are most likely to promote efficient governance, and only partially on an assertion of enterprise democracy for its own sake.

Conceptions of the public interest in the field of social and economic policy very largely depend for their articulation on forms of intervention which take the corporation as the object of regulation. How companies are owned and controlled has a vital impact on the way they respond to regulatory interventions. The crucial variables here include whether the firm is held in the public or the private sector; if in the private sector, whether its ownership is dispersed or concentrated; and to what extent non-shareholder constituencies, such as employees, creditors and customers, have important ownership claims alongside those of the shareholders. Since the 1980s, the shift from public to private ownership, the increasing focus on shareholder interests, and the decentralisation and fragmentation of organisational forms, have led to fundamental realignments in the role and objectives of corporate management, with far-reaching effects for employees, customers and communities. The resulting tensions are especially visible at the point where corporate governance norms interact with those of alternative and, to some degree, competing influences, including those of utility regulation, inter-firm contracting and industrial relations.

In this chapter we study a case of just this type. We look at the governance arrangements used in the construction of the Terminal 5 building ('T5') at London's Heathrow Airport.[1] The T5 project was one of enormous complexity, because of the multiple sets of contractual relationships involved, and one of considerable financial and reputational risk for the client, the airport operator BAA. BAA put in place a governance structure which avoided the problems which similar construction projects in the United Kingdom, such as those on the Jubilee underground line extension and the new Wembley Stadium, had encountered. The delays and cost overruns on which these earlier projects had foundered were not repeated at T5. Governance arrangements were a part of T5's success. T5 saw the adoption of an innovative framework for inter-firm contracting (the T5 Agreement) and a new framework collective agreement for the conduct of industrial relations on multi-firm construction sites (the Major Projects Agreement). Both of these agreements contained an explicit commitment to relational and deliberative forms of governance.

Section II sets out a theoretical framework based on different reflexive approaches to governance. We argue for a systemic analysis which distinguishes between social learning within and between social sub-systems. Section III sets out the systemic context to the T5 project, by which we mean the role played by corporate governance norms, utility regulation, norms of inter-firm contracting and industrial relations in shaping the T5 Agreement and the Major Projects Agreement. Section IV looks at the way in which these agreements operated in practice and section V assesses the outcomes of the project and its aftermath. Section VI concludes.

---

[1]   We draw on a more detailed account of the T5 project in Deakin and Koukiadaki (2009), which contains an account of the data collection methods which were used and provides details of relevant sources.

II.   THEORETICAL FRAMEWORK

'Internalist' approaches to governance stress the importance of communicative processes, dialogue and deliberation in the emergence of enduring solutions to collective action problems. They may be contrasted with 'externalist' conceptions of governance which place emphasis on incentive structures of the kind associated with formal contractual devices for risk allocation. Within the frame of the REFGOV project, Jacques Lenoble and Marc Maesschalck identify different models of 'reflexive' governance, which they term:

(1) the *new-institutional economic* approach;
(2) the collaborative-relational approach;
(3) the 'pragmatist' approach; and
(4) the 'genetic' approach (Lenoble and Maesschalck, chapter one, above).

They consider each one of these approaches as going beyond the previous one. In the fourth approach, building on the others, a thorough-going reframing of interests and identities on the part of the collective actors is seen to be an essential step in the realisation of successful governance processes.

We draw here on the theory of reflexivity which informs the REFGOV project to develop a theoretical model which clarifies the role played by deliberation at intra- and inter-systemic levels in generating collective learning. In adopting a systems theory approach, we aim to amplify the insight of Lenoble and Maesschalck that it is necessary to move beyond approaches based on a model of contract as a purely ex ante incentive structure.

The *new institutional* stream in economics has directly influenced a number of significant bodies of work in the contractual governance area. Lenoble and Maesschalck argue that the main characteristic of this approach is the suggestion that efficiency can be enhanced through the external ordering of behaviour. Institutions put in place incentive structures which are considered, in themselves, to be sufficient for ensuring coordination. The criterion of 'success' of this mode of governance refers to the extent to which 'co-ordinated self-regulation' can by itself lead to 'optimal' institutional design in contractual arrangements. Coordination in a new-institutionalist perspective is not spontaneous, but instead requires external 'hierarchical framing' (Brousseau 1999) or some mode of external integration, that is, 'integrated coordination' (Marengo and Dosi 2005). This is the sense in which new-institutional economics is said to adopt an 'externalist' conception of learning and, as a result, an 'externalist' conception of governance (for a critical review, see Lenoble and Maesschalck 2010: part 2).

The *collaborative-relational* approach depends, by contrast, on the significance of dialogue among the relevant actors or stakeholders. In the context of corporate governance, emphasis is placed on the need to promote communication, deliberation and participation among key stakeholders with interests in the organisation in question. The conjecture is that institutional design will be incomplete, ex ante, and that effective coordination, in addition to or perhaps in substitution for institutional structures, involves the conscious development of processes and mechanisms for collective learning among the actors. Law has here a function as responsible for providing a resource of information about solutions to bargaining problems and assisting the parties to reach contractual cooperation (Deakin and Carvalho 2010). The criterion of 'success' of this mode of governance refers to the extent to which, in spite of conflicting notions of meaning within each sub-field, a common understanding or some form of consensus can be achieved through dialogue.

The third approach, *experimentalism*, goes a stage further in suggesting a role for more specific mechanisms such as benchmarking, monitoring and audit (Dorf and Sabel 2002) or cognitive reframing (Argyris and Schön 1996) as bases for collective learning. According to Sabel (2005), the test of a cooperative mechanism is its capacity to lead to effective changes in behaviour by developing processes that, in incorporating discussion of the new possibilities produced by cooperation, reinforce the process of cooperation under way and thus decrease uncertainty in its continuation. What is sought, in this approach, is twofold social learning: the social learning that results directly from participating in the cooperative search for solutions within a process of local experimentation, and the learning that results from evaluating and comparing different local solutions at the level of the framing mechanisms. Through a shared will to 'internalise' the conditions for success of the learning operation, these approaches aim at building agreement concerning the nature of governance problems and how to address them. The criterion of 'success' of this mode of governance refers to the extent of development of the capacities of stakeholders to actively engage and participate in social dialogue and experimentation, and thereby to contribute to the process of learning.

In the *pragmatist* approach, learning is viewed as a continuous and active process of adaptation and construction in which knowledge is developed through a permanent feedback loop between the system and its environment. According to Argyris (1974: 365), learning is defined

> as the detection and correction of errors, and error as any feature of knowledge or of knowing that makes action ineffective. Error is a form of mismatch: it is a condition of learning, and matching is a second condition. The detection and correction of error produces learning and the lack of either or both inhibits learning.

The potential of organisations to learn through feedback from the consequences of their actions has been developed by Argyris and Schön (1996) through the concepts of single- and double-loop learning. Single-loop learning implies a general tightening and improvement in current procedures and changes in existing organisational rules, largely at programme level. This process is compatible with an 'optimization' strategy in line with a new-institutionalist approach to governance; here, the objective is to search for an optimum in an already pre-structured space of solutions (Peschl 2008: 139). Any activities pursued add to the knowledge base or firm-specific competencies or routines of the organisation without altering, however, the nature of its activities. The parties are expected to articulate their purposes and goals and simultaneously control their environment in order to ensure achievement of those goals (Argyris 1974).

By contrast, in double-loop learning, which puts into practice a kind of meta-learning strategy, the features of learning expand to include the rethinking of existing rules according to why things are being done; it involves understanding the reasons for current rules and then questioning these reasons. Hence, an original set of dynamics becomes feasible in the whole process of learning as organisations start to change the framework of reference (Peschl 2008: 138). There is also the potential for triple-loop learning (Swieringa and Wierdsma 1992), which leads to questioning the rationale for the organisation as a whole, particularly the mixture of internal desires and identity, and the relationships with the external environment. The solutions found have the potential to bring forth fundamentally new knowledge and insights or understanding through reflection, that is, a process of radically questioning the premises and studying their implications for the organisation and for the dynamics of learning through an invitation for dialogue between the parties.

In emphasising the importance of dialogue and reflection, these reflexive analyses are compatible with the notion of learning which has been developed by systems theory. Beginning with the idea of the operative closure of social systems, systems theory suggests that 'the system can only deal with its own internal construct of the environment' (Teubner 1993: 74); hence the influence of one system on another can only be understood through 'translation' of the discourse of the former into the specific terms used by the latter. The role of social systems then is to 'contribute to the emergence of forms of *meaning* through which the complexity of the world can be understood' (Deakin and Carvalho 2010, emphasis in original). Intra-systemic learning is a function of the operation of the system's internal 'working parts', which ensures its self-reproduction over time. Inter-systemic learning is inherently more problematic. Because systems are operatively closed, they cannot *directly* influence one another. However, because systems are 'cognitively open', each one is capable of *indirectly* influencing the evolutionary path of the other. Institutional devices which allow for deliberation across system boundaries — which we term 'systemic deliberation' for short — can play a role in bringing about a more or less productive form of what systems theorists refer to as 'structural coupling' (Luhmann 1995, 2004; Teubner 1993).

Our notion of 'systemic deliberation' focuses primarily on processes of decision-making and control, and on procedures and structures that provide overall direction *across* social subsystems. It thereby offers a way to identify instances of structural coupling by which systems interact with their environment. An understanding of the empirical complexity of the context of governance structures is important here. In order for a 'systemic deliberative' approach to work, it is essential that feedback mechanisms exist within a context of subsystems which are of approximately equal power or legitimacy at the level of the discourses to which they give rise. Successful mechanisms are those which observe a 'principle of reciprocity', according to which influences are capable of running both ways, and not simply from one 'dominant' subsystem to another.

An 'externalist' or new-institutionalist approach to governance would evaluate contractual arrangements according to the criterion of incentive alignment, that is to say, on how far incentive structures were aligned with, and likely to bring about, strategies which will maximise the aggregate wellbeing of the parties. By contrast, a reflexive approach, looks to see how far contractual arrangements are capable of promoting both intra- and (above all) inter-systemic learning in the sense that we have described them. Empirical work can provide a context to test these different conceptions of governance. With this point in mind, we now turn to our case study of T5.

III.   THE SYSTEMIC CONTEXT OF THE T5 PROJECT

In large construction projects, contractual relations are shaped by a number of institutional influences. These do not remove from the contracting parties the scope for autonomous action, but by framing contractual interactions in a certain way, they may make it more or less difficult, as the case may be, for them to arrive at a basis for cooperation.

In the context of Terminal 5, the first such influence to consider is that of the *corporate governance* system in a narrow sense, that is, the set of rules and practices governing the ownership and control of business organisations. Core institutions of corporate governance in the United Kingdom, in particular those relating to takeover regulation and board structure, tend to place the interest of shareholders above those of other corporate stakeholders, such as employees and creditors (Armour et al 2003: 531). However, the shareholder interest is qualified to a certain extent by the leeway given to boards, as a matter of both law and practice, to take into account a wider range of concerns as long as, in doing so, they continue to serve the goal of maximising shareholder returns over the long-term. Recent corporate governance reforms, contained in section 172 of the Companies Act 2006, have required directors to consider the interests of a wider range of corporate constituencies when considering how to discharge their fiduciary duty to act in the best interests of the company. This change affects, in principle, the way that the board takes strategic decisions affecting its future. Section 172 embodies the concept of 'enlightened shareholder value' which was defined by the Company Law Review Steering Group in the early 2000s as placing the board under a duty 'to achieve the success of the company for the benefit of the shareholders by taking proper account of all the relevant considerations for that purpose', including a proper balanced view of the short and long term, the need to sustain effective ongoing relationships with employees, customers, suppliers and others, and the need to maintain the company's reputation and to consider the impact of its operations on the community and the environment. (Company Law Review Steering Group 2000)

It is not clear how far the change made to the law in 2006 has brought about a change in the practice of boards, in particular since no stakeholders other than shareholders have any standing to enforce directors' fiduciary duties, and even shareholders have very limited rights to bring derivative actions on the company's behalf. To some degree, however, section 172 can be thought of not so much as a prescriptive change, but as a restatement of the way many boards of UK-listed companies were already behaving at the point when the reform of UK company law was underway. As we shall see, it is compatible with the strategic decision-making undertaken by BAA when formulating the T5 project.

There are, however, other pressures in the UK system which more clearly lead to a prioritisation of shareholder concerns. Largely unaffected by the 2006 Act, the City Code on Takeovers and Mergers[2] continues to underpin a market for corporate control in which managerial under-performance leads to shareholder exit and consequent changes in ownership and control. Owing to these pressures and to executive remuneration arrangements which link pay to financial performance, senior managers have largely internalised the goal of maximising shareholder returns (Pendleton and Gospel 2005: 62). The strong orientation towards a norm of shareholder primacy has a number of implications. First, UK firms generally prefer mergers and joint ventures instead of relational contracting as a means to achieve coordination with their suppliers (Lane 1997). Secondly, they may find it difficult to develop long-term 'partnership arrangements' with their workforces (Edwards 2004: 526). In these respects, UK corporate governance practice more closely resembles an 'externalist' or new institutionalist conception of governance than one based on systemic deliberation between stakeholders. As we shall see, the operation of the UK takeover market played a significant role in the unfolding of the T5 project.

The UK approach to *utility regulation* is based on coordination through bilateral contracting between the regulator and the dominant regulated firm, which is in almost all cases an enterprise that was privatised in the 1980s or 1990s after having previously benefited from a legal monopoly. Regulatory decision-making since the start of the period of privatisation paid minimal attention to the interests of suppliers and of the workforce (Prosser 1999: 208). At the same time, there is evidence that firms which operate in sectors where services and products for end users are regulated in the interests of ensuring quality and reliability of supply sometimes have stable and active relationships with suppliers and are committed to employment security, career opportunities and human

---

[2] Takeover Panel (2006) *The City Code on Takeovers and Mergers*, 8th edn, May 2006 since then periodically updated, available at www.thetakeoverpanel.org.uk.

capital development. Deakin et al (2006: 155) found evidence that the regulation of product and service quality, of the kind observed in most utility sectors and in certain parts of manufacturing and services, favoured the emergence of stable labour-management partnerships. This was because, in these markets, profitability was linked to the ability of companies to maintain a high and consistent quality of products and services for end users. To that extent, utility regulation operated as a countervailing force to the pro-shareholder tendency of corporate governance norms. There is evidence of this effect at work in the T5 case.

Large-scale construction projects such as T5 necessarily give rise to horizontal and vertical *contracting between firms* of some complexity. A key issue in inter-firm relations is the need for high levels of coordination of interdependent activities that are performed by separate employing organisations covering engineers, surveyors, contractors and employees, all engaging in a complex process of contracting and sub-contracting. New institutionalist conceptions of multi-firm contracting, based on transaction-cost economics (eg Williamson 1985) and game theory (eg Axelrod 1990), stress the role played by expost adjustment of contractual expectations, suggesting that contracts serve as a 'framework' for the performance of agreements. However, these approaches still tend to overlook 'either the social learning processes within longer-term relationships (transaction-costs economics) or the dimension of the social embeddedness of interorganisational relations (game theory)' (Bachmann 2003: 8). Complex organisational relationships with long-standing divisions between disciplines and organisations and accepted ways of working may hinder the development of forms of cooperation and communication links between firms themselves (Harty 2005: 521). At T5, as we shall see, a critical issue was how to promote governance structures that could encourage the building of consensus regarding the nature of the challenges faced by the parties, notwithstanding these potential barriers to cooperation.

Finally, we consider the *industrial relations* context of T5. In the context of large projects and as a result of multi-firm arrangements it is very common to come across situations in which workers employed by different organisations, or by agencies, work alongside each other at the same workplace, often employed on quite different terms and conditions, leading thus to a blurring of organisational boundaries (Grimshaw et al 2005). This fragmentation is partly the result of the traditional conception of the legal framework surrounding the employment relationship as involving a single employer and a single employee. Common law rights and duties as well as statutory employment regulation are largely predicated upon the notion of an 'employee', as legally defined, working for a single employer. As a result, in multi-employer workplaces, 'worker voice typically becomes fragmented and divided, and in some cases muted altogether' (Marchington and Rubery 2005: 138). But the absence of deliberation between management and labour is also the result of the confinement of site-level collective bargaining to wages, hours and terms and conditions of employment; such bargaining does not extend to the core areas of managerial 'prerogative' (Wedderburn 1986:

chapter 4). This problem has been accentuated by a steep fall in the proportion of employees covered by collective agreements, declining union membership rates, and contraction in the scope of bargaining (Kersley et al 2006). From 2004, legislation in the form of the Information and Consultation of Employees Regulations (ICER) came into force, requiring all firms above a certain size to have information and consultation mechanisms in place. ICER derives from the EC Information and Consultation Directive of 2002,[3] the roots of which lie in the codetermination-based models of employee representations found in many continental European systems. ICER falls a long way short of mandating the codetermination practices of particular national systems, but in its emphasis on forms of social dialogue which go beyond distributive bargaining, it has the potential to make a significant impact on British industrial relations practice. The representative structures put in place under ICER, as in other information and consultation laws, are designed for single-employer units, and so cannot be easily adapted to workplaces where subcontracting as well as the use of agency and casual or self-employed labour are the norm. British employers make widespread use of flexible forms of employment, and the construction sector in the United Kingdom is one of the most fragmented in organisational terms. There is also only limited adherence by construction employers to national-level collective agreements. Nevertheless, another of the sectors involved in the T5 project, electrical contracting, is one in which multi-employer national bargaining has remained relatively strong. It is distinctive both in the scope of application of its agreements and in the standards that it sets and there has been continuity in support for the collective agreement and for the Joint Industry Board (JIB) (Gospel and Druker 1998: 249). As we shall see, this variant of national level collective bargaining was to play a major role in the governance of industrial relations at T5.

IV.   THE CONSTRUCTION OF T5: THE ROLE OF INTRA- AND INTER-SYSTEMIC LEARNING

A.   Corporate Governance and Utilities Regulation in the Making of the T5 Agreement

When the T5 project started, the principal client, BAA Plc, was the United Kingdom's dominant airport operator. The company had been privatised by the 1986 Airports Act and listed on the FTSE 100 index of the London Stock Exchange (LSE). The 1986 Act also introduced the economic regulation of airport charges by the Civil Aviation Authority (CAA), which imposed price caps on the aeronautical charges levied by BAA on airlines using Heathrow, Gatwick

---

[3] EC National Information and Consultation Directive 2002/14/EC [2002] OJ L 80, 23.3.2002

and Stansted airports. In February 2006, when the project was nearing comple-tion, BAA was approached by Groupo Ferrovial, a leading partner in a consortium, which declared an interest in acquiring it through merger or takeover. In June 2006, Ferrovial officially took control of BAA after gaining 83 per cent of its shares. In August, BAA was de-listed from the LSE and the company name was subsequently changed from BAA Plc to BAA Ltd, signifying its conversion from a public to a private company. The takeover by Ferrovial did not affect BAA's status as a regulated utility. However, BAA's conversion from a regulated utility and listed Plc, which was then taken over in a bid mostly funded by debt, influenced its approach to the construction of T5 at each of the relevant stages of the project.

At the beginning of the T5 project, BAA saw itself in a situation where the project's failure would be reputationally disastrous, bearing in mind its position as both a utility, subject to regulatory pressure for service improvements, and a listed company required to meet shareholder expectations (Wolmar 2006). In other projects, including the construction of the new Wembley football stadium and the extension of the Jubilee line on the London underground, legal costs had formed a substantial proportion of budget overruns. There had also been widespread bankruptcies among suppliers forced to absorb the costs of late completion. Penalties imposed on suppliers for late performance, in accordance with construction contracts of the traditional type, had failed to protect the ultimate clients from significant financial and reputational losses. On the basis of the experience gained from these projects and from its own experience of failures in the construction of underground lines at Heathrow (Brady et al 2008: 34), BAA's solution to those challenges was to create a customised, legally binding contract — called 'the T5 Agreement' — between itself and its 60 suppliers, which also formed the basis for agreements between these 'first-tier' contractors and their own subcontractors. The principles underlying the T5 Agreement were drawn in large part from the influential report 'Rethinking Construction' (1998) in which BAA's Chief Executive Officer Sir John Egan had played a prominent role. A fundamental aspect of the T5 Agreement was BAA's understanding that 'the client always bears the risk' (Wolmar 2006; see also Brady et al 2008). In contrast to the traditional penalty clause approach to construction contracts, under the T5 Agreement BAA assumed the residual risks of the project and the ultimate responsibility for any cost overruns, while committing itself to making payments for savings made by suppliers that qualified for a share of a reward fund. Equally importantly, the T5 Agreement was explicitly aimed at encouraging collaborative behaviour, which was designed to improve BAA and partners' working in integrated project teams (Wolmar 2006). In addition, BAA had the power to monitor the performance of contractors and subcontractors, to set quality standards and, where necessary, to engage directly with suppliers; this was a much more proactive role than was normal in construction contracts of this kind.

The formulation of the T5 Agreement can be seen as the outcome of learning which was both intra- and inter-systemic. BAA's perceptions of the dangers of relying on traditional forms of contractual risk allocation were based in part on its own experience of earlier construction work at Heathrow. It also drew on industry practice, as just explained. This explanation, focusing on intra-systemic learning, is, however, only a partial one. BAA was subject to external influences which, in this case, favoured the emergence of an innovative contractual solution. Corporate governance pressures meant that BAA, as a listed company, was under pressure to deliver shareholder value. The capital cost of the T5 project was not far removed from the total equity value of the company in the early 2000s. Thus, the project was one with the potential to put the company's future on the line. But in part because of the very high stakes involved, BAA was able, at least at the outset of the project, well before the Ferrovial bid, to persuade its shareholder base (which then consisted largely of UK-based pension funds and other institutional investors) to take a long-term view of their holdings.

BAA also had the support of the airport regulator in the approach it was taking. Two changes made to the airports price cap review for the period 2003–08 provided the background for the conclusion of the T5 Agreement: first, the caps imposed allowed Heathrow to increase its charges in real terms by 6.5 per cent, per annum, reflecting the considerable capital spend on T5 during the 2002–08 period (Starkie 2008: 69); and, secondly, the regulator introduced for the first time into the Heathrow cap a 'trigger' which would reduce the maximum allowable charge if BAA failed to achieved certain capital project milestones, such as T5, on time (Wolstenholme et al 2008: 11).

The context of the T5 Agreement was therefore a measure of productive 'coupling' between the systems of corporate governance and utilities regulation. An 'enlightened' or long-term approach to shareholder value dovetailed with the regulator's willingness to allow BAA some flexibility over pricing and charging in return for adherence to quality standards and adherence to the timetable for the completion of T5. In this way, interests that could have been directly in conflict with one another — an exclusive focus on shareholder value, on the one hand, and a rigid application of the price capping regime, on the other — were reconciled. The learning process which informed T5 was, in this sense, inter-, as well as intra-, systemic.

B. Performance of the T5 Agreement and Related Contracts

i. *Multi-Firm Contracting at T5*

The scale, complexity and high cost of the construction of T5 make it a prime example of a contractual 'megaproject' (Flyvbjerg et al 2003). Construction commenced in September 2002; phase one of the project was completed in March 2008. At any one time, the project employed up to 8,000 workers, and as many as 60,000 people were involved in the project over its lifetime. T5 was structurally allowed to operate as a separate business unit within BAA, enabling it to develop a distinctive operating model for the identification and management of risks (Doherty 2008: 250).

The way the T5 Agreement structured inter-firm contracting in practice is subject to conflicting interpretations. On the one hand, it can be seen as an illustration of the value of putting in place an ex ante framework for contracting which efficiently anticipates the contingencies faced by the parties and deals with them accordingly — a view compatible with a new institutional or 'externalist' conception of governance. The critical move was BAA's acceptance that while it could use penalty clauses to shift certain liabilities on to the suppliers in the event of late or defective performance, it could not shift certain residual risks, in particular reputational ones. This perception informed the major *formal* innovation of the T5 Agreement, namely the pooling of liabilities arising from late performance between BAA and groups of suppliers engaged on particular parts of the project. Costs arising from overruns were shared by the suppliers collectively, with BAA taking out insurance policies to cover certain project-wide liabilities. If the work was completed ahead of schedule, the suppliers qualified for bonuses for 'exceptional performance'.

However, the formal dimensions of the Agreement, while important, are only part of the story. Alongside the formal incentive structures which the Agreement put in place, the relational and deliberative elements of the project also need to be considered. In order to ensure that the project met the constraints imposed on it, emphasis was placed on the effective diffusion of information, the use of frameworks, benchmarks and measurement and the operation of integrated teams working. Integrated team working, which was designed to enable suppliers to work effectively as part of coordinated teams and focus on meeting the project's objectives not only in relation to the traditional time, budget, and quality measures but also in relation to safety and environmental targets, was regarded by BAA's senior managers as a fundamental ingredient to the success of T5 (Doherty 2008: 263). The performance of the key suppliers was reviewed by BAA twice a year, and more regularly if problems arose. In addition, integrated forums operated throughout the project's duration in which key suppliers came together with BAA to review performance against targets and discuss future delivery challenges. These mechanisms were seen by managers in both BAA and the suppliers as helping to create a common framework of understanding that allowed both sides to assess any shortcomings and to adjust their strategies accordingly.

ii. *Industrial Relations at T5*

BAA did not directly employ any of the workers involved in construction at T5 and was not a party to collective agreements relating to the construction project. However, BAA set out an industrial relations policy for work being done on the

T5 site, and this was incorporated in the T5 Agreement; as such it was contractually binding on the parties to it. The relevant principles included, among others, the use of direct labour in preference to casual forms of employment or self-employment, with limited provision for agency work to meet peaks in demand; the negotiation of local agreements which were to be no less favourable than existing national and sectoral agreements; the establishment of comprehensive structures for basic wage rates and for productivity-related bonuses and allowances; and the 'cascading' of agreed terms and conditions and employment quality standards to second-tier subcontractors and suppliers, together with arrangements for the monitoring of their performance.

These principles were reflected in the two main sets of collective agreements that governed the site: the Hourly Paid Employees Agreement which governed the civil engineering side of the project, and the Major Projects Agreement (MPA) and Supplementary Project Agreement (SPA) which together governed the provision of mechanical and electrical (M&E) services on T5. The second of these sets of agreements, the MPA and SPA, is the focus of our analysis here. At the time of the conception of the T5 project, the parties to the MPA were the principal employers' associations in the M&E sectors — the Electrical Contractors' Association (ECA), the Association of Plumbing and Heating Contractors (APHC), the Heating and Ventilation Contractors' Association (HVCA), 'the Electrical Contractors' Association of Scotland (SELECT), and the trade union representing workers in the M&E industries, Unite (previously Amicus).

The MPA was an 'umbrella' collective agreement intended specifically to apply to large construction projects. Each of the existing collective agreements, that is, the JIB agreement in electrical contracting, the agreements for plumbing and for heating and ventilation and the National Agreement for the Engineering and Construction Industries (NAECI) that covers part of the engineering industry, contributed aspects of the model used in the MPA. T5 was the first and (so far) only case in which the MPA has been applied, and was a trigger for its adoption and development.

In October 2001, a meeting took place between ECA officials and BAA managers at which BAA stressed the desire to avoid having a multiplicity of collective agreements applying to the site. On the part of Unite, there was strong support at national officer level for a single agreement. Following negotiations, the SPA was agreed between Unite and the principal contractors on the M&E side at T5, namely AMEC, Balfour Kilpatrick and Crown House Engineering, in November 2003.

In line with the T5 Agreement, the MPA and SPA contained provisions setting out a pledge on both sides to implement integrated team working. In return for the union's approval of this form of 'functional' labour flexibility, the MPA and SPA committed the employer side to a system of productivity-related bonuses that, in practice, delivered levels of pay substantially above the standard rates for the relevant trades. In addition, these agreements put in place new deliberative mechanisms, the MPA Forum in the case of the MPA and the T5 Joint Council in the case of the SPA, which combined negotiation over pay and conditions with a broader conception of social dialogue based on regular information exchange and consultation over strategic decision-making.

Consultative meetings took place on a frequent basis between individual shop stewards (lay union representatives) and the management of each supplier and between the stewards and representatives of all suppliers at Joint Council level. In addition there was informal consultation between industrial relations managers at site level and a number of union officers including 'designated representatives' whose role was set out under the SPA. The role of designated representatives was similar to that of traditional 'convenors' or senior shop stewards, but, exceptionally, their functions were defined with the aims of promoting the MPA in mind, and not exclusively in terms of protecting their own members' interests. Under clause 20 of the MPA, their responsibilities, which had to be carried out 'in cooperation with Management', included '[developing] on the project … an environment of social partnership' and '[promoting] industrial relations harmony and the avoidance of recourse to unofficial actions', as well as more traditional goals such as '[ensuring] the maximum take-up and compliance with Trade Union membership'.

The MPA Forum and the Joint Council operated as loci for the incorporation of employee interests into decision-making processes of the project and for monitoring the operation of the MPA and SPA with a view to adapting them to the evolving requirements of the T5 project. Annual reports on the T5 project were prepared by the MPA Forum which included specific references to lessons learned from the operation of certain provisions of the MPA and SPA, including those relating to the timing of implementation of the agreements, productivity issues, and training plans. An independent auditor was appointed to provide a monthly report to the Joint Council, ensure compliance with the terms of the MPA and SPA and provide advice and guidance to incoming contractors new to the T5 arrangements.

The success of the agreements in providing a framework for the resolution of disputes at T5 can be seen in the way an issue relating to the use of agency workers was resolved towards the final stages of the project. The MPA and SPA committed the employers to making limited use of agency labour to cover peaks and troughs in demand, and to ensure that agency workers received equal treatment, from the point of view of terms and conditions of employment, with comparable directly-employed workers. The employment of agency workers was nevertheless resisted by the unions on the grounds that workers supplied by agencies, even if employed on equal terms to those of the regular workforce, generally did not receive training, and were more difficult to recruit into membership of the union. In the final phases of the project, a change in the law governing the taxation of agency workers led to greater numbers of them being employed through intermediary companies which the unions regarded as legal shams. The issue of whether this type of agency work contravened the MPA and SPA was eventually resolved in the union's favour after the four-stage dispute resolution procedure set up under the agreements was invoked. This procedure was unusual in allowing for disputes to be taken 'off site' if not initially resolved and referred to procedures specific to the MPA rather than being settled at the level of the relevant national collective bargaining procedures.

Industrial relations at T5 exemplified elements of governance which can be described as relational (the open-ended nature of the social dialogue), experimental (through the role of benchmarking and audit) and pragmatist (the 'double-loop' or meta-level learning involved in the refinement of the MPA and its adaptation to the context of T5 through the SPA). Most of the learning generated through the MPA and SPA was intra-systemic in nature, in the sense that it was confined to the immediate industrial relations settings in which those agreements operated. There is also evidence of inter-systemic learning at the level of the interface between the corporate governance and industrial relations systems. The 'enlightened shareholder value' approach adopted by BAA in its investor relations helped to provide the context for the adoption of the MPA at T5. Although BAA was not a party to the MPA or SPA, the industrial relations approach it set out in the T5 Agreement provided an important part of the background against which the MPA emerged and was then applied at T5. The parties to the MPA were aware of BAA's commitment to a stable industrial relations environment and the explicit promotion of a labour-management partnership.

V. THE OUTCOME OF THE T5 PROJECT AND ITS UNCERTAIN AFTERMATH

The T5 project met a broad range of objectives, which included enhancing productivity, reduction of costs, and promoting a high quality of end project, while preserving above-industry average labour standards. The project was completed on time and on budget, avoiding the cost overruns and delays of the Jubilee Line and Wembley Stadium projects. The opening of the terminal building in March 2008 proved, in the short-term, to be a near-disaster, as the malfunctioning of the baggage-handling system led to highly-publicised cancellations of flights in the first few days of its operation. This failure was completely unconnected to the construction process and occurred after the engineering and construction firms involved in it, and their workforce, had almost entirely left the site. Most of the reputational damage associated with the baggage-handling issue was sustained by the terminal's user, British Airways. Within a week of opening, the system was working as expected and the terminal has gone on to operate successfully.

The T5 project can also be regarded as having met its industrial relations goals. First, the objective of an above-industry average health and safety record was achieved. There were two fatalities, against an industry average of six for a project of this size. In terms of major injuries, 600 were expected. This was the equivalent to the *reportable* incidences (that is, both major and more minor ones) and overall T5 was three times better than the industry average (Doherty 2008: 112). Secondly, industrial relations stability was provided. No days were lost to industrial action on the M&E side of the project. Thirdly, while employers and the trade union thought that there had been scope for further productivity improvements, no use was made of the provisions in the MPA and SPA for reduction or suspension of productivity-related bonuses paid to the workforce (see Baker Mallett 2005, 2008). In repeated employee surveys, over 75 per cent of the workforce felt that T5 was the safest site they had worked on and over 60 per cent thought it was a good place to work (Doherty 2008: 106). Absenteeism and turnover were substantially below the norm for the construction sector. There was less accord in other issues, mainly the use of agency labour on site, although, as we have seen, a resolution of kinds to this issue was arrived at.

What role did the governance structures of the T5 Agreement and MPA/SPA play in these outcomes? At first sight, multi-firm construction projects such as T5 look like an unlikely candidate for arrangements capable of promoting 'systemic deliberation'. This, at least, is the conventional picture. The experience of T5 suggests, however, that this is not an inevitable outcome. As we have seen, the structures put in place at T5 challenge conventional understandings of what governance structures could achieve in the UK context, where similar projects have failed in the past under conditions of short-termist pressures from shareholders, antagonistic inter-firm contracting, and adversarial industrial relations. In the case of T5, corporate governance and utilities regulation not only encouraged the adoption of a relational approach to contracting, but they also contributed, as explained above, to the successful application of the arrangements at the level of multi-firm contracting and industrial relations on the T5 site. This success, as we have seen, was achieved via the inclusion in the T5 Agreement of governance structures which allowed for the pooling of risks between the different parties. However, the success of the project was also made possible by the participation of parties with multiple interests in the design of the project from its inception.

The aftermath of the project has, however, been less successful, in the sense that it has proved hard to replicate elsewhere the arrangements which worked well at T5. First, despite an expansion of the membership of the MPA in October 2007 to include representatives of the thermal insulation contracting industry, efforts to promote the MPA as the model for the completion of the London Olympic Games and Paralympic Games in 2012 were unsuccessful. The high set-up costs of the MPA and the pooling of risks between client and contractors did not win government approval in this critical case (Prior 2008). Short-term financial interests set the benchmark by which the public authorities measured and assessed the possibility of using the MPA for the 2012 sites. Secondly, it is uncertain whether the MPA will even be applied in future BAA projects, in particular the plan for a new Heathrow East Terminal to replace the ageing Terminals 1 and 2.

Why did Ferrovial take a very different approach to the Heathrow East project from that which BBA had taken with regard to Terminal 5 a decade or so earlier? New constraints arising in the operation of utility regulation affecting BAA were part of the problem. In 2008 the CAA reduced the financial return BAA was to be allowed to make between 2008 and 2013 (CAA 2008) and the Competition Commission (CC) made a provisional decision to force BAA to sell two of its three London airports and one of its Scottish airports (CC 2008).

Further background to this uncertainty was formed by financial difficulties faced by Ferrovial, and in particular by its need to service the debts it took on when it completed the takeover of BAA in 2006. The takeover illustrates the limited degree to which, once a bid for control is mounted, the board of a listed company can have regard to 'enlightened shareholder value'; its principal duty under the Takeover Code is to get the best price it can for the shareholders (see Deakin et al 2004). As a listed company with dispersed and predominantly institutional shareholder ownership, BAA had operated with a certain degree of autonomy with regard to strategic decision-making. Its board and management had thereby been freed to take a long-term view of the T5 project. Once Ferrovial mounted its bid for the company in 2006, the sole issue for the board (as the Chairman at the time put it) was whether shareholders were getting the best possible deal. In turn, most of BAA's shareholders were ready to sell once Ferrovial's offer gave them a substantial premium over the pre-bid price. Following the takeover, BAA ceased to be a widely-held, listed company and became a wholly owned subsidiary of Ferrovial. In order to buy out the existing shareholders, Ferrovial had taken on debts which, before long, were in excess of BAA's assumed asset value. Under these circumstances it is not surprising that Ferrovial seemed to be opting in the course of 2008–09 for a low-commitment, low-cost option with regard to the new Heathrow East terminal project.

VI.   ASSESSMENT

The T5 study suggests that governance structures based on deliberation and on the inclusion of multiple stakeholders can successfully emerge even in a context, such as that of the United Kingdom, where pressures on firms to prioritise shareholder value are strong. What makes T5 particularly distinctive as a case study in governance is the presence alongside 'intra-systemic learning', that is, learning within different sub-systems, of inter-systemic learning, that is, the possibility for learning in the sense of error correction to spill over from one systemic context to another. The functional differentiation of subsystems is an expression of societal complexity and thus, in a sense, an unavoidable consequence of the highly articulated division of labour which characterises modern market economies. Learning across the social subsystems that we have identified in this study — corporate governance (narrowly construed to refer to company-shareholder relations), utility regulation, inter-firm contracting and industrial relations — is therefore inherently problematic. Yet, mechanisms of 'structural coupling' exist to make this kind of meta-systemic learning possible. These mechanisms take the form of institutional devices and discursive techniques which mediate between the separate subsystems. The practice of boards taking decisions by reference to 'enlightened shareholder value' is an example of this, as it seeks to insert into corporate governance discourse a perspective on the value of cooperation between stakeholder groups that would otherwise be absent. It thereby opens up a route for the language and practice of industrial relations 'partnership' to become relevant within the context of relations between managers and shareholders. Conversely, the industrial relations practice of 'information and consultation' takes social dialogue between managers and worker representatives beyond the distributive concerns which have traditionally shaped collective bargaining, and introduces the possibility of joint decision-making aimed at the realisation of joint goals.

The distinctive success of T5 was, we suggest, the result in large part of the opportunities for inter-systemic deliberation to which its distinctive governance arrangements gave rise. The T5 Agreement successfully integrated inter-firm contracting arrangements with those governing industrial relations while, for a brief period, flexibility in utility regulation was matched by the willingness of shareholders to take a long-term view of their investments. Yet, the aftermath of T5 also illustrates just how precarious these arrangements were. Even as the project was nearing completion, the shareholders cashed in their holdings, and the priority for BAA's new owners was paying down the debts incurred in the takeover. This set in chain a series of events which was to see the abandonment of flexibility by the regulator and a return to pre-T5 practices with respect to inter-firm contracting and industrial relations.

The difficult aftermath of T5 is an indication of the limits on inter-systemic deliberation which characterise the wider British corporate governance environment. We suggested earlier that to be successful, inter-systemic learning must involve two-way flows between the different subsystems (the 'principle of reciprocity'). Within the T5 project, this was achieved, thanks to the integrative mechanisms just referred to; in the aftermath of T5, the principle of reciprocity was violated, and a more familiar picture re-emerged, namely one of the dominance of financial considerations over others. The financial aspects of UK corporate governance, which are epitomised by the role played by the Takeover Code and related market for corporate control in directing boards and managers to prioritise shareholder concerns, were remarkably little affected by the other changes which were taking place more widely within company and labour law. Corporate mergers and takeovers are still dictated by short-term financial considerations, with little or no scope for boards to take a long-term view of corporate strategy, and few opportunities for workers and other stakeholders to exercise voice within the takeover process. The 'long shadow' cast by the Takeover Code (Deakin et al 2004) is nowhere more evident than in the uncertain prospects for BAA under Ferrovial's ownership at the end of the 2000s.

6

The Democratic Experimentalist Approach to Governance: Protecting Social Rights in the European Union

OLIVIER DE SCHUTTER

I. INTRODUCTION

T HERE ARE TWO ways in which the development of European integration through the EU interacts with the protection of fundamental rights
(De Schutter 2007). First, the transferral of powers to the European Union
(EU) entails the risk that these powers will be exercised in a way that does not
comply with the requirements of fundamental rights. This issue has been largely
discussed since the 1970s, when it became evident that the European Communities would have impacts going beyond their stated economic purposes, and that
the law they developed could affect economic operators in ways that could have
an impact on their basic rights. It is this concern which the European Court of
Justice and, later, the European Court of Human Rights, sought to address: both
jurisdictions arrived at the conclusion that, unless appropriate checks are provided, the extension of the competences of the EC, and now of the EU, could
affect fundamental rights, and that it was their duty to protect the potential
victims of such developments.

Secondly, economic integration within the EU may also create incentives for
the EU Member States to adopt legislation or policies that are considered
desirable in order to benefit the most from the opportunities created by market
integration or in order, at least, not to be put at a disadvantage as a result of such
integration. Such legislation or policies may not correspond to what would be
most effective to promote the full realisation of human rights. But, in the view of
the national authorities, they may nevertheless be seen as justified if the benefits
outweigh the costs to human rights. Even though it would be allowable for the
state to adopt certain measures that improve the protection of human rights, that
state could refrain from doing so, in particular, where this would lead companies

to relocate their activities elsewhere, exercising their freedom of establishment within the EU and the possibility to provide services or ship goods abroad, from whichever Member State they choose to operate.

This describes, in the most stylised way, the problem known as 'regulatory competition'. Although they are traditionally tasked to protect fundamental rights, courts are ill-equipped to address this problem effectively. Courts may, of course, intervene on the rare occasions when regulatory competition leads states to undermine basic rights in such a way that violations are denounced. They provide, in that sense, a minimum — or groundfloor — protection. However, such occasions are very unusual. Far more frequent are situations in which national law-makers — or, in the context of collective bargaining, employers — invoke the requirements of maintaining or achieving 'competitiveness' vis-à-vis foreign companies in order to justify, for instance, loosening certain requirements of labour law, of consumer protection, or of environmental regulations, as such requirements are stipulated in domestic rules.

The traditional approach to this question has been based on a crude dichotomy between 'deregulation' (at domestic level) or 're-regulation' (at European level), corresponding respectively to the 'negative' and 'positive' dimensions of European integration (Scharpf 1999: chapter 3). This simplification has been unhelpful and the source of unnecessary confusions. First, by seeing 'negative integration' as a potential source of 'deregulation' at domestic level, it does not make a distinction between the situation in which the requirements of the internal market (particularly the four fundamental freedoms) impose on governments to remove certain disproportionate or discriminatory regulations, that might constitute unjustifiable obstacles to the exercise of free movement, and the situation in which the internal market functions merely as an incentive to deregulate, in order to help achieve a competitive advantage on the other Member States and, in particular, to be more attractive to increasingly mobile capital. Yet, this distinction is essential: in the latter situation, the choice in favour of deregulation is done at domestic level, and it is the result of power struggles between actors competing to define the national public interest; in the former situation, overcoming 'deregulation', as imposed by 'negative integration', requires collective action at EU level, which may be much more difficult to achieve taking into account the multiple veto points that exist and the difficulty of achieving agreement in an enlarged Union with increasingly diverging conceptions of the role of the state in the market.

Secondly, such a model assumes more or less explicitly that governments will define their positions (both as regards domestic regulations and regulations adopted at EU level) on the basis of the interest of the companies located under their jurisdiction, which they will seek to reward, and on the basis of the need to attract new companies to establish themselves on their territory. This is a very crude assumption, and it will be in some cases unrealistic. In fact, the available evidence is rather that governments sometimes hide behind the requirements of EU integration to condemn certain undertakings (less competitive than those located in other Member States), while defending others (improving their competitiveness by adapting, where necessary, the regulatory framework, or providing tax incentives): as noted by Young, 'politicians found it convenient to use the single market and the constraints from "Brussels" as cover for changes in domestic policies and as a justification for both inaction and action at home' (Young 2005: 111). Indeed, according to the theory of comparative advantage on which international trade is premised, while firms compete against one another, countries don't: all countries gain by each country specialising in the production of the good or the provision of the service in which it has a comparative advantage. This implies that the interests of the country as a whole and those of its industries may not converge, where the said industries are less competitive than the industries of other states. Of course, many governments will act in order to protect their industries whichever the efficiency losses involved, notwithstanding the theoretical gains from the international division of labour. However, whether or not they do so is a question of political economy that depends on the ability of economic actors to capture the political decision-making process: it must be examined empirically, rather than assumed theoretically.

Thirdly, the 'deregulation/re-regulation' approach is oversimplifying also in that the only alternative to a state exercising its regulatory functions at domestic level seems to be the establishment of a 'super-state' at European level, as if the scenario of a European Welfare State were a realistic possibility. There are areas, of course, in which the EU has been attributed competences which it may exercise in order to move in this direction — and workers' rights are the subject of an important EU body of law. However impressive these advances though, they still remain far from constituting the first steps towards a European Welfare State, or towards the EU as an organisation dedicated to the promotion and protection of social rights. In fact, that scenario is so remote that the alternative is a demobilising one, not one that truly shows the direction of reform.

Instead, I ask here which alternatives exist both to the risk of deregulation at domestic level (as a result of regulatory competition) and to the chimera of re-regulation at European level (which is often unrealistic). My interest is in situations in which either the EU has no competence to take action, or in which there is no political will to do so — situations in which, in other terms, 're-regulation' at EU level is not a realistic option. Are we then condemned to the blind mechanisms of regulatory competition? Or are other possibilities open? It is striking that Fritz Scharpf, the main expositor of the 'deregulation/re-regulation' approach, mentions 'political imitation' as a possible factor weighing against the pressure exercised on national regulators by 'regulatory competition' (in areas such as process regulations or taxation of mobile factors or households where such competition may exist), but then states that such 'political imitation' will not be considered further in his examination of the regulatory competition debate (Scharpf 1999: 90–91). Why not? How could such communication across jurisdictions be organised in order to ensure that it works for the benefit of an improvement in standards — a 'race to the top', rather than a 'race to the bottom', as in the regulatory competition scenario?

The reader familiar with the general theme of this book will have no difficulty recognising the homology between the attempt to overcome the 'deregulation/re-regulation' dichotomy through mechanisms that promote learning across jurisdictions, and the more general questions of governance that the book addresses. 'Regulatory competition' may be said to result in coordination through price signals, without any attempt to act collectively; in contrast, 're-regulation' consists in finding agreement on new rules, based on a shared understanding of the European public interest. However, in neither of these two branches of the alternative does learning truly take place. Here, taking the protection of the rights of workers as an example, I try to identify what learning-based approaches to governance can bring to a debate that has originated with the European Economic Community itself. My answer is that such approaches broaden our political imagination, but that more work needs to be done to ensure that the alternatives that are offered lead in fact to optimal outcomes, that truly could ensure that the political preferences of the actors, as reflexively redefined, translate into political action. In this perspective, the issue is less *at which level* social rights are being defined, than *how* this definition takes place, through which procedures, including which actors, and on the basis of which re-framing through deliberation.

II.   THE 'REGULATORY COMPETITION' DEBATE AND SOCIAL RIGHTS: THE ORIGINS

We should begin, perhaps, by recalling the understanding of the relationship between social rights and the common market that was dominant when the European Communities were established. In 1955, acting at the request of the Governing Body of the International Labour Office, a group of experts chaired by the Swedish economist Bertil Ohlin examined the 'Social Aspects of European Economic Co-Operation'. They concluded that the improvement of living standards and labour conditions in the common market should essentially result from the functioning of the market itself, both because of the equalisation of factor prices this would lead to (since wages would be led to rise in labour-abundant countries, as a result of those countries exporting more labour-intensive goods), and because of the productivity gains to be expected from a more efficient international division of labour (Ohlin et al 1955).

That conclusion was based to a significant extent on what was already known at the time to trade specialists as the Heckscher-Ohlin theorem. The theorem, as expounded in the 1933 book by Ohlin, *Interregional and International Trade*, affirms that a country will specialise itself in the production of goods that intensively uses its relatively abundant factor of production, and will import the commodity that intensively uses its relatively scarce factor of production (Ohlin

1933[1]). It follows that trade liberalisation can be a partial substitute for factor mobility and that it will lead in time to factor price equalisation, since the reward for the abundant factor increases and the reward for the scarce factor decreases. The theorem thus offers a fundamentally optimistic view of the benefits of international trade: in this approach, trade flows are caused by differences in endowment factors, and their overall net effect is positive, since in each trading country, the most abundant factor will reap greater rewards than in a situation of autarky.

This optimism was largely mirrored by the Ohlin group of experts. The experts expressed their faith in the ability of international trade to lead to an increase in the standards of living benefiting all categories of the population and conducive, in time, to better and more equal social conditions across the EU. Yet, the experts at the same time clearly acknowledged that these results hold 'when account is taken of the strength of the trade union movement in European countries and of the sympathy of European governments for social aspirations, to ensure that labour conditions would improve and would not deteriorate' (Ohlin et al 1955: paragraph 210). In addition, they emphasised that this 'equalisation in an upward direction' of labour standards could be facilitated if all European countries joined the international conventions adopted by the International Labour Organisation or the Social Charter, then under negotiation within the Council of Europe: the experts considered that it would be useful

> to consider what steps might be taken to promote the more widespread application of the provisions of these Conventions by European countries and thus add to their effectiveness as instruments for solving certain of the social problems connected with closer European economic co-operation' (Ohlin et al 1955: paragraph 273, vi).

Finally, they noted that the establishment of freer international markets 'may be expected to foster the development of international contacts among trade unions and employers' organisations representing the same industry in different countries', something which might assist in 'safeguarding the workers' right to a fair share in the benefits of increasing productivity' while at the same time 'reducing the risk of excessive increases in money wages, costs and prices which otherwise might lead to inflationary pressure in certain countries' (Ohlin et al 1955: paragraph 215).

This essentially optimistic view about the social impacts of European economic integration formed the European version of what JG Ruggie later referred to as the 'embedded liberalism' characteristic of the post-World War II international economic order (Ruggie 1982). In this view, the reduction or elimination of trade barriers between modern Welfare States should serve to enhance the redistributive capabilities of each state vis-à-vis its own citizens, thus leading the

---

[1] Ohlin attributed his views to the influence of an article published in 1919 by Professor E F Heckscher, under whom Ohlin had studied. See Samuelson 1948 and Flam and Flanders 1991.

regulatory state at domestic level to complement trade liberalisation at international level: the gains from trade should benefit the Welfare State, just like the Welfare State should protect the losers from international trade, thus ensuring that international trade remains a politically desirable option. This, however, presupposes that the Welfare State should not be obliged to renounce its regulatory functions under the pressure of trade liberalisation. It also assumes that in their domestic policies, states are not primarily motivated by the need to improve their international competitiveness — that they are not mutating from Welfare States to what Hirsch calls 'national competitive States' (Hirsch 1995).

The Ohlin group of experts were perhaps aware, more than their conclusions seem to suggest, of these limitations. In referring to a floor of rights set at international level, to the need for social dialogue at national level, and to the constitution, at least to some degree, of a transnational movement of workers and employers in order to ensure some form of cross-country comparisons, they were in effect stating the three pre-conditions for economic integration to lead to improved social conditions. One of them, the Frenchman Maurice Byé, found this to be imbalanced. Accusing his colleagues of 'over-optimism', he noted that the danger of their attitude was that 'it gives nations the illusion that they will both enjoy the advantages of European unification and remain fully free to take independent decisions. Any such hope', he remarked,

> would involve a contradiction. Moreover, it could not be shared by all social groups. The more sceptical, weak or fearful elements would weigh any argument based on a long term approach, no matter how perfect and how logical, against immediate threats to their existence (Ohlin et al 1955: 139).

III.   THE DEBATE REVIVED: THE DEBATE ON SERVICES IN THE INTERNAL MARKET

Recent developments in the area of the free provision of services in the EU have given a renewed urgency to the debate. In January 2004, the European Commission proposed a new Directive on services in the internal market (European Commission 2004a). At the core of the Directive, was the so-called 'country of origin principle'. This principle, which specific, sectoral directives had already relied upon,[2] would have ensured that a service provider wanting to supply services to clients in another Member State would in general be subject only to

---

[2]   See eg, art 2(1) of Council Directive (EEC) 89/552 of 3 October 1989 on the coordination of certain provisions laid down by law, regulation or administrative action in Member States concerning the pursuit of television broadcasting activities [1989] OJ L298/23 (as amended by Council Directive (EC) 97/36 [1997] OJ L202/60) ; or art 3(1) of Council Directive (EC) 2000/31 of 8 June 2000 on certain legal aspects of information society services, in particular electronic commerce, in the internal market ('Directive on electronic commerce') [2000] OJ L178/1. The lead author of the proposal of the Commission on the Directive on electronic commerce, Emmanuel Crabit, was also closely involved within the Directorate General internal market in preparing the proposal for a Directive on services in the internal market (see Crabit 2000).

the rules and regulations of the Member State where it had been established. The country of origin principle was defined in the proposal of the Commission as implying that

> Member States shall ensure that providers are subject only to the national provisions of their Member State of origin which fall within the coordinated field [i.e., which concern any requirement applicable to access to service activities or to the exercise thereof] (article 16(1), al 1).

This principle was to cover all national provisions relating to access to and the exercise of a service activity, 'in particular those requirements governing the behaviour of the provider, the quality or content of the service, advertising, contracts and the provider's liability' (article 16(1), al 2). As stated in the extended impact assessment accompanying the proposal (European Commission 2004b: 23–24):

> The barriers affecting the freedom to provide services require mainly that Member States refrain from applying their own rules and regulations to incoming services from other Member States and from supervising and controlling them. Instead they should rely on control by the authorities in the country of origin of the service provider. This would remove the legal uncertainty and costs resulting from the application of a multitude of different rules and control measures to which cross-border service providers are currently subject.

The proposal for a Directive on services in the internal market formed part of a series of initiatives aimed at improving competitiveness and promoting growth within the EU, in order to transform the EU into the most competitive and dynamic knowledge-based economy in the world by 2010, as called for by the March 2000 Lisbon European Council.[3] The adoption of a strategy for the elimination of the obstacles to the free movement of services formed an inherent part of this project. The proposal for a Directive on services in the internal market was motivated, primarily, by a desire to encourage economic growth by promoting the development of cross-border activities by reducing the administrative burdens weighing on service providers and by increasing legal certainty. The Commission considered that there was no risk of social dumping entailed in the country of origin principle: the Community *acquis*, the Commission stated, 'ensures that the minimum working conditions, including minimum salaries of the country to which the workers are posted, have to be respected' (European Commission 2004b: 36). On the contrary, it was added, innovation in services and competitiveness would be improved, and net employment would increase, since 'the posting of skilled or white collar workers would help the process of job creation through the transfer of know-how into local markets which in turn is likely to raise productivity and investment levels' (European Commission 2004b: 36).

---

[3] Presidency Conclusions, Lisbon European Council (24 March 2000) para 17.

The reference to the Community *acquis* was, in particular, to the 1996 Posted Workers Directive.[4] This Directive was adopted following a series of cases which raised the question of which regulations the host state could impose on workers posted on a temporary basis on their territory, for the performance of contracts by service providers established in another Member State and whose business activities, including as regards the employment relationships, are therefore regulated by the state of establishment.[5] In order to ensure that the posting of workers in transnational provision of services would not encourage social dumping, the Posted Workers Directive imposed an obligation on the host Member State to ensure at a minimum that service providers established in another Member State comply with the rules pertaining to

(a)   maximum work periods and minimum rest periods;
(b)   minimum paid annual holidays;
(c)   the minimum rates of pay, including overtime rates, but excluding supplementary occupational retirement pension schemes;
(d)   the conditions of hiring out workers, in particular the supply of workers by temporary employment undertakings;
(e)   health, safety and hygiene at work;
(f)   protective measures with regard to the terms and conditions of employment of pregnant women or women who have recently given birth, of children and of young people; and
(g)   the equality of treatment between men and women and other provisions on non-discrimination (article 3(1)).

In principle, in order to be imposed on the service provider established abroad, the rules relating to these areas should be stipulated by law, regulation or administrative provision. However, the Directive provides that, as regards the construction sector, they may also be contained in collective agreements or arbitration awards which have been 'declared universally applicable'.

When it was presented in 2004, the proposal for a Directive on services in the internal market was presented as fully preserving the Community *acquis* in the area of the posting of workers. Indeed, article 17 of the proposed Directive stated that the country of origin principle did not apply to matters covered by the Posted Workers Directive. And, while article 24 of the proposal for a Directive on internal services in the internal market contained 'specific provisions on the posting of workers', it did seem to preserve the full integrity of the system established by the Posted Workers Directive: it merely stated that the Member State of posting should in principle 'carry out in its territory the checks,

---

[4]   Council Directive (EC) 96/71 of 16 December 1996 concerning the posting of workers in the framework of the provision of services ('Posted Workers Directive') [1997] OJ L18/1.
[5]   See in particular Case C-113/89 *Rush Portuguesa Lda v Office national d'immigration* [1990] ECR I-1417; Case C-272/94 *Criminal proceedings against Guiot* [1996] ECR I-1905.

inspections and investigations necessary to ensure compliance with the employment and working conditions applicable under Directive 96/71/EC', the imposition of certain types of obligations being excluded; and that the Member State of
origin of the service provider should ensure that both its authorities and those of
the Member State of posting receive certain information necessary to ensure full
compliance with the legal requirements imposed on the service provider.

There was a clear risk, however, that the principle of the country of origin not
only would be moving beyond the case law of the European Court of Justice on
the freedom to provide services,[6] but that in addition it would in fact entirely
reverse the system of the Posted Workers Directive. In this Directive, the list of
rules contained in article 3(1) of the Directives constitutes a *minimum* protection
the host state is obliged to provide. Once the Posted Workers Directive becomes a
derogation to the principle of the country of origin, these rules come to define
instead the *maximum* degree of protection a state may offer: in the system
envisaged by the 2004 proposal for a Directive on services in the internal market,
while the matters 'covered' by the Posted Workers Directive, as listed in article
3(1) of this instrument, were 'excluded' from the application of the principle of
the country of origin principle (article 17 (5)), all the other aspects of the
employment contract were to be regulated by the law of the state of establishment rather than by the law of the host state. Although the proposal of the
Commission did provide for the possibility of certain case-by-case derogations to
the principle of country of origin (article 19), none of them is really relevant to
the protection of posted workers, and they seem to be premised, rather, on the
need to ensure an adequate protection of the recipient of services, rather than of
those working for the service providers themselves. For some, this opened the
way to social dumping, if we understand by this expression the choice of
employers to work under a set of rules aimed at the protection of workers which
allows them to be more cost-effective than potential competitors operating on
the same market (De Schutter and Francq 2005; Blanpain 2006). The timing was
particularly ill-chosen: in May 2004, 10 new Member States were to join the EU,
and there were strong fears that the protection of workers was significantly
weaker in those countries, giving the employers in those countries an unfair
advantage in the internal market if they were authorised to provide services
following the regulations imposed on them in the state of establishment only,
with the exception of a minimum set of rules imposed by the state of posting in
the areas listed in article 3(1) of the Posted Workers Directive.[7]

---

[6] In a case concerning the legal basis of Directive 94/19 of the European Parliament and the
Council of 30 May 1994 on deposit-guarantee schemes ([1994] OJ L 35/14), the Court in fact
explicitly denied that there existed a general principle of supervision by the home state of the service
provider offering services in another Member State: see Case C-233/94 *Germany v European
Parliament and Council of the EU* [1997] ECR I-2405 [64].

[7] See in particular, expressing this concern, Vaughan-Whitehead 2003.

Perhaps unsurprisingly, the proposal presented by the European Commission led to strong reactions from a number of sides. On 9 February 2005, the European Economic and Social Committee (EESC) adopted an opinion on the proposal, making a series of suggestions for amendment of the draft Directive.[8] Regarding the country-of-origin principle, the EESC warned that this would lead to regulatory competition and thus to a lowering down of employment, environmental and consumer protection standards, in the presence of widely differing legal, welfare and healthcare systems within the EU (see paragraph 3.5.3.). Rejecting a weakening of existing social protection, wage or safety standards at the workplace as a result of the Directive, the Committee recommended a two-stage transition period, and that Member States be entitled to lay down employment conditions that would apply in their countries to relevant employees, immigrants or posted workers. The EESC regretted a certain ambiguity in the way the proposal of the Commission described its relationship to the Posted Workers Directive, and stated its view that

> Workers from another Member State must receive exactly the same treatment as workers from the country in which the work is being done. This is quite clear from the anti-discrimination perspective that underpins the EU treaties. Wages and working conditions are therefore in all significant aspects to be governed by the rules applying in the country in which the work is being carried out. Control of compliance with these rules in all significant aspects must, to be effective, take place at the place of work. The Services Directive must therefore make clear that the objective of the Posting of workers Directive is to protect workers and that under this directive it is fully permissible to have better rules than the mandatory minimum requirements for workers in a certain country (paragraph 3.6.1.2.).

On 16 February 2006, following one year of discussions, the European Parliament in turn adopted a resolution requesting that the proposal be significantly amended.[9] It recommended in particular that provisions be inserted specifying that the Directive

> shall not apply to or affect labour law, i.e any legal or contractual provision concerning employment conditions, working conditions, including health and safety at work, and the relationships between employers and workers. In particular it shall fully respect the right to negotiate, conclude, extend and enforce collective agreements, and the right to strike and to take industrial action according to the rules governing industrial relations in Member States. Nor shall it affect national social security legislation in the Member States (article 1(7) of the text as amended).

It also recommended that it 'shall not be interpreted as affecting in any way the exercise of fundamental rights as recognised in the Member States and by the Charter of fundamental rights of the European Union, including the right to take industrial action' (article 1(8)). The Parliament also proposed to replace the

---

[8]   [2005] OJ C221/113.
[9]   Doc EP 369.610, P6_TA(2006)0061, 16 February 2006.

principle of the country of origin by a reaffirmation of the freedom to provide services, implying that no restriction to that freedom shall be allowed which does not comply with the principles of non-discrimination, necessity, and proportionality (article 17(1)). In addition, it proposed to explicitly state the primacy of the Posted Workers Directive over the Directive on services in the internal market (article 3(1)), and the insertion of a provision recognising that the provisions of this latter directive on the freedom to provide services

> do not prevent the Member State to which the provider moves from imposing requirements with regard to the provision of a service activity, where they are justified for reasons of public policy, public security, environmental protection and public health. Nor do they prevent Member States from applying, in conformity with Community law, their rules on employment conditions, including those laid down in collective agreements (article 17(3)).

In sum, rather than the revolution proposed by the European Commission through the country of origin principle, the Parliament proposed to reaffirm the case law of the European Court of Justice, and to facilitate the exercise of the freedom to provide services by a series of measures which the initial proposal of the Commission already contained (such as the establishment of single points of contact or administrative cooperation between the authorities of the state of establishment and those of the state where the service is provided).

Taking into account these concerns, the European Commission put forward another proposal in April 2006. The new proposal was substantially revised and followed, for the most part, the requests of the Parliament. It became Directive (EC) 2006/123EC on services in the internal market.[10] The Directive explicitly states that it does not affect the Posted Workers Directive, and that therefore it 'should not prevent Member States from applying terms and conditions of employment on matters other than those listed in Article 3(1) of Directive 96/71/EC on grounds of public policy' (recital 86). Indeed, the Directive should not affect labour law applied in accordance with national and Community law (article 1(6)), and as proposed by the Parliament, the primacy of the Posted Workers Directive is explicitly affirmed (article 3(1)(a)). Although it contains a number of rules on administrative simplification, which aim to facilitate the exercise of freedom to provide services, the country of origin principle has disappeared: instead, as proposed by the Parliament, the principle of free provision of services is reaffirmed, which implies that any restrictions are allowable only insofar as they comply with the principles of non-discrimination, necessity and proportionality (article 17).

---

[10] Council Directive (EC) 2006/123 of 12 December 2006 on services in the internal market [2006] OJ L376/36.

IV. THE 'REGULATORY COMPETITION' SCENARIO AND THE COURT OF
JUSTICE (I): LAVAL

It is the balance established by the 1996 Posted Workers Directive and the 2006
Directive on services in the internal market that the recent case law of the
European Court of Justice seemed to put in jeopardy. In *Laval un Partneri Ltd*,[11]
the Court was asked by the Swedish Labour Court to deliver a preliminary ruling
in a case opposing a Latvian contractor, Laval un Partneri Ltd, to a Swedish trade
union. Laval intended to use Latvian posted workers on a construction site in the
Swedish town of Vaxholm, for the renovation and extension of school premises.
It intended to pay these workers less than the minimum amount stipulated in a
collective agreement concluded between, on the one hand, the Swedish building
and public works trade union, in its capacity as the central organisation representing building workers, and the central organisation for employers in the
construction sector (Sveriges Byggindustrier). This collective agreement imposed
a number of pecuniary obligations for the employers bound. These obligations,
including on the hourly wage and other matters referred to in article 3(1), first
subparagraph, (a) to (g) of the Posted Workers Directive such as working time
and annual leave, went beyond those set out in the applicable Swedish legislation;
some of them related to matters not referred to in that article. Agreeing to the
terms of this collective agreement would have extended the same obligations to
Laval. However, Laval had signed collective agreements in Latvia with the Latvian
building sector's trade union, of which 65 per cent of its workers were members.
None of the members of the Swedish trade unions parties to the collective
agreement concluded with the Sveriges Byggindustrier were employed by Laval.
Laval therefore considered that it should not conclude another, separate collective
agreement for work to be performed in Sweden. A social conflict followed the
refusal of Laval to agree to the terms of the collective agreement proposed by the
Swedish unions. It led ultimately to other trade unions boycotting all Laval's sites
in Sweden. In February 2005, the town of Vaxholm requested that the contract
between it and Baltic be terminated. A month later, Laval was declared bankrupt.

It is not necessary here to go into a detailed discussion of the answers of the
Court of Justice to the questions it was referred by the Swedish courts. Essentially,
the Court concludes that posted workers may not be protected through the
legislation of the state of posting beyond the level of protection which must be
guaranteed to these workers under article 3(1), first subparagraph, (a) to (g) of
the Posted Worker Directive (paragraph 81). As to the question of whether the
collective action resorted to by the Swedish unions was in violation of article 49
EC, which guarantees the freedom to provide services, the Court takes the view
that

---

[11]   Case C-341/05 *Laval un Partneri Ltd* [2007] ECR I-11767. For useful commentaries, see Ganesh
2008 and Deakin 2009.

the right of trade unions of a Member State to take collective action by which undertakings established in other Member States may be forced to sign the collective agreement for the building sector – certain terms of which depart from the legislative provisions and establish more favourable terms and conditions of employment as regards the matters referred to in Article 3(1), first subparagraph, (a) to (g) of Directive 96/71 and others relate to matters not referred to in that provision – is liable to make it less attractive, or more difficult, for such undertakings to carry out construction work in Sweden, and therefore constitutes a restriction on the freedom to provide services within the meaning of Article 49 EC (paragraph 99).

While acknowledging that the right to take collective action is a fundamental right recognised under Community law (paragraphs 90–91), and thus may constitute an overriding reason of public interest justifying, in principle, a restriction of one of the fundamental freedoms guaranteed by the EC Treaty (paragraph 103),[12] the Court notes that, here, the obstacle to the freedom to provide services created by the collective action launched by the Swedish unions cannot be justified with regard to the objective of improving social protection, since,

> with regard to workers posted in the framework of a transnational provision of services, their employer is required, as a result of the coordination achieved by Directive 96/71, to observe a nucleus of mandatory rules for minimum protection in the host Member State (paragraph 108).

Collective action thus cannot seek to impose obligations on employers beyond the obligations the host state must impose in accordance with article 3(1) of the Posted Workers Directive: the Court concludes that the blockade imposed by the Swedish unions on the construction side of the company's subsidiary violates Community law and should not be allowed.

For our purposes, it is another question submitted to the European Court of Justice in *Laval* that is most interesting. This question concerned the Swedish Law on workers' participation in decisions (the MBL),[13] a provision of which prohibited taking collective action with the aim of obtaining the repeal of or amendment to a collective agreement between other parties. In 1989, it was held by the Swedish labour courts that such prohibition extended to collective action undertaken in Sweden in order to obtain the repeal of or amendment to a collective agreement concluded between foreign parties, in a workplace abroad, if such collective action is prohibited by the foreign law applicable to the signatories to that collective agreement. This reading of the MBL was given in a dispute concerning working conditions for the crew of a container ship named *Britannia*, flying a foreign flag. In reaction, and with a clear intention to combat what they saw as a risk of social dumping, the Swedish legislature adopted the 'Lex

---

[12] See eg, joined cases C-369/96 and C-376/96 *Arblade* [1999] ECR I-8453 [36]; Case C-165/98 *Mazzoleni and ISA* [2001] ECR I-2189 [27]; joined cases C-49/98, C-50/98, C-52/98 to C-54/98 and C-68/98 to C-71/98 *Finalarte* [2001] ECR I-7831; Case C-36/02, *Omega* [2004] ECR I-9609 [35].

[13] Lagen 1976: 580 om medbestämmande i arbetslivet ou medbestämmandelagen.

Britannia', limiting the scope of the principle expounded in the *Britannia* judgment. The 'Lex Britannia' entered into force in 1991. It provided, inter alia, that the prohibition to resort to collective action to undo an existing collective agreement shall apply only if an organisation commences collective action by reason of employment relationships falling directly within the scope of the Swedish Law. In practice, the 'Lex Britannia' thus authorised collective action against foreign service providers only temporarily active in Sweden, even in circumstances where such service providers had concluded a collective agreement in their home state and where the foreign legislation prohibited unions from using collective action to question the terms of the agreement reached. This, the Court of Justice considered, amounted to a form of discrimination prohibited under the EC Treaty:

> national rules, such as [the 'Lex Britannia'], which fail to take into account, irrespective of their content, collective agreements to which undertakings that post workers to Sweden are already bound in the Member State in which they are established, give rise to discrimination against such undertakings, in so far as under those national rules they are treated in the same way as national undertakings which have not concluded a collective agreement (paragraph 116).

The obvious risk is that such a mandated mutual recognition of collective agreements will allow employers to establish themselves in states in which wages and social advantages are relatively low and unions relatively weak, and to use the collective agreement concluded with the local unions as a shield against any collective action by the unions in the state of posting, aimed at questioning the terms of the collective agreement reached in the state or origin. It is precisely this consequence that the 'Lex Britannia' sought to avoid: as remarked by the European Court of Justice, the 'Lex Britannia'

> is intended, first, to allow trade unions to take action to ensure that all employers active on the Swedish labour market pay wages and apply other terms and conditions of employment in line with those usual in Sweden, and secondly, to create a climate of fair competition, on an equal basis, between Swedish employers and entrepreneurs from other Member States (paragraph 118).

But this intention — to combat 'social dumping' — does not appear to the Court to correspond to the grounds of public policy, public security or public health which are limitatively enumerated in article 46 EC, applied in conjunction with article 55 EC (now respectively articles 49 and 55 of the Treaty on the Functioning of the European Union (TFEU)), as justifying derogations from the freedom to provide services guaranteed in article 49 EC (now TFEU). The 'Lex Britannia' thus violates EU law.

V.   EVALUATING LAVAL

Laval has been widely denounced as encouraging 'social dumping' by employers and 'regulatory competition' between states. The notion of 'social dumping' may of course be given various definitions, ranging from situations in which an employer deliberately violates existing legislation in order to achieve a competitive advantage, to situations where practices as regards working conditions and wages comply with the applicable labour legislation and simply reflect different levels of productivity between workers, without entailing any distortion of competition (on these various definitions, see Vaughan-Whitehead 2003: 325–27).[14] As employed here, it refers to the practice of companies to locate their activities in the state, and thus under the regulatory regime, that will make compliance with social regulations least costly, in order to be the most competitive in the internal market. 'Regulatory competition' in turn refers to the choice of states to regulate wages and other working conditions in order to ensure that the companies established under their jurisdiction will not be placed at a competitive disadvantage as a result of higher labour costs being imposed on them than would be justified by the productivity of their workers, in comparison to companies established in other Member States which compete for the same markets.

It deserves notice that there are few restrictions to the potential 'abuse of the right to establishment' in EU law, when a company decides to reincorporate in a Member State other than its state of origin in order to benefit from a more favourable regulatory environment. In *Centros Ltd*, the Court expressed the view that

> the fact that a national of a Member State who wishes to set up a company chooses to form it in the Member State whose rules of company law seem to him the least restrictive and to set up branches in other Member States cannot, in itself, constitute an abuse of the right of establishment. The right to form a company in accordance with the law of a Member State and to set up branches in other Member States is inherent in the exercise, in a single market, of the freedom of establishment guaranteed by the Treaty.[15]

Although the Court added that this should not be seen as an obstacle to the adoption by states of measures aimed at preventing fraud, for instance where it is established that the formation of the company intends to evade obligations towards private or public creditors,[16] the case was widely seen as promoting regulatory competition in corporate law in the EU.[17] *Centros* was reaffirmed in a case in which a company incorporated in the Netherlands was denied by the German courts the capacity to be a party to legal proceedings in Germany

---

[14]   For a discussion of these various definitions, see Vaughan-Whitehead 2003: 325–27.

[15]   Case C-212/97 *Centros Ltd* [1999] ECR I-1459 [27].

[16]   Case C-212/97 *Centros Ltd* [1999] ECR I-1459 [38].

[17]   See Ebke 2000; Looijestijn-Clearie 2000; Roth 2003; Siems 2002; Deakin 1999.

without reincorporating in Germany, a restriction to freedom of establishment which the Court considered a violation of the rules of the EC Treaty on freedom of establishment.[18] Finally, in *Kamer van Koophandel en Fabrieken voor Amsterdam v Inspire Art Ltd*, decided in 2003, the Court considered that it was not abuse of the right of establishment to seek to circumvent the more demanding conditions imposed under Dutch company law by incorporating in the United Kingdom, even if almost all the activities of the company do in fact take place in the Netherlands:

> the fact that a company does not conduct any business in the Member State in which it has its registered office and pursues its activities only or principally in the Member State where its branch is established is not sufficient to prove the existence of abuse or fraudulent conduct which would entitle the latter Member State to deny that company the benefit of the provisions of Community law relating to the right of establishment.[19]

It is against this background that we can understand why, when it examined the initial proposal of the Commission for a Directive on the services in the internal market, the European Parliament favoured the addition of a recital in the preamble:

> The place at which a service provider is established should be determined in conformity with the case law of the Court of Justice according to which the concept of establishment involves the actual pursuit of an economic activity through a fixed establishment for an indefinite period; this requirement is also fulfilled where a company is constituted for a given period or where it rents the building or installation through which it pursues its activity. According to this definition which requires the actual pursuit of an economic activity at the place of establishment of the service provider, a mere letter box does not constitute an establishment. In cases where a provider has several places of establishment it is important to determine from which place of establishment the actual service concerned is provided; in cases where it is difficult to determine from which of several places of establishment a given service is provided, this is the place where the provider has the centre of his activities relating to this particular service (proposed recital 41).

The insertion of this recital aimed at avoiding the phenomenon of 'letter box' companies, established in one Member State with the sole purpose of working under its regulatory framework, and even if the activities of the company do not in fact present any real connection to the state of incorporation. The Court itself has subsequently agreed that restrictions on the freedom of establishment could be justified in exceptional circumstances 'on the ground of prevention of abusive practices', for instance in order to 'prevent conduct involving the creation of

---

[18] See Case C-208/00 *Überseering BV v Nordic Construction Company Baumanagement GmbH ECR* [2002] ECR I-9919.

[19] Case C-167/01 *Kamer van Koophandel en Fabrieken voor Amsterdam v Inspire Art Ltd* [2003] ECR I-10155[139]. See Wymeersch 2003; Kersting and Schindler 2003.

wholly artificial arrangements which do not reflect economic reality, with a view to escaping the tax normally due on the profits generated by activities carried out on national territory'.[20]

However, the main safeguard against the risk of companies relocating in order to escape certain onerous regulatory requirements and hire workers under the terms of a domestic legislation less protective of the rights of workers, stems from the fact that, for a number of EU Member States, the state of incorporation is not the decisive factor for purposes of determining the state of establishment: instead, they rely on the 'real seat' doctrine, which presupposes that the company is considered to be established where it concentrates its activities or has its main place of business, and thus creates a link between the 'nationality' of the company — the law under which it operates — and its 'residence', its principal place of business.[21] A company will therefore not be authorised to rely on its freedom of establishment in order to develop activities in one Member State while remaining governed by the law of the Member State of origin (where the company was initially incorporated), solely in order to benefit for the more favourable regulatory provisions of the latter. This is illustrated, for instance, by the *Cartesio Oktató és Szolgáltató bt* judgment of 16 December 2008.[22] The Hungarian law applicable did not allow a company incorporated in Hungary to transfer its seat abroad while continuing to be subject to Hungarian law as its personal law. This in practice obliged the company wishing to convert itself into a company governed by the law of another Member State, first to cease to exist as a Hungarian company. The Court refused to treat this as a disproportionate restriction to the freedom of establishment of companies: instead, it took the view that it is up to the national law of the Member State of incorporation to decide whether a company may transfer its registered office or its actual centre of administration to another Member State without losing its legal personality.

'Regulatory competition' in the EU is therefore not unbridled. Certain restrictions are imposed on companies seeking to incorporate themselves under the laws of the Member State that impose the lightest burdens. These restrictions in turn diminish the pressure on states to relax their regulatory standards, since the clearest instances of abuse — such as the setting up of 'letterbox' or 'front' subsidiaries[23] — may be reacted to by states. Nevertheless, within these broad limitations summarised above, companies may choose where to establish themselves and, thus, under which rules to provide services across the EU. What are the consequences? Some have noted the disciplining virtue that could result from 'regulatory competition', in the meaning which has been referred to: states will act more rationally, it has been suggested, if some degree of horizontal economic

---

[20] Case C-196/04 *Cadbury Schweppes and Cadbury Schweppes Overseas* [2006] ECR I-7995 [55].
[21] This constitutes a notable difference with the United States, where incorporation is decisive (see Charny 1991).
[22] Case C-210/16 *Cartesio Oktató és Szolgáltató bt* nyr.
[23] Case C-196/04 *Cadbury Schweppes and Cadbury Schweppes Overseas* [2006] ECR I-7995 [68].

competition is organised, obliging them to offer the best 'fit' of regulation combined with well-educated workforce and other advantages to the companies locating their activities under their jurisdiction.[24] However, there are also instances in which 'regulatory competition' may lead to sub-optimal outcomes: in what may be understood as one form of the prisoner's dilemma, states will legislate, not in accordance with the 'real' preferences of the domestic constituency (ie, what that constituency would have chosen in the absence of competition from other jurisdictions), but taking into account the need to attract companies (or to stem their relocation abroad) as a source, primarily, of employment creation. The notions of 'social dumping' and of 'regulatory competition' both suggest the risk of a 'race to the bottom' in the presence of a variety of regulatory regimes coexisting in an area in which the factors of production are mobile and in which mutual recognition of these regulatory regimes is established.[25] A decisive question for the future direction of social rights in the EU is whether such a 'race to the bottom' is likely, and whether *Laval* encourages such an evolution.

What does *Laval* stand for, under this dynamic perspective? In substance, the European Court of Justice considers that the *minimum* (or 'mandatory') rules which the host Member State must impose compliance with on its territory in fact should be treated as the *maximum* level of protection that state may grant to workers posted on its territory: any further restriction to the freedom to provide services is likely to impose a disproportionate burden on the service provider, and collective action seeking to force that service provider to agree to more favourable terms of employment are considered to constitute an abuse of the right to resort to collective action. This turns the Posted Workers Directive on its head. It also amounts to choosing, among the different objectives pursued by the Posted Workers Directive, the freedom to provide services above the other two objectives — the protection of the rights of workers and the policy space of the host state. It is also premised on the idea that the application of any legislation at the place of posting which differs from the legislation imposed on the service provider in the state of establishment is per se a restriction on the freedom to provide services, *whether or not the legislation of the state of establishment provides an equivalent level of protection to workers.*

Thus, *Laval* reflects an understanding of mutual trust in the transnational provision of services in the EU which may be called 'blind': it is not conditional on the state of establishment of the service provider guaranteeing workers with a level of protection of their rights equivalent to that ensured in the host Member

---

[24]   See eg, Trachtman 1993: 51–53. For a comparison between the United States and the EU debates on regulatory competition, see also Barnard 2000: 57–78.

[25]   The notion of the 'race to the bottom' was apparently introduced Cary 1974: 666. However, the idea is already expressed with great clarity by Justice Brandeis, in *Liggett Co v Lee* 288 U.S. 517, 559 (1933) (Brandeis, J, diss), where he makes reference to the 'race of laxity' between states as businesses would move to the states with the least demanding regulatory requirements.

State. In the view of the Court, it does not matter whether or not the foreign service provider is bound, in the Member State of establishment, by rules ensuring a protection of workers equivalent to that they would be guaranteed by the extension to those workers of collective agreements concluded in the state of posting by the local unions for the benefit of the local workforce. It is in that sense that *Laval* may be said to organise regulatory competition between the EU Member States.

This also derives from the second part of the judgment, which concerns the allegedly discriminatory character of the Lex Britannia adopted in 1991 by the Swedish legislature in order to combat 'social dumping'. The Court takes the view that it is discriminatory not to apply a rule prohibiting collective action aimed at setting aside collective agreements already concluded between labour and management to collective action against service providers established in another Member State. The assumption appears to be that collective agreements concluded abroad must be trusted in principle to offer a sufficiently high level of protection of workers. Whether such trust should be blind or should instead be seen as a rebuttable presumption that the protection of workers is sufficiently robust, is not clear. The Court notes at one point that the Lex Britannia 'fails to take into account, *irrespective of their content*, collective agreements to which undertakings that post workers to Sweden are already bound in the Member State in which they are established'.[26] This suggests that collective agreements which are insufficiently protective of workers may not shield the foreign service providers having concluded them from having to face collective action by Swedish unions. However, the remainder of the judgment of the Court does not refer back to this proviso, and suggests instead that the EU Member States should trust collective agreements concluded in another Member State as ensuring a level of protection equivalent to collective agreements concluded under their own jurisdiction.

VI.   THE 'REGULATORY COMPETITION' SCENARIO AND THE COURT OF JUSTICE (II): VIKING

Laval was decided on 18 December 2007, but it does not stand alone. It may be replaced in a broader context in which the European Court of Justice increasingly appears to favour an interpretation of the requirements of Community law that seeks to encourage competition between the national regulatory systems, and that treats with suspicion any attempt by the Member States to limit the impacts of such competition on the protection of workers (Eliasoph 2008). In *International Transport Workers' Federation and Finnish Seamen's Union v Viking Line*

---

[26]   Case C-341/05 *Laval* [2007] ECR I-11767 [116] (emphasis added).

ABP and OÜ Viking Line Eesti ('Viking'),[27] decided only a few days before *Laval,*
the International Transport Workers' Federation (ITF) and its local affiliate, the
Finnish Seaman's Union (FSU), resorted to collective action in order to prevent
Viking, a Finnish ferry boat operator, from re-flagging a Finnish vessel as an
Estonian vessel in order to escape the application of Finnish employment laws
and the applicable collective agreement. The Court considered that such collective action, in the form of a strike and a boycott, should be treated as a restriction
to the freedom of establishment recognised under article 43 EC, since it has

> the effect of making less attractive, or even pointless, [...] Viking's exercise of its right to
> freedom of establishment, inasmuch as such action prevents both Viking and its
> subsidiary, Viking Eesti, from enjoying the same treatment in the host Member State as
> other economic operators established in that State (paragraph 72).

The Court acknowledged that the right to take collective action for the protection
of workers is a legitimate interest which, in principle, justifies a restriction of one
of the fundamental freedoms guaranteed by the Treaty, and that the protection of
workers is one of the overriding reasons of public interest recognised in its case
law.[28] However, even if they pursue a legitimate aim compatible with the Treaties
and are justified by overriding reasons of public interest, restrictions to freedom
of establishment are only acceptable insofar as they are suitable for securing the
attainment of the objective pursued and do not go beyond what is necessary in
order to attain it. While the Court recognised the legitimacy for unions to seek to
safeguard the rights of *current* employees of the vessel, it expressed the view that
any collective action going beyond that objective would be disproportionate:
resorting to strikes or boycotts to avoid reflagging would be unacceptable, in the
eyes of the Court, if it were established that the jobs or conditions of employment
at issue were not jeopardised or under serious threat. Such is the case, in
particular, if the company concerned has agreed to a binding undertaking that
the reflagging would not result in terminating the employment of any person
employed by them at the time it is made, even if such undertaking does not
include the renewal of short-term employment contracts or prevent the rede-
ployment of any employee on equivalent terms and conditions.[29] In other terms,
collective action by unions may seek to protect the acquired rights of existing
employees: it would be abusive if it served, instead, to discourage the exercise of

---

[27]   Case C-438/05 *International Transport Workers' Federation and Finnish Seamen's Union v Viking
Line ABP and OÜ Viking Line Eesti ('Viking')* [2007] ECR I-10779.

[28]   Referring to the social provisions of the EC Treaty, the Court also noted that 'the Community
has thus not only an economic but also a social purpose', which implied that 'the rights under the
provisions of the Treaty on the free movement of goods, persons, services and capital must be
balanced against the objectives pursued by social policy, which include, as is clear from the first
paragraph of article 136 EC, inter alia, improved living and working conditions, so as to make
possible their harmonisation while improvement is being maintained, proper social protection and
dialogue between management and labour' (para 79).

[29]   See [82] of the judgment and the 10th question referred to the European Court of Justice by the
Court of Appeal (England and Wales) (Civil Division).

freedom of establishment by companies seeking to relocate themselves to benefit from a more favourable regulatory environment.

The distinction between these two purposes of resorting to collective action was put forward by AG Poiares Maduro in the opinion he delivered in the *Viking* case. It was justified as follows:

> collective action to persuade an undertaking to maintain its current jobs and working conditions must not be confused with collective action to prevent an undertaking from providing its services once it has relocated abroad. The first type of collective action represents a legitimate way for workers to preserve their rights and corresponds to what would usually happen if relocation were to take place within a Member State. Yet, that cannot be said of collective action that merely seeks to prevent an undertaking that has moved elsewhere from lawfully providing its services in the Member State in which it was previously established' (paragraph 67).

This latter form of collective action, in the view of the Advocate-General, 'entirely negates the rationale of the common market' (paragraph 68). However, these two criteria are not equivalent. From the viewpoint of the 'common market', what matters is whether or not the collective action functions as an obstacle, or at least as a disincentive, to relocate activities in another EU Member State, whether the action seeks to preserve existing jobs in one Member State or whether it seeks to go beyond that and to ensure that further investments will lead to more jobs being created in that Member State. Conversely, collective action that seeks to protect employment in one plant is unrelated to the establishment of the common market if the competing plant where relocation is envisaged is situated in the same Member State, and it does not matter in that regard if the collective action concerns existing (acquired) rights of workers or the hiring or conditions of employment of new workers.

What is even more disturbing, however, is that collective action is more important, rather than less, in a transnational context, where it seeks to constitute a counterweight to the exercise by companies of their freedom of establishment. The reason for this is simple: whereas social legislation can be set at national level, through the normal political process, the same may not be possible to achieve at the EU level, in part because of the limited competences of the EU in the area of social rights, and in part because of the difficulty of achieving the required consensus between EU Member States in this domain. AG Poiares Maduro rightly recognises the importance of transnational collective action which, he states, 'in principle constitutes a reasonable method of counter-balancing the actions of undertakings who seek to lower their labour costs by exercising their rights to freedom of movement', particularly taking into account 'the fact that workers have a lower degree of mobility than capital or undertakings' (paragraph 70). However, he adds that:

> A policy of coordinated collective action could easily be abused in a discriminatory manner if it operated on the basis of an obligation imposed on all national unions to support collective action by any of their fellow unions. It would enable any national

union to summon the assistance of other unions in order to make relocation to another Member State conditional on the application of its own preferred standards of worker protection, even after relocation has taken place. In effect, therefore, such a policy would be liable to protect the collective bargaining power of some national unions at the expense of the interests of others, and to partition the labour market in breach of the rules on freedom of movement (paragraph 71).

This is a paradoxical result. Allowing for transnational collective action to constitute a 'counter-weight' to the free movement of companies only insofar as it preserves the freedom of each national union to choose whether or not to join the action, seems to negate the idea of collective action altogether, the very purpose of which is to strengthen the bargaining position of all workers by imposing a collective discipline across the workforce. The possibility of collective action must be commensurate to what is at stake — the disciplining of economic actors that operate transnationally. Lord Wedderburn made the point forcefully already in 1973:

> The true correlative to an international agreement securing the right to capital the right to move and, therefore, organize across the boundaries of national states would be an agreement securing to collective organizations of workpeople the right to take common action in negotiating, bargaining with and, if need be, striking against the multinational enterprises. [...] It is not true free movement of labour but free international trade union action which is the true counterpart to free movement of capital (Wedderburn 1973: 249).

It is only the possibility of transnational collective action that can restore the balance between the position of employers (and shareholders), on the one hand, and workers, on the other hand, taking into account the important obstacles to the exercise by workers of their freedom of movement. Transnational collective action already allows us to move beyond the alternative of deregulation (negative integration) and re-regulation (positive integration through law), that has classically structured the debate on the relationship between the economic and the social dimensions of European integration. However, the idea of equalising the bargaining power of each side remains insufficient. It still expresses an almost physicalist idea of competing forces, when what we need is a deliberative idea about how to shape the European public interest. How can this be achieved?

VII.   BEYOND REGULATORY COMPETITION AND RE-REGULATION: LEARNING

A.   The Promise of Democratic Experimentalism

The idea of 'regulatory competition' is premised on the view that states will seek to create a regulatory environment as favourable as possible to the undertakings established under their jurisdiction, in order to attract them, as a source of capital mobilisation and employment creation, transfers of technologies, and fiscal revenues, for the state concerned (Simmons, Elkins and Guzman 2006). However, this is in fact a highly reductionist view. It impoverishes our understanding of states' behaviour just like the idea of the *homo economicus*, in classical economics, impoverishes our understanding of the behaviour of the individual. It underestimates the complexity of decision-making processes at domestic level and, in particular, the weight of workers' unions in our advanced Welfare States. It is precisely the reality of the contest of the definition of the 'public interest' in each state that is ignored when the national preferences of each state are pre-defined, or depoliticised, based on a view of governments as systematically seeking to attract foreign capital by creating a regulatory environment favourable to the undertakings established on their territory. Instead, while it is acknowledged that 'social policy regulations that have (or are perceived as having) the effect of reducing profits and hence capital incomes are [...] vulnerable to increased capital mobility', the 'race to the bottom' in this area 'will at least be impeded by the political commitment of national governments to social policy purposes and by the resistance of unions and other groups that would suffer from deregulation and setbacks' (Scharpf 1997: 524).

There is thus a relative autonomy of domestic politics from regulatory competition between states: while actors at the domestic level can seek to justify their positions by relying on arguments based, for instance, on the risk that undertakings will relocate their activities, or on the need to protect workers from the risks of 'social dumping', the position of the state as a whole will depend on the ability of each of the competing groups to push towards the compromise most favourable to their respective constituencies (Menz 2003; Esty and Geradin 2000). This is not to say that states cannot be treated as 'rational actors', for instance to describe their position in international negotiations. For instance, the 'liberal intergovernmentalist' model of international negotiations adopted by Andrew Moravcsik takes as its departure point 'the assumption that states act rationally or instrumentally in pursuit of relatively stable and well-ordered interests at any given point in time' (Moravcsik 1998:18), a methodological approach he also refers to as the 'unitary-actor assumption'. However, Moravcsik rightly distinguishes the formation of national preferences as a separate and contested moment, noting that his 'rationalist framework of international cooperation' does not assume that states are 'unitary in their internal politics'. Quite the contrary in fact:

> National preferences – the underlying 'states of the world' that states seek to realize through world politics – are shaped through contention among domestic political groups. The unitary-actor assumption maintains only that once particular objectives arise out of this domestic competition, states strategize as unitary actors vis-à-vis other states in an effort to realize them (Moravcsik 1998: 22).

In contrast, many regulatory competition scenarios adopt a reductionist view of the formation of the political preferences of each state. Not only do they seem to assume, without justification, that the interests of the business community will be systematically prioritised above those of workers or of the public as a whole. They also underestimate the potential role of what has been referred to above as 'political imitation' — ie, of the process through which each state seeks inspiration from the others, in making decisions of its own. Communication between jurisdiction matters, not only because it may lead to a 'race to the bottom' in certain areas, as states observe each other and do not wish to have their competitiveness undercut by the regulatory choices made in other states, but also because 'best practices' can be shared, and relied upon by various groups within the state, to force a 'race to the top'.

Indeed, at the core of the idea of democratic experimentalism, as pioneered in particular in the work of Ch Sabel and J Zeitlin,[30] is the intuition that governance in multi-level (or federal) entities should be conceived in order to encourage local experiments (the search, in each sub-unit, of innovative solutions to the problems to which all units are confronted), combined with a pooling of the results following such experiments (on the basis of the evaluation made of those experiments). In this view, the combination of decentralised experimentation with the pooling of information and evaluations performed jointly should allow all sub-units of the system to benefit from the progress in understanding made in local settings. Such collective learning may potentially result in the empowerment of groups at the domestic level, whose inability to propose credible alternatives may otherwise lead to their marginalisation from the political process. It is precisely the potential of such collective learning that is underestimated in the scenarios of 'regulatory competition' that assume that states act with the main or even the sole purpose of enabling undertakings established on their territory to increase their competitiveness: such scenarios simply ignore the reality of democratic self-determination, and the potential role, in the formation of domestic policy preferences, of political imitation.

However, democratic experimentalism and the collective learning that it seeks to encourage, only have chances of succeeding if certain institutional conditions are fulfilled, both at EU and at national level. Essentially two sets of conditions can be identified. One set of conditions relate to building the capacity of the actors, particularly the normative and organisational resources they have at their disposal to take part in democratic decision-making. Another set of conditions relate to the progressive elucidation of the European public interest.

B.   Enhancing Capacities

The capacity of actors in domestic political processes to effectively learn from developments in other jurisdictions and to define their positions on that basis cannot be merely assumed: it must be affirmatively created. One means to facilitate this is to establish, within each Member State, an institution specifically

---

[30] See in particular Sabel and Zeitlin 2008; Sabel and Zeitlin 2010. For previous contributions in this direction, see also Dorf and Sabel 1998; Sabel and Cohen 1997; Gerstenberg and Sabel 2002.

tasked with examining responses given to certain problems in order jurisdictions, with providing a causality analysis identifying the factors explaining the successes and failures of these experiments, and with discussing whether the solutions developed elsewhere could inspire similar developments in the local jurisdiction concerned. The existence, within the 'receiving' jurisdiction, of an agency specifically dedicated to the understanding of such foreign experiments and to assessing whether the transposition of such experiments would be desirable, could greatly contribute to overcoming bureaucratic inertia and the resistance of policy-makers who, in the face of uncertainty about whether change will be rewarding, might otherwise prefer to opt for the perpetuation of routines — for choice without search. In that sense, the reception structures may be more or less favourable to mutual learning: the wide diffusion of foreign policy experiments to a broad range of actors, as well as the establishment of expert bodies or think tanks whose mission it is to draw the attention of policy-makers to the need to explore those solutions, could greatly contribute to the success of mutual learning as one possible result of evaluation. Alternatively, in the absence of such a specialised learning institution or in combination, the transnational organisation of networks — such as through the establishment of global or European unions — may promote such learning, by the exchange of experiences across jurisdictions that such networks allow.

Whether through specialised agencies or through transnational networks of actors, learning across jurisdictions requires the performance of solid, appropriately contextualised causality analysis. Indeed, contextualisation both of the solutions developed in other settings and of the problems encountered in the 'receiving' jurisdiction seems necessary for learning to be successful. Solutions developed elsewhere cannot simply be presumed to be transposable to any other context: instead, what makes one approach successful in any particular situation will depend on a full range of factors which may or may not be present in the context in which that solution is being replicated. In what may be seen as one version of the 'garbage can' logic of decision-making (Cohen et al 1972), the available solutions risk predetermining the understanding of the problem to be addressed, rather than the problem being diagnosed independently of which solutions offer themselves. Therefore, any attempt by a 'receiving' jurisdiction to borrow from solutions developed elsewhere to similar policy problems should be preceded by an attempt to identify the conditions which allowed those particular solutions to be effective where they were first introduced, and by a diagnosis of the reasons why the approaches currently in place in the receiving jurisdiction have failed, which should be conducted independently of the existing catalogue of alternative policies. While foreign experiences may shed light on certain problems in the 'receiving' jurisdiction which might otherwise have been underestimated or ignored, they should not be seen as a substitute for the analysis of those problems under the specific circumstances in which they have arisen. The risk of such 'decontextualized learning', in which solutions are prescribed irrespective of local conditions (Hemerijck and Visser 2006: 42), is especially high where the analysis of policy options is sectorialized, ie where this analysis focuses on discrete areas of public policy, defined relatively narrowly, and thus detached from the analysis of the background conditions which may play a role in the success or failure of the policy options which are experimented.

C.   The European Public Interest

What makes the idea of democratic experimentalism as a source of collective learning particularly attractive is that it breaks down the classical principal-agent relationship, as well as the distinction between means and ends. In this learning-based model of governance, there is no predefined EU-wide 'public interest' to be simply implemented by a combination of EU and domestic policies. Instead, the 'sub-units', the Member States, constantly redefine the aims of European integration as they experiment with different policies: these policies serve not as mere instruments in the service of some higher ideal, but as searching devices that contribute to defining the objectives pursued. However, this shift — away from Rousseau, if you wish, and embracing the pragmatist politics of Dewey — leaves open the question of how different experiments, conducted within each sub-unit, are to be evaluated, and how collective action at EU level should be conceived and could be made to emerge.

For policies developed within each jurisdiction to be a source of learning, they should be evaluated. This does not necessarily presuppose that the evaluation criteria have to be set in advance, in the form of a predefined grid of indicators; but it does require that the basis on which each experiment is evaluated is made explicit and can be subject to open deliberation and critique. The 2001 White Paper on European Governance lists both participation and accountability — along with openness, effectiveness, and coherence — among the five principles of good governance (European Commission 2001: 10). Evaluation of course, contributes to the effectiveness of EU policies, but it may also stimulate democratic debate and promote accountability. Provided with the results of an evaluation of the achievements of the Member State concerned in a particular policy area, opposition political parties, civil society organisations, the media, and the public at large, not only will be better equipped to request explanations from decision-makers, and to critically gauge the justifications offered for pursuing particular policy options; they will also be more motivated to invest in any participatory mechanisms proposed to them. The broad discussion of alternatives to the dominant solution may provide public officials with an incentive to revise their routines. This may compensate at least partly for their fear that, by exploring those alternatives, they will betray established expectations and threaten acquired positions, which may be costly in electoral terms — especially since, as noted by

March and Olsen, voters tend to sanction mistakes, more than the failure to explore untested opportunities, leading policy-makers to be generally risk-averse.[31]

In the area of fundamental rights, and of social rights in particular, the Fundamental Rights Agency set up in 2007 could constitute a mechanism to promote collective learning between the Member States, by ensuring that their experiences in the field of fundamental rights are compared and that best practices are identified and their diffusion, perhaps, encouraged. The Impact Assessment Report appended to the proposal put forward by the European Commission on 30 June 2005[32] initially justified the establishment of the Agency by the finding that

> Although the Member States have developed various strategies, policies and mecha-
> nisms to respect and mainstream fundamental rights when implementing Union law
> and policies, there is a lack of systematic observation of how the Member States do this.
> Such a lack represents a missed opportunity, as the potential for sharing of experiences
> and good practices and mutual learning is not met.[33]

Thus, a discussion should be organised at EU level — and possibly, with the Fundamental Rights Agency acting as a clearing house for information and exchanges of best practices —, on the lessons to be drawn from successes and failures of experiments conducted within each Member State. This is also vital for another reason. It seems to be required for the very possibility of collective action to develop at the EU level, where decentralised approaches appear unsatisfactory in the presence of problems with important cross-border dimensions, in which the efforts of each state can only be successful if combined with those other states. It would, of course, not be compatible with the purpose of a decentralised and experimentalist approach to problem-solving, to identify 'the Union' as a 'principal' in charge of deciding which problems should be addressed at the level of the EU rather than at the level of the Member States. Yet, in the absence of a procedural solution to the question of the allocation of competences between the Union and the Member States, the risk may be that the national authorities will only explore the possibilities which appear to them satisfactory in the decentral-ised framework under which they operate, and in the absence of any certainty about the choices which will be made by the other sub-units. In this scenario, their 'freedom to experiment' by an inventive use of their margin of appreciation in the face of ambiguously defined objectives without any specification as to the means, might turn out to be purely illusory: as well highlighted by the concept of

---

[31]   March and Olsen 1995: 227. In that sense, 'Democratic institutions (…) are both arranged to speed up and slow down learning from experience and adaptation' (March and Olsen 2001: 13).

[32]   Proposal for a Council Regulation establishing a European Union Agency for Fundamental Rights and Proposal for a Council Decision empowering the European Union Agency for Fundamen-tal Rights to pursue its activities in areas referred to in Title VI of the Treaty on European Union (COM (2005) 280 final of 30.6.2005).

[33]   SEC(2005)849 of 30.6.2005, p 8.

regulatory competition, this freedom vis-à-vis rules set from above by the 'principal' may be constrained by the choices made in other jurisdictions, given the high degree of interdependency between choices of each national jurisdiction in the internal market.

The allocation of competences between the Member States and the Union cannot be defined according to some pre-defined formula, or according to boundaries clearly delimited once and for all. Indeed, it is precisely the reverse that is suggested here: that a mechanism be set up in order to identify the problems which might need to be addressed collectively, on a case-to-case basis, and in clear acknowledgement of our incapacity to anticipate all the situations where such collective action might be required.[34] The principles of subsidiarity and proportionality that guide the exercise by the EU of its competences in the areas in which it shares its competences with the Member States could also guide the deliberation about what tools should be developed at EU level in order to broaden the range of alternatives explored at Member State level, and thus promote democratic self-determination by ensuring that choices made at state level will not be determined by the risks of regulatory competition. However, these principles are useful signposts because they are vague and open, and not because they are prescriptive or because they provide some sort of formula to calculate what is in the European public interest — for they do not. Subsidiarity is useful not for what it says, but for what it is silent about. In a learning-based understanding of governance, it should be conceived as 'active', in the sense identified by Pierre Calame:

> … because the interests guaranteed by the higher levels are expressed not through the implementation of uniform rules applying to isolated individuals but through the formulation of obligations regarding the results to be achieved. These obligations to achieve certain results are addressed to a community of partners: national civil servants, local government officials, private-sector businesses and voluntary associations. They force those involved to work in partnership and create a permanent learning process focusing on appropriate and meaningful action: action is no longer judged in relation to its outward forms but in relation to the way it is devised and implemented locally, with reference both to the aims pursued (. . .) and the specific circumstances of each context (Calame 2001: 229).

VIII.   CONCLUSION

We are not fatally entrapped in the apparent dilemma between a decentralised protection of social rights, with the associated risk of regulatory competition and a 'race to the bottom', and re-regulation at EU level, leading to the super-imposition of a European Welfare State over and above the national Welfare

---

[34] For such a procedural understanding of the principles of subsidiarity and proportionality guiding the exercise of powers shared between the Union and the Member States, see De Schutter 2005: 340–42 ; and Weatherwill 2003: 46.

States. The evaluation of each Member State's successes and failures can both promote learning across jurisdictions, and encourage actors at domestic level to redefine their position in the light of experiments launched elsewhere. This can strengthen accountability at domestic level. It can accelerate the identification of innovative solutions and of swift responses to new problems. It can also lead to identify where collective action is required at EU level: in order for the range of choices at domestic level to be truly expanded, these choices should not be based on considerations of efficiency and competitiveness, in disregard of the European public interest and of the possibility for states to coordinate with one another and to make progress in one agreed direction. In order to achieve this, simply encouraging local experimentation shall not be enough. The pooling of lessons from local experiments, and the organisation of a deliberation about how they should be evaluated, should constitute both a disincentive for the adoption of beggar-thy-neighbour policies, and a source of enhanced accountability. The establishment, within each EU Member State, of an institution specifically dedicated to the analysis of policies conducted in other states, as well as the strengthening of transnational networks, could accelerate learning across jurisdictions, and favour policy imitation. The systematic collection of information about best practices and their analysis at EU level, by an institution such as the Fundamental Rights Agency, could also constitute a useful tool for that purpose. Learning shall not happen by accident. It can be promoted by design. Institutions matter: without an appropriate institutional framework, actors will be tempted to prefer negotiation and interest-group politics, when what we expect is that they justify their positions in the light of the broader European public interest. The risk is, otherwise, that European politics will look like the picture drawn by public choice theorists: this would be defeat for experimental politics, and for all, a missed opportunity.

Part III

Towards 'Genetic' Reflexive Governance

From Collaborative to Genetic Governance: The Example of Healthcare Services in England*

PETER VINCENT-JONES AND CAROLINE MULLEN

THIS CHAPTER PROVIDES both: (a) an overview of contemporary healthcare governance in England in terms of the four main REFGOV approaches to social learning; and (b) preliminary results from a more specific case study of the genetic approach, focusing on the changing role of non-governmental organisations (NGOs) in health and social care networks.

The chapter shows how two dominant governance approaches (the neo-institutional economic and the collaborative/relational) have developed in parallel with twin strands of healthcare modernisation since the 1970s. These reform strands have entailed bureaucratic restructuring and the introduction of quasi-markets and competition on the one hand, and democratic renewal through the introduction of systems of patient and public involvement (PPI) on the other hand. The example of service commissioning in healthcare quasi-markets is used to illustrate how the deficiencies of the purely neo-institutional economic approach are rooted in its externalist conception of social learning, while the limitations of the collaborative and relational approach lie in the multiple failures of PPI to provide adequate deliberative fora, to develop capacities on the part of citizens and stakeholders for contributing to social learning, and to ensure receptiveness on the part of commissioners of services to inputs from citizens and stakeholders. Emphasising the need to establish such basic conditions of reflexive governance, we consider how the democratic experimentalist and pragmatist approaches might build on these foundations further dimensions of reflexivity in decision-making by key actors in healthcare networks.

The chapter then illustrates the further gains to be achieved by the genetic approach with reference to the ongoing NGO case study. We show how the current economic and political climate requires fundamental reconsideration by

* An earlier version of this chapter was presented at a workshop on Reflexive Governance, University College Dublin, 23 April 2009. Thanks to the participants for their comments, and to Tammy Hervey for acting as discussant for the chapter.

NGOs of how they serve the interests they represent, and how they position themselves strategically in relation to government and other actors. Against this background the empirical research focuses on the development of capacities for social learning involving one charitable organisation in England, with particular attention to evidence of cognitive reframing and fundamental identity transformation.

I. INTRODUCTION

According to the theory of reflexivity informing this book, the public interest in healthcare is dependent on social learning processes involving specific kinds of communication, deliberation and reflection on the part of actors engaged in the organisation and provision of the services in question. Social action that fails to incorporate the economic, democratic and pragmatist elements associated with such learning will be incapable of resolving governance problems to the satisfaction of those involved in collective action to the greatest extent possible. Stated in positive terms, the attainment of reflexivity requires that actors have the capacities and competencies to participate in and contribute to social learning; that they communicate and interact in relational and deliberative ways; that they engage in and learn from experimentation through collaborative forms of joint inquiry; and that their learning is informed by cognitive processes entailing the adjustment and redefinition of frames, representations and collective identities. While the concepts in this formulation may be familiar (governance, reflexivity, social learning, the public interest), their articulation in the legal-philosophical theory developed by Lenoble and Maesschalck and their collaborators at the *Centre de Philosophie du Droit* (CPDR) is distinctive. In order to help differentiate this social learning perspective from others, and to clarify the current authors' interpretation and application of it in the healthcare context, two preliminary points are in order.

First, the principal focus is on social action rather than on legal or regulatory frameworks. Reflexivity as a quality of governance refers ultimately to a particular kind of orientation on the part of actors in decision-making and problem-solving, both individually and in relation to other actors.[1] This is not to deny the

---

[1] The term 'orientation' is used here to refer to the particular stance adopted by the actors performing decision-making and problem-solving functions. By contrast, Lenoble and Maesschalck use 'approach' to describe a theory of governance, or way of theorising about governance: 'From among the various current disciplinary approaches, we have identified four approaches within the theory of governance that ... inquire into the question of the conditions for good governance in terms of collective learning' (Lenoble and Maesschalck 2010: pt II, ch 6, s 1 §1). Similarly, earlier in the same book, three 'successive stages' in governance theory are differentiated (Lenoble and Maesschalck 2010: pt II, Introduction). Corresponding with the main REFGOV approaches to social learning, we distinguish four social action orientations: economic; collaborative and relational; pragmatist (comprising both democratic experimentalism and Shönian pragmatism); and genetic.

fundamental role of the state and supra-national authorities such as the European Union (EU) in constituting the institutional and organisational environment in which social action occurs. The recent modernisation of the National Health Service (NHS) in England has led to increasing complexity in the nature and composition of healthcare networks (see Annex A).[2] New classes of actor (service commissioners, foundation trusts) have been created or refashioned from pre-existing entities. Service providers that have historically been excluded from participation in the NHS have been encouraged to compete for NHS business. Patient and public interests have been recognised and views represented by very different bodies (Patient and Public Involvement Forums, Local Involvement Networks). New regulatory agencies (Monitor, the Care Quality Commission (CQC)) have been established or adapted to oversee the operation of the developing quasi-market. Commissioners and providers of services have been made subject to various legal duties to involve patients and the public, and to respond to reports and recommendations made by regulators. A major purpose of the present research is to explore how reflexive governance may be facilitated or impeded by such institutional and organisational features.

Secondly, social action in healthcare networks is conceived in terms of social learning, rather than of rationalist or technocratic decision-making. Instrumentalist problem-solving models are particularly inappropriate in this public service context due to the inherent complexity of health services, the extent of structural reform, and the rapid pace of NHS reorganisation. While social learning must necessarily take account of economic considerations, it must also (in order to be effective in satisfying the expectations of those engaged in the collective action) incorporate democratic and pragmatist elements. Neither the nature of governance problems nor the interests of actors can be assumed to be fixed. Rather they are negotiated, defined and redefined through collective engagement in various communicative, experimental and cognitive practices. In this conception, social learning is characterised by a fundamental openness to the need for revision of basic assumptions underpinning the provisional goals and problem-solving strategies of the organisation (Argyris and Schön 1978). While the parameters of social action are environmentally determined, the way in which governance issues are addressed depends ultimately on the specific capacities and dispositions of the actors and stakeholders in healthcare networks.

We begin by identifying the dominant approaches to healthcare governance in England, together with their limitations (section II). In section III, we explore the collaborative and relational foundations of reflexive social learning, before proceeding to consider further experimentalist and pragmatist dimensions including ultimately the genetic approach. In section IV, we outline a case study of the

---

[2] Since devolution there has been significant policy divergence in the organisation of healthcare within the United Kingdom. On the contrasting reform paths in the English and Welsh NHS, see Hughes and Vincent-Jones 2008.

genetic approach, focusing on the changing role of NGOs in health and social care networks. Finally, some suggestions are made in section V as to regulatory reforms that might help facilitate the development of conditions of increased reflexivity in the governance of this human service sector.

II.   DOMINANT GOVERNANCE APPROACHES AND THEIR LIMITATIONS

Following widespread acknowledgement of the failure of the market to satisfy the public interest in healthcare, the NHS was founded in 1948 based on the principle that services should be provided free at the point of use and funded from general taxation. The role of the state was significantly extended beyond securing the formal institutional framework and enforcement machinery for guaranteeing market exchange, as envisioned in neo-classical economic theory. Hospitals that had previously been run by local councils or voluntary bodies were nationalised and reorganised on a regional basis, under the ultimate control of the Secretary of State in a system of centralised planning. In the 1970s the modernisation of the NHS took two directions, one concerned with combating inefficiencies associated with bureaucratic organisation, while the other addressed the limitations of traditional democratic processes in ensuring adequate accountability for the management of the service. Linked with these concurrent reform trajectories there have emerged two dominant theoretical approaches to governance, respectively the neo-institutionalist economics approach and the collaborative and relational approach. While it is not suggested that actors in healthcare networks consciously adopt one or other (or a combination) of these approaches, corresponding social learning orientations may nevertheless be discerned through empirical observation of their practical decision-making and problem-solving activities.

A.   Economic Reform and the Neo-Institutional Economics Approach

From the 1970s, welfare state institutions that had been created in response to market failure were themselves increasingly perceived as failing. Public choice and agency theories drew attention to the untrustworthiness of state employees and the need for tighter management and discipline within public organisations (Casson 1991: 246). Of greater significance, the new institutional economics (in particular transaction cost theory) focused on the need to harness economic incentives in public services through new forms of purchaser choice and provider competition (Richards and Rodrigues 1993). An early experiment with competition in the NHS 'internal market' in the 1990s was succeeded by a more developed form of quasi-market organisation, involving the commissioning by NHS bodies of services from competing providers on behalf of patients. Most recently, elements of the governance model employed in the UK utilities sectors have been introduced into healthcare, with an enhanced role for competition and individual choice, and issues of supply and demand including price, availability, and quality being subject to regulation by independent agencies in accordance with statutory frameworks established by the state.[3]

A key role for the state in quasi-market and regulated market forms of public service organisation is to correct deficiencies in the operation of market forces by adjusting economic incentives. Service improvement is dependent on overcoming various obstacles to responsiveness including monopoly power, bounded rationality, asymmetric information, externalities and agency (Department of Health (DH) 2006c: paragraph 2.4). Given appropriate institutional structures, the assumption is that actors in healthcare networks will adopt solutions to governance problems that maximise efficiency and minimise transaction costs, in the context of other goals and constraints determined by regulation. For example, commissioners of services such as Primary Care Trusts (PCTs) and local authorities will be motivated to improve tendering and contracting procedures. Through increasing competition and appropriate regulation, service providers will have incentives to develop 'new models of care' and 'smoother pathways of care' that are more responsive to the needs and preferences of patients and service users (DH 2006c: paragraph 1.14). Patients will contribute to the overall improvement of services through the 'Patient's Choice' scheme, which together with increased supply-side competition will enhance efficiency by changing referral patterns and resource flows. The decision-making orientation of actors in healthcare networks is supposed to be conditioned by this institutional framework, which steers social behaviour in ways that better address contemporary governance problems in the public interest to the general benefit of society.

Two main limitations may be identified with this 'externalist' institutional theory and associated social learning orientation. First, the approach remains rooted in neo-classical assumptions concerning the fixed nature of individual preferences, the 'natural' competencies of actors, and the nature of economic rationality. Even on narrow economic criteria, numerous barriers to efficiency remain in spite of institutional reform. A growing body of empirical evidence has revealed structural problems with quasi-market organisation, similar to those that occur in real markets (Propper and Bartlett 1997). Such problems, and the associated absence or ineffectiveness of appropriate incentives, pose major difficulties for a social learning model based solely on economic calculation. Secondly, this approach tends to ignore the need for decision-making (in order to satisfy the general interest to the greatest extent possible) to take account of a wider range of criteria, interests and values, requiring public participation and democratic deliberation. The attempt to promote conditions of success of social learning through the hierarchical restructuring of economic interaction can only ever be partially successful. This brings us

---

[3] The main economic reforms, including the introduction of NHS foundation trusts, the expanded role for the independent sector in service provision, the sharpening of incentives through 'payment by results', the introduction of increased patient choice, and the new system of regulation under the Care Quality Commission, are summarised in Annex B.

to the collaborative and relational approach to governance, which focuses attention on the 'internal' organisation of the learning operation.

B.   Democratic Renewal and the Collaborative/Relational Approach

The second strand of NHS modernisation has aimed to increase the involvement of patients and the public in healthcare governance.[4] Limited citizen representation was achieved through the creation in 1974 of Community Health Councils (CHCs). By the end of the 1990s such bodies were considered as failing due to a combination of lack of consistency in working practices and an inability to reflect the diversity of local communities (Tritter and McCallum 2006: 158). The foundations of the modern framework for 'patient and public involvement' (PPI) were laid at the turn of the century. From 2001, NHS bodies were required to 'involve and consult' patients and the public in the planning of services, in decision-making affecting their operation, and in the development and consideration of proposals for changes in their provision. Legislation in 2002 provided for the abolition and replacement of CHCs by Patient and Public Involvement Forums (hereafter 'Forums') for each PCT and NHS Trust in England.

A further wave of PPI reform began in 2007. This second phase was prompted by New Labour's decision after three years in office to continue with the Conservatives' policy of increasing competition and provider pluralism, reversing its earlier commitment in the immediate aftermath of the 1997 General Election to a programme of NHS modernisation involving bureaucratic restructuring and performance management. The Local Government and Public Involvement in Health Act 2007 provided, first, for the abolition of Forums and their replacement by Local Involvement Networks (LINks) from 31 March 2008. Whereas Forums had a limited role in representing patient and public interests in respect of health services provided by a single NHS Trust, the remit of LINks covers both health and social care and extends across an entire local authority area. Secondly, the 2007 Act narrowed the scope of the 'duty to consult', requiring only that 'users of services' be 'involved (whether by being consulted or provided with information, or in other ways)'. The range of issues on which users must be involved is limited to those which would affect the user's experience of the service, or the choice of service available.[5] Thirdly, duties are imposed under the 2007 Act on 'services-providers' to reflect upon and explain what they have done differently in response to reports and recommendations made by LINks, and on service commissioners similarly to show what they have done in response to consultations required to be undertaken with users of services.

---

[4]   For details see (Vincent-Jones et al 2009).

[5]   This appears to preclude wider citizen involvement in more fundamental issues of how services are provided and by whom (for example by public or independent providers). The effect of the reform is arguably to limit the role of patients and public to that of consumers rather than citizens (*cf* Tritter and McCallum 2006: 161).

The PPI system is intended to lead to a very different decision-making orientation on the part of actors in healthcare networks to that associated with neo-institutional economics. What distinguishes the collaborative and relational approach is 'the idea that the conditions of success of the learning operation require an aggregative and deliberative shaping of the communicative competencies of the various stakeholders' (Lenoble and Maesschalck 2010, part II, chapter 6, section 1 §1). The implication is that governance problems must be addressed by maximising dialogue and deliberation among all parties with interests or stakes in the issues in question. This requires the opening of channels of communication between key actors, and the development of appropriate venues and fora for the participation of patients and the public in order that they may effectively become involved in and contribute to social learning. Receptiveness to the ideas and experiences of citizens is therefore a necessary condition of social learning at this level. However, there are significant weaknesses in the institutional and organisational framework of PPI in altering the behavioural orientation of NHS commissioners and service providers in ways that open up decision-making processes to a wider range of stakeholder influences.

First, on past experience, the problem with the legal duty to involve patients and the public in practice is that consultations tend to be insincere and tokenistic. Many NHS bodies have been suspected of seeking to avoid their statutory duties or interpreting narrowly the range of situations in which they are required to consult, often with the collusion of the Department of Health. The House of Commons Health Committee concluded its review of the original consultation duty:

> Too often it seems to the public that decisions have been made before the consultation takes place. Too often NHS bodies have sought to avoid consultation under Section 11 about major issues. Unfortunately the Department of Health has supported those NHS organisations in trying to limit the scope of Section 11 (House of Commons Health Committee (HCHC) 2006–07, paragraph 271).

As has been seen, the revised duty to 'involve' patients and the public in service planning and decision-making under the 2007 Act is narrower than the original duty, precluding public engagement on the matter of how (and by whom) services are provided. It might of course be argued that the reduced scope for consultation is of little consequence, given the Government's own reluctance to observe the terms of the original wider duty and its ineffectiveness in practice. However, what is important about the failure of this aspect of PPI is the attention drawn to the limits of *law* (or at least the limits of this *form* of law) in changing the *behaviour* of key actors in the healthcare environment. The legal framework by itself is incapable of facilitating the conditions necessary to promote a sufficiently receptive and deliberative orientation on the part of the relevant actors.

Secondly, LINks might be argued to offer better prospects for increasing patient and public involvement in decision-making. Each LINk is free to decide its governance structure and membership, which may include both voluntary organisations and individuals. LINks may therefore engage a greater number and broader range of participants than either of their predecessors (Forums or CHCs). The Department of Health maintains that 'every LINk should be established in a way that is inclusive and enables involvement from all sections of the local community, especially those who are difficult to involve or seldom heard' (DH 2006b: 4). LINks will obtain views from citizens and service users about health and social care needs and experiences, and convey those views to organisations responsible for commissioning, providing, and managing local health and social care services. By representing the views of patients and the public in this way, LINks may compensate for the reluctance or inability of commissioners and service providers to consult with the public directly. Furthermore, the power to make reports and recommendations about how local care services could or ought to be improved implies a proactive role in conducting investigations and shaping agendas, beyond gathering and conveying information about needs and preferences. It is too soon to know how far LINks will take advantage of the opportunities provided by their wider remit. Their success in enhancing receptiveness will depend on a twofold communicative process, involving both the obtaining of views of patients and the public, and the representation of those views to relevant bodies such as commissioners and service providers. There is no guarantee that such communication will occur, or that any information conveyed to decision-makers will be understood or taken into account in practice (although there is an incentive in this respect in the statutory requirement that healthcare bodies must respond to the reports and recommendations made by LINks).

In sum, while the deficiencies of the purely neo-institutional economic approach are rooted in its externalist conception of social learning, the main limitation of the collaborative and relational approach has been the failure in practice to promote receptiveness on the part of decision-makers to inputs from patients, the public and other stakeholders.

C.   A Dominant Approach, or Approaches?

The foregoing sections have traced twin trajectories of NHS modernisation with distinct theoretical bases and rationales. A consensus has emerged among the major political parties over how the public interest in healthcare should be maintained, based on the continuing commitment to a service which is free at the point of delivery and funded from general taxation. Economic reforms directed at increasing efficiency through quasi-market competition and individual choice are being combined with reforms aimed at enhancing patient and public voice in democratic processes, reflecting the pressures on European societies to increase both the efficiency of public services and the participation of citizens in decision-making affecting healthcare (Council of Europe 2000). In tandem with these strands of economic and democratic reform there have developed respectively neo-institutional and collaborative/relational governance approaches, which together serve to structure the decision-making and problem-solving orientations of key players in healthcare networks.

The combination of approaches is illustrated by the governance issues confronting PCTs and local authorities in their role as purchasers of services in health and social care quasi-markets. Prior to tendering, contracts have to be planned and specified with regard to future contingencies and the allocation of risk. Government guidelines for public contracting generally follow the prescriptions of textbook transaction cost economics on public procurement. Contract design is supposed to be carefully matched to the circumstances. 'Arm's length' contracting is suited to low-risk situations where the activity is not critical to the purchaser's strategic objectives, there are many suppliers, and the costs of changing to another provider would be low. At the other extreme is a form of 'partnering', considered suited to situations in which the service is critical to the client's strategic objectives, where requirements are changing, and where the market is evolving and relatively under-developed. However, while contracting for simple public services such as refuse collection or building cleaning may be amenable to such straightforward economic analysis, the problems are much greater in human services sectors such as social care and healthcare. These services are likely to be difficult to specify prior to tendering. The commissioning authority then has to select among competing providers in the public, private and voluntary sectors. While transaction cost theory is clear about the factors that ideally need to be taken into account in decision-making, in practice problems of monopoly power, asymmetric information, bounded rationality, and opportunism make these processes hazardous. At this point the inherent limitations of the neo-institutional economics approach to governance and its associated social learning orientation become apparent. The problems are so complex and the uncertainties so great that the issues cannot satisfactorily be addressed solely through economic rationality.

More fundamentally, purchasers cannot avoid taking account of collaborative/ relational factors beyond narrow economic calculations based on efficiency. Quasi-market contracting implies a trilateral rather than a bilateral relationship, with the services being purchased on behalf of 'third party' consumers. This gives rise to a further set of governance problems, concerning the responsiveness of purchasing decisions to the needs and preferences of service recipients and citizens. Here PCTs are engaged in a different form of social learning (and of the means of satisfying the public interest in healthcare governance) based on communications with patients and the public. The importance of the collaborative and relational dimension is evident also in the relationship between the commissioner and the service provider. The emphasis on 'partnering' reflects the acknowledgement in government discourse of the importance of trust and cooperation in economic exchanges, and of the need to avoid damaging these aspects of relational contracting through an exaggerated and distorted ideal of competition (Vincent-Jones 2006).

III.   FROM COLLABORATIVE/RELATIONAL TO GENETIC GOVERNANCE

It has been established that key actors in healthcare networks such as commissioners and service providers cannot properly discharge their quasi-market responsibilities without being receptive to inputs from patients and the wider public. We now consider in greater depth the specific nature of the potential contribution of patients and the public to social learning processes.

A.   Collaborative and Relational Foundations

At least two democratic rationales for PPI may be distinguished. A first notion is that PPI should enhance the influence of patients and the public in matters of policy-making, planning and implementation by allowing them a voice in directly determining decisions. In this conception 'citizen participation is a categorical term for citizen power' (Arnstein 1969: 216[6]). In the 'ladder' ranking different degrees of citizen participation and non-participation, citizen control is presented as the pinnacle of involvement. The aim of PPI here is to transfer a degree of power and therefore control from managers and professionals to citizens. The problem with this conception is that it leaves relatively little scope for communicative and deliberative processes that, according to the foregoing theoretical analysis, are essential pre-conditions of effective social learning. The struggle to increase user involvement entails 'a contest between two parties wrestling for control over a finite amount of power. Involvement is conceptualised in competitive terms: "a zero-sum game" ' (Tritter and McCallum 2006: 158). However, there is no reason to believe that complex governance problems can be resolved any better by citizens rather than managers and professionals, or that the public interest will be any better served by such a transfer of power.

In the second conception the purpose of PPI is to facilitate patient and public voice in contributing to deliberation which informs, but does not necessarily determine, decision-making (Mullen 2008: 399). This model of democratic engagement opens up a space for social learning, drawing on the unique experiences of patients as co-producers of human services. User involvement here entails 'constructive dialogue aimed at reshaping the relationship between patients, healthcare professionals and the public . . . as a catalyst to more widespread cultural change' (Tritter and McCallum 2006: 158):

> The key contribution users make arises from their distinct personal experience and non-medical or technical frame of reference; it is asking questions that health professionals have not considered. One aim of user involvement may be to break down boundaries, share experience, and build understanding. This suggests not a hierarchy of knowledge – relevant professional versus irrelevant lay – but rather a complementarity between forms of knowing, set within a willingness to acknowledge differences (Tritter and McCallum 2006: 164).

---

[6]   http://lithgow-schmidt.dk/sherry-arnstein/ladder-of-citizen-participation.pdf.

While many questions of health policy, planning and implementation raise difficult technical issues, these frequently cannot be separated from social and ethical considerations of value, including how values should be interpreted in decision-making (see Mullen 2008: 397–98). For example, the decision whether a surgery should be relocated or merged at the cost of reduced accessibility for a small section of a community must take account of matters such as finance, measurement of health gain, knowledge of transport systems, and accessibility. However, these technical issues are in practice intertwined with other dimensions such as the value that should be given to preserving life, or the priority that should be accorded the protection of minority interests weighed against the benefits to a majority (Weale 2006: 38). Due to the fact that technical knowledge cannot be neatly separated from social and ethical considerations, it cannot be assumed that such dilemmas are most appropriately addressed by professionals. Patients and the public may contribute to social learning by raising what would otherwise be unconsidered questions or ideas, drawing on their particular experiences, knowledge and understandings (see Weale 2006: 40; Martin 2008; Levitt 2003: 23; Mullen 2008: 404–08).

Dialogic involvement may accordingly be understood as a form of democratic engagement drawing on people's ideas and questions to test and challenge decision-making on existing or proposed policy, planning or practices. In this conception, citizens and service users should be entitled to expect from decision-makers a reasoned response to relevant matters raised, which may lead to further queries or questions, to which further responses should in turn be provided. Where no relevant response can be given, the decision should be reconsidered. Conversely, where responses can be provided, or where plans or practices are altered and developed in order to enable a response, then it is plausible to maintain that the decisions have some defensibility (Mullen 2008). The notion of 'defensibility' avoids the simplistic assumption that the purpose of deliberation is to reach consensus (Dent 2006: 457). The aim instead is to develop proposals and practices that are more defensible than they would otherwise be, in the sense of requiring reasoned responses to different forms of patient and public input.

While this analysis is right to emphasise the active contribution of citizens in deliberative processes, it remains confined within a discourse of democratic legitimacy, with the notion of 'defensibility' being used to justify the decision ultimately reached as the most legitimate possible in the circumstances. In REFGOV perspective, by contrast, the role of dialogue following patient and public input is to maximise the potential for social learning. Nevertheless, patient and public voice is an essential precondition of 'good' governance on either criterion. Effective dialogue presupposes mutual communication (speaking and listening) on the part of decision-makers and other stakeholders in healthcare networks. This implies that citizens have, or can acquire, relevant knowledge or understanding, and also that they have or can develop the capacity to articulate views on healthcare issues in order to contribute ideas and challenges. LINks clearly have a potential role to play in such capacitation, as collective actors representing the views or interests of individual patients and members of the public. They have a further capacity-building role in providing fora or methods of debate which maximise the input of relevant ideas, questions and challenges within the deliberative process, drawing upon the widest possible range of experience, knowledge and understanding (Mullen 2008: 407).

B.   Democratic Experimentalism

The dialogic and deliberative elements of social learning so far considered are necessary conditions of reflexive governance, but they are not by themselves sufficient. A further requirement is that decision-makers remain open to the nature and definition of issues, rather than attempting to find solutions to problems that are fixed in advance. Such openness may be regarded as particularly important in light of challenges posed by the complexity of NHS reorganisation and the frenetic pace of reform. Rational-technocratic assumptions are a feature not only of narrow economic approaches to governance, but also of some democratic models that see the purpose of public engagement in terms of the aggregation of fixed individual preferences, or the provision of citizens with a voice in directly determining decisions.[7] Both democratic experimentalism and Schönian pragmatism avoid such rationalism, but in very different ways. These social learning approaches are considered respectively in the present and subsequent sections.

Democratic experimentalism describes a form of social learning in which actors engage continually in processes of joint inquiry, benchmarking and peer review. For Sabel, 'learning by monitoring' is an experimentalist practice involving the 'creation of institutions that make discussion of what to do inextricable from discussion of what is being done', such that 'discrete transactions among independent actors become continual, joint, formulations of common ends in which the participants' identities are reciprocally defining' (Sabel 1994: 138). While originally used to analyse the superior performance of Japanese production systems in private industry, this perspective is arguably applicable to English healthcare governance which is similarly characterised by a form of vertical disintegration and the breakdown of hierarchy as the instrument of collective problem-solving. The actors in this context (commissioners and service providers, regulators and rule-makers, patients and citizens) may also be seen as collectively engaged in 'a continuous discussion of joint possibilities and goals' in which 'their understanding of their situation is limited'. Democratic experimentalism requires that groups of such actors

> jointly specify what they believe they understand so as to expose and begin exploring the limits of that understanding. Just as in a conversation they must accept the

---

[7]   For example, where citizens are asked in a questionnaire to answer 'yes' or 'no' to a question, or to select from among a limited range of options.

possibility that their views of themselves, or the world, and the interests arising from both – their identities, in short – will be changed unexpectedly by those explorations (Sabel 1994: 145).

A recent strand in socio-legal contract scholarship suggests that vertical disintegration of the supply chain in many industries is being accompanied by new forms of 'contracting for innovation' that are distinct from the collaborative mechanisms of relational contracting (norms of reciprocity, expectations of future dealing, etc) (Gilson et al 2009). The contractual relationships between commissioners and providers of services in health and social care networks may similarly be analysed in terms of the scope for such iterative collaboration.

Iterated co-design is a further key feature of this pragmatist theoretical perspective, emphasising collaboration between those responsible for designing and implementing policy. This notion implies that 'government should intervene less, and above all less directly, in civil society'. Rather:

> the state should encourage or require civil society actors to supervise themselves in the provision of services or rules, and limit its own intervention to monitoring the self-supervision of civil society actors: Instead of issuing detailed regulations, or specifying how services are to be provided, the state would set general goals, monitoring the efforts of appropriate actors to achieve those goals by means of their own devising. The state would intervene only when the efforts of the latter fall short (Sabel 2004).

While this vision will be familiar to advocates of a more 'responsive' approach to public services regulation (Vincent-Jones 2006),[8] in England the NHS remains a highly centralised public bureaucracy. The limited autonomy accorded parts of the NHS is accompanied by the constant threat of government intervention for failure to meet centrally determined performance targets. To the extent that social learning in the experimentalist sense requires collaboration, trust and cooperation between the Government and decentralised authorities, these qualities may

---

[8]   The principal relational condition of responsive public service governance is sensitivity on the part of regulators to the circumstances in which regulation occurs. In particular, responsive regulators need to exercise fine judgment as to whether a more or less interventionist response is required, depending on the capacity of regulatees for self-regulation. Regulatory sensitivity implies the existence of some degree of cooperation between regulators and regulatees in all forms public services governance. In the case of 'contracting regimes', this quality is necessary both in the hierarchical regulatory relationship between central government and public agencies, and in the contractual relationship between such agencies and the other contracting party. Lack of regulatory sensitivity on the part of central government may be expected to have a negative impact on the capacity of public agencies to perform their contractual regulatory roles responsively. Regulatory sensitivity further implies not only the general avoidance of adversarial relations and the minimum use of legitimate force, but also the existence of active collaboration and partnership in regulatory relationships. This applies to the design and modification of contracting regimes as well as their practical operation. For the argument that contracting regimes need to be designed and managed from the 'bottom up', with greater involvement of professional groups and other stakeholders from the outset, rather than imposed from the 'top down' in pursuit of the Government's pre-determined policy agendas — see (Vincent-Jones 2006).

be lacking in the English context (see the discussion of trust as an essential element of reflexive governance in the energy sector in chapter four by Prosser et al, earlier in this volume).

There is greater scope for experimentalist practices involving recently corporatised semi-autonomous foundation trusts and new entrants to markets for healthcare services such as Independent Sector Treatment Centres (ISTCs) and NGOs. Due to their relative autonomy from the NHS hierarchy, such groupings may better resemble the federated or networked bodies described by Sabel:

> Once a service is being provided, initial rules are in place, or production begins, continuous monitoring detects errors and breakdown, uses these findings to trigger searches for the root causes of design or other flaws that escaped earlier examination... Taken together routines such as benchmarking, simultaneous engineering, continuous monitoring, error detection and root cause analysis define methods for choosing provisional, initial goals and revising them in the light of more detailed, partial, proposals arising from efforts to implement them (Sabel 2004: 11).[9]

By contrast with traditional hierarchical approaches to problem-solving, 'search networks' serve as devolved pragmatist institutions that work by finding others in similar situations and providing comparative information on methods and relative performance (Sabel 2005).

Benchmarking may be defined simply as the comparison of practices, systems or organisations according to accepted standards or indicators. While international benchmarking of healthcare systems was pioneered by the Organisation for Economic Co-operation and Development (OECD) in the 1980s, the use of this technique at the national level began a decade later as part of the Government's New Public Management drive for increasing efficiency and service quality (Waite and Nolte 2005). Other forms of benchmarking have developed recently at the initiative of various groups of actors in healthcare networks. Benchmarking may be used by government as a tool for driving up standards through performance metrics and rankings, or by organisations performing similar roles or located in the same sector as a more collaborative mechanism for joint improvement and dissemination of best practice (Northcott and Llewellyn 2005). A further distinction may be drawn between 'indicator' and 'ideas' benchmarking, the former associated with league tables and 'star-ratings' while the latter focuses on organisational learning and process improvement (Northcott and Llewellyn 2005: 423). There exists in this regard a fundamental ambivalence in New Labour policies which emphasise the value of collaboration and

---

[9] 'Put another way, the routines make it routinely possible to correct ends through the exploration of means and vice versa ... So we can think of these new institutions as pragmatist in that they systematically provoke doubt, in the characteristically pragmatist sense of an urgent suspicion that their own routines – habits gone hard, into dogma – are poor guides to current problem solving' (Sabel 2004: 11).

service improvement on the one hand, while pursuing competition and penalising poor performers on the other hand. Exemplifying the obstacles to iterated co-design just discussed, the suspicion is that: 'as long as benchmarking metrics are employed for political purposes, the more desirable results of this tool will be difficult to achieve' (Northcott and Llewellyn 2005: 431).

In any event, benchmarking can only operate effectively as an experimentalist mode of learning if it is accompanied by internal reflection by members of the organisation on its methods and processes. There is little evidence that state-imposed benchmarking is having this effect (Waite and Nolte 2005). The current scheme in the NHS, 'Essence of Care', is a supposedly new benchmarking approach launched by the Department of Health in England in 2001 to provide incentives for continuous quality improvement in areas such as privacy and dignity, nutrition and hygiene. In practice the use of this 'tool kit' is patchy, with NHS managers tending to focus their efforts on quantitative rather than qualitative aspects, and on measurability of comparative performance data (Ellis 2006: 377). There appear to be significant problems of regulatory ineffectiveness and unintended consequences, for example the encouragement of a short-term culture of box ticking, deflection of attention from aspects of healthcare which are more important but more difficult to measure, and perverse incentives to alter recording methods to achieve higher rankings at the expense of actual performance improvement (Waite and Nolte 2005: 444). Such problems with this form of performance management apply across the whole field of public services regulation in England (see Vincent-Jones 2006: 160–64).

C.   Cognitive Reframing and the Genetic Approach

Schönian pragmatism avoids the rationalist tendency in traditional problem-solving models by focusing on specific processes of cognitive reframing as further essential conditions of effective social learning. In order to break out of repetitive and defensive patterns of thinking associated with 'single-loop' learning, individuals and organisations must engage in 'frame reflection' involving 'double-loop' learning. Whereas in the former learning mode the response to intractable governance problems is to search for further solutions within a given set of governing variables, the latter includes the capacity to question those variables and thereby alter the framing of the problem: 'Double-loop learning occurs where error is detected and corrected in ways that involve the modification of an organisation's underlying norms, policies and objectives' (Argyris and Schön 1978: 3). This capacity critically to reflect on and reconceptualise problems and the assumptions on which they are based clearly adds a new dimension to the social learning approaches so far considered. Through this orientation, organisations within healthcare networks will perform their roles successfully to the extent that learning is able to take place through forms of inquiry which 'resolve incompatible organisational norms by setting new priorities and weightings of norms, or by restructuring the norms themselves together with associated strategies and assumptions' (Argyris and Schön 1978: 18). On the other hand, organisations are predicted to fail where their fundamental assumptions and routines become self-reinforcing, and single-loop learning inhibits the detection and correction of error (Argyris 1982: 8). In these cases decision-making may remain trapped within the dominant paradigm of technical rationality (Schön 1983).

According to Lenoble and Maesschalck, the theoretical advance offered by the genetic approach over Schönian pragmatism is the further specification of an institutional mechanism capable of facilitating the actors' engagement in the frame-reflective processes associated with double-loop learning. Rather than being taken for granted, in the genetic approach the capacity for cognitive reframing and self-representation is conceived:

> as the product of an operation of 'terceisation', that is, as the product of an operation that requires, as part of the process of self-construction, the invocation of a third element whose externality makes possible the actor's construction of her or his image – the image that will enable her or him to identify herself or himself (and her or his interests) in a given context for action (Lenoble and Maesschalck 2010: part II chapter 6 section 2).

Through such terceisation (or 'differentiation'[10]), the actor forms an *identity* comprising both a reconstructed relationship with the past (reflectability) and an anticipated relationship with the future (destinability). Only by remaining 'simultaneously open to anticipation and retrospection', are actors able to adapt to new challenges and overcome 'defensiveness' and other routines that serve as obstacles to the cooperative resolution of the most difficult governance problems.

The case study example of the genetic approach (Lenoble and Maesschalck 2010: part II chapter 6) focuses on the problem of collective bargaining in the context of liberalisation of the Belgian electricity sector. At the turn of the century two labour movement cultures stood in opposition to one another, such that two possible paths of action existed and an impasse arose between two opposing visions of the kind of collaboration that should be sought with other actors in the electricity sector. The strategic options for the unions were either to adopt a defensive posture and attempt to preserve traditional benefits and rights, or to 'resituate action in line with the new rules of the game, i.e. *learn a new role*'. In adopting the latter option, the unions rebuilt their collective identity and assumed a new position on the basis of a critical examination of past impasses that might imperil current action. The new strategic positioning entailed the *linking* of the unions' interests with those of citizen-consumers in the liberalised service sectors, thereby overcoming the polarisation of positions that previously had entailed the subordination of the latter to the former.

---

[10]   See Lenoble and Maesschalck 2010: pt II ch 6 s 2 §1.

The underlying purpose of this case study is to show how collective action strategies vary according to the deployment by the actors of an experimentalist analysis, a Schönian pragmatist analysis, or a genetic analysis. It is not here being claimed that the actors *themselves* conceive of their approach to governance problems literally in these terms (or even in terms of social learning). The important point is that alternative orientations and strategies can be discerned from the actors' internal communications (distinct from external communications, or publicity or campaigning statements):

> The question we are asking is . . . how to analyse the various possible approaches on which participants in this collective action have been able to base, and will be able to base, their redefinition of strategies for action, in the climate of new constraints on collective action that changes in the regulatory context present them with (Lenoble and Maesschalck 2010: part II chapter 6 section 3).

The methodological implication is that the precise nature of the social learning orientation adopted by any given actor is a matter for empirical testing. The genetic analysis 'makes it possible to discern whether a terceisation mechanism is at work, and if so, how; and how it is playing a part in the process of collective identity-making' (Lenoble and Maesschalck 2010: part II chapter 6 section 2).

Bearing in mind that the approaches to social learning should be seen as supplementary rather than alternative, it cannot be the case that every governance problem is so intractable as to require a genetic approach for its effective resolution. The dominant approaches to social learning in the healthcare context (section II of this chapter) are 'dominant' precisely because they characterise the *routine* decision-making and problem-solving activities of actors in healthcare networks. Returning to the example of the role played by PCTs and local authorities in commissioning services on behalf of patients and the public in competitive quasi-markets, the performance of this purchasing function necessarily entails social learning operations combining neo-institutionalist and collaborative/relational approaches. Thus, while the process of tendering and award of contracts involves economic calculation, it is also informed by democratic considerations. Contracts for health services cannot be specified or managed without close attention to the views and preferences of patients and the public. Where the issues surrounding commissioning are particularly complex or contentious, the satisfaction of the general interest may be dependent on both the capacity of patients and the public to advance ideas and challenges, and on the readiness of decision-makers to respond appropriately and to revise plans and policies in the light of these and other inputs. Building on these foundations, the attainment of reflexivity in the commissioning role may further require that PCTs and local authorities engage in experimentalist inquiry in collaboration with other public purchasing agencies and other stakeholders, for example involving practices such as benchmarking, and that they avoid rationalist-technocratic preconceptions in the framing of problems and the search for solutions to them.

Beyond this, however, it appears unlikely in this example that a genetic element in social learning is necessary in order to achieve full reflexivity. In addition to the system-wide survey of the conditions of social learning in healthcare networks already provided, therefore, what is needed is a case study specifically illustrating the genetic approach and testing the REFGOV hypothesis with regard to tercei- sation.

IV.   CASE STUDY: NGOS IN HEALTHCARE NETWORKS

This section accordingly presents initial findings of a case study of the genetic approach in the human services context, focusing on the changing role and identity of NGOs in health and social care networks in England. The NGOs involved in the study are charitable organisations established and run for the benefit of particular groups of patients and carers (the organisations' beneficiar- ies). These independent sector bodies have no choice other than to adapt in the face of multiple scientific and technical developments in health and social care research, and radical reforms which are destabilising the policy frameworks in which they operate. In order to meet the challenges of a rapidly shifting environment in a way that satisfies the normative expectations of their members and beneficiaries, NGOs may need to construct new identities in a 'context for action' and learn new roles (Lenoble and Maesschalck 2010 : part 2 chapter 6 and chapter one of this volume). The first question for the study is whether these bodies are engaging in novel forms of action in the public realm which might indicate that identity transformation is occurring. Assuming this to be the case, the second question is how any such transformation can be understood in terms of processes of self-capacitation or geneticisation.

By contrast with the threats to the position of the labour unions in Belgium as portrayed by Lenoble and Maesschalck, the main problem for NGOs in England is arguably how to make the most of the opportunities presented by the new institutional and organisational environment. New Labour's enthusiasm for engaging the energies of the 'third sector' in human services has created a potential for NGOs to strengthen their position in healthcare networks, in particular by influencing policy-making at national level, by involvement in planning the commissioning of public services (Improvement and Development Agency (I&DEA) 2008), and by bidding for and winning social care and health service contracts in competition with NHS and private sector bodies. However, these opportunities are accompanied by new challenges. The extension of the role of NGOs to include the quasi-market provision of (publicly funded) services directly to client groups has led to tensions with their traditionally independent public service mission (Carmel and Harlock 2008). Furthermore, closer ties with government in the making and development of policy create dilemmas over the extent to which NGOs feel able to challenge government in promoting the interests of the particular service user groups they represent (Craig et al 2004).

Our case study examines the approaches used by a number of charities (working in the fields of cancer care and support, and in mental health) in their efforts to adjust to changing environmental conditions. We investigate the empirical question of the nature of the social learning orientation or orientations adopted by NGOs in this context, through examination of their work in seeking to influence government policy in health and social care, and their role in developing and providing publicly funded services. This research will test the REFGOV hypothesis by focusing specifically on the actors' capacities (collaborative/relational, Schönian pragmatist, and genetic), with particular attention to any transformation of their collective identity for action and evidence of terceisation.

In relation to the development and provision of services, we consider whether any organisational changes can be understood as transformation of collective identity 'in a context for action', and if so how these transformations impact on the NGOs' ability to develop and provide services in a way that meets the normative expectations of their members. We investigate these questions by studying changes and developments in how the NGOs:

(a) perform contract bidding and service providing functions (taking account of problems of developing new expertise and skills, establishing trust and coop- eration with new contracting partners, and the role of the Compact between the Government and the voluntary sector in enhancing relationality);
(b) involve patients and the public in contract specification and management, including the extent and form of dialogue and deliberation with these and other stakeholders; and
(c) engage in experimentalist and collaborative practices such as joint inquiry, peer review, and benchmarking in developing expertise and solutions appro- priate to the new service providing role.

In relation to influencing health and social care policy, we again consider whether changes in the NGOs' representation of their interests can be understood as transformation of collective identity for action, and examine how this transfor- mation impacts on the NGOs' ability to fulfil the normative expectations of their members to the greatest extent possible. These questions are addressed by studying developments and changes in:

(a) choices made by each NGO of issues on which to focus (involving examina- tion of why these issues have been selected rather than others, what are the 'public interest' grounds for the selection, and whether the interests are sectional or general within the group);
(b) the degree of receptiveness of policy-makers to inputs from NGOs (includ- ing the nature of any subsequent deliberation or dialogue);
(c) the analysis of the issues by NGOs following the Government's response or lack of response to their input, including whether the Government response

is considered reasonable (any such change could indicate collective identity transformation initiated by government response to the NGO);

(d) the Government's position, including any evidence of increased receptiveness to NGO input following the initial exchange; and

(e) the strategy on the part of NGOs (including changes in the way in which they advance their argument, or their priorities).

Work on the empirical case study is ongoing at the time of writing in January 2010. In this section, therefore, we report on preliminary findings of the study of just one of the charities, concerned with the interests of people with mental illness, their carers and families. In recent years the organisation (which we shall call MENTHEAL) has undergone significant changes in its approach to service development and capacity to provide services, and in its approach to policy and campaigning. The following paragraphs offer an interpretation of developments in the organisation's work, based on initial analysis of interviews with staff working in the areas of service development and design, and campaigning and policy development ('SD' and 'CP' respectively in the following).

A.   Organisational Capacity for Provision of Public Services

SD showed MENTHEAL's awareness of the necessity for substantial organisational change in adapting to a policy environment which had shifted from statutory grant funding to contract commissioning. Since contract tendering began in the 1990s, there has been increasing recognition of the benefits of competing for large scale contracts which treat *'whole populations of need'*. The decision to bid for such contracts was motivated also by the concern to avoid over-reliance on working in partnership with bigger organisations. This sort of partnership might be with an NHS Trust which, on winning the contract, could subcontract part of the service to a voluntary organisation. While NHS Trusts and local authorities have some incentive to form partnerships with charitable bodies in order to *'build a bridgehead'* with the voluntary sector, MENTHEAL believes that such arrangements may present a risk to the organisation's independence.

SD suggested that MENTHEAL has recently reached several milestones in the organisational development needed to create the capacity to bid for large scale contracts. The potential difficulties of such development, including problems of practical positioning and of securing accountability for and reflection on the changes taking place, have been recognised. The problem of market positioning is illustrated by the example of therapy services which, until very recently, MENTHEAL had little experience of delivering. SD described how an unmet need for these services had been identified through patient surveys. This development work enabled the organisation to bid for and win contracts for these publicly funded services when the opportunity arose. SD was aware of the potentially negative impact of tendering for large scale contracts on the organisation's rationale as a body representing the interests of people suffering mental illness and their carers. The risk for charitable bodies in this regard was that they might become '*redefined because of mission creep*', and become a '*casualty of contracting*'. There was recognition more generally of the dangers of '*unintended consequences of change*', and of the need to manage internal tensions within the organisation. SD indicated that mitigating these risks has involved reflection both on the environment that has prompted change, and on the mode of adaptation to that environment. Care is being taken to ensure that development and growth are consistent with MENTHEAL's mission, rather than simply following '*government prescription*'.

SD maintained that the successful management of change is dependent on both good charity governance and systematic business processes. Systems are required to help promote accountability and ensure that staff hold the organisation in trust, with different sections and departments (including regional offices) sharing a sense of ownership in the organisation and its development. '*Emotional intelligence*' can assume particular importance when changes are not implemented smoothly (for instance, if regional sections disagree with decisions made by the centre). SD explained that cooperation between different parts of the organisation could not simply be expected, so development processes included the use of methods by which internal issues and concerns could be raised and explored. Any development is subject ultimately to a test of whether it is consistent with, or can be grounded in, the organisation's charitable objects.

Even where changes are grounded in the ways described above, it was acknowledged that organisational development can have unforeseen effects on the relationship with beneficiaries and service users. SD reported a view that, although a charitable organisation may feel that it is retaining its independence, bidding for large contracts would inevitably affect service users' perceptions of the organisation. Voluntary bodies need therefore to strive to remain distinctive in the way in which they deliver services, and to set clear limits as to how far they will '*dance in tune*' with commissioners. Expansion of the organisation's role in service provision also affects the nature of relationships by changing the profile of the people to whom services are provided. While anyone receiving a service from MENTHEAL could be described as a beneficiary of the organisation, they are not all members of the organisation. The relationship or 'contract' with service users who are members will be different from that with non-member service users. SD maintained that care was needed to ensure that both types of service user are appropriately treated, and their relationship with the organisation protected. MENTHEAL seeks to achieve this by methods of self assessment and 'value audits'. Value audits are described as an internal audit involving a structured method of providing evidence (SD commented that the organisation had previously used an internal quality standard, but that this had been found to be unhelpful, especially in conjunction with other forms of accountability and reporting that were required of contract providers).

B.   Decisions on Bidding for Contracts and Designing Services

MENTHEAL recognises that as an independent charity, it is free to decide what public services to take on. SD maintained that the decision whether to bid for public service contracts should involve consideration of consistency of the proposed course of action with the organisation's mission, in the same way as decisions on organisational development. The scope for influencing a service was a key factor in deciding whether or not to bid for a contract to provide it. If there was considered to be little scope, MENTHEAL would not bid for that service. Such scope is limited, however, by the fact that NHS contracts apply the same inflexible rules for any potential provider (whether public, private or third sector). These rules are performance-related, involving particular quality indicators relating to volume, outcomes and clinical measures. In this respect, contracts differ from block grants. Despite this lack of flexibility, SD suggested that there is some potential for innovation, especially during the tendering processes in which there may be opportunities to shape the design of services. This potential is increased where services put out to tender are supposed to be concerned with development and learning. MENTHEAL also uses other strategies to facilitate innovation in service design. One approach is to seek grant funding which, although requiring accountability to funders, imposes fewer restrictions than contracts. A further approach is to build margins into funding structures thus enabling innovative projects to be conducted (for example, the organisation prioritises such projects involving service-users).

SD estimated that since 50 per cent of their bids were successful, there was a need also to take account of the cost to the organisation of bids for contracts that might not be secured. The decision-making process here involves discussion among staff, and signing off by the organisation's board. SD emphasised that MENTHEAL seeks to enhance its decision-making in this context through conscious reflection on its previous mistakes.

C.   Campaigning and Influencing Policy

CP indicated that MENTHEAL has a clear sense of its identity as a '*service user and carer-led*' organisation which exists for the benefit of mental health service users and their carers. This identity informs the organisation's approach in selecting issues on which to campaign and/or take up with policy-makers. Some campaigning issues have been initially identified through, for instance, focus groups involving the organisation's beneficiaries and service user testimonials. CP explained that policy initiatives by government would also have a direct influence in determining issues taken up in the organisation's campaigning and policy work. Decisions on such matters are made by the organisation's public affairs team and need to be approved by the board of trustees, with the involvement of service users in both cases.

CP explained how the role of service users and carers can go beyond simply suggesting issues on which the organisation might focus in its campaigning activities and attempts to influence policy. This extended role might include involvement in discussions as to how policy should develop and why it should develop in particular ways. One such example was the use of a 'policy proofing' panel examining criminal justice, commissioned by the Government, including the participation of people with direct experience of the criminal justice system. The panel heard policy proposals, gave their opinion of how they would work in practice, and offered views as to the form the policy should take. A further example concerned the organisation's involvement in an NHS programme of events in which service users and carers were asked how policy should develop. MENTHEAL is a member of the Programme Board organising these events, and is also tasked with drawing conclusions and making recommendations in light of discussion at them. Such examples indicate the emphasis that the organisation places on ensuring that service users and carers can engage proactively in policy development. However, at this stage in the research, questions remain about the processes by which different individuals' ideas and arguments are taken into account in the recommendations made following such debate. The issue here is not so much whether individuals are enabled to make their point (in this regard, CP highlighted the role of facilitators in drawing out each individual's positions and reasoning). Rather it concerns how the organisation develops recommendations from the ideas and discussion at the event (in other words, how are recommendations determined on the basis of the points and arguments made within the debate?).

CP indicated that the organisation, and service users and carers, have varying success in influencing policy development. MENTHEAL's engagement with politicians and policy-makers has undoubtedly created conditions which might help gain such influence. Building on ongoing relationships, the organisation has been able to persuade politicians and policy-makers to attend meetings, to secure commissions (such as running the criminal justice policy proofing panel), and to occupy positions such as involvement in the NHS programme described above. Through such activities the organisation has been able to raise concerns in areas where it considers that its views have not been adequately taken into account. More broadly, CP explained that a requirement of continued service user engagement is that this is not tokenistic, and that recognition of this point acts as an incentive for policy-makers to listen to opinions of service users and carers.

Successfully presenting a case to policy-makers can be, but is not necessarily, dependent on the capacity to make a good argument. Such an argument might be a result of reasoning combined with the presentation of evidence. One example of successful use of evidence involved the organisation demonstrating that while people being prescribed a particular drug should have been routinely tested for diabetes, these tests had not been occurring. MENTHEAL secured amendments to legislation which provided mechanisms to help ensure this routine testing took place. Nevertheless, the organisation has also experienced situations in which policy-makers have failed to take account of reasoned arguments, and discussion has resulted in stalemate.

D.   Developing Awareness of Civil Rights

CP described how MENTHEAL is currently developing a 'civil rights approach' which will increasingly form the basis of the organisation's campaigning. In advocating and explaining this approach, the organisation draws expressly on the experiences of the civil rights movements in 1960s America, and of the Suffragettes in Britain. MENTHEAL considers that there remains substantial public misinformation about mental health illness, and that the current treatment of people suffering from such illness amounts to discrimination. This discrimination is reflected in social attitudes which are prejudiced against people with mental health problems. Discrimination also occurs when public services treat people with mental health illness as a patient group with multiple problems, rather than viewing the 'problem' as occurring when services fail to meet people's needs. For the organisation, adopting the civil rights approach means developing campaigns which make the case for tackling discrimination against people suffering mental health illness.

The approach also aims to empower service users through training on how to deal with media and politicians, so that they can more effectively make their case directly. In this respect, individual empowerment through the civil rights approach may have a positive effect on people's recovery from mental illness. The reasoning is that developing the capacity of service users to articulate their experiences and opinions in debate with policy-makers and politicians will enhance their ability to '*use their direct experience as a powerful means of changing things*'. This in turn means that service users feel that they have made a contribution to influencing policy, and this will have a beneficial impact on their recovery. CP explained how the civil rights approach has affected the relationship with politicians more generally. The suggestion is that, since service users are held to be '*experts in the system*', politicians view their involvement as a credible way of developing policy. However, there is evidence that politicians also support service user involvement in policy discussion because they find that service users' case studies can reinforce their own arguments and positions.

The adoption of the civil rights approach is consistent with the organisation's self-identity as existing in the interests of, and being led by, service users and carers. In particular, it seems consistent with MENTHEAL's emphasis on enabling service users and carers to put forward ideas, accounts and opinions. However, such an approach would not *necessarily* follow from a position of being a '*service user and carer-led*' organisation, so its adoption appears to have been the result of a deliberate decision.

E. Provisional Conclusions

Although the discussion above is based only on initial findings of the case study, it is plausible to maintain that MENTHEAL has been, and is still, undergoing significant change. The discussion on provision of public services showed how the organisation considers expansion of its capacity to take on large-scale contracts as necessary to retaining its independence. In this sense, it can be suggested that the organisation believes that such expansion is *a condition* it must fulfil in order to satisfy the normative expectations of its members and beneficiaries to the greatest extent possible. The organisation recognises potential difficulties that this expansion presents to its mission, and uses forms of reflection and deliberation in seeking to mitigate these difficulties. This can be seen in the account of internal debate over the potentially damaging effects of any proposed developments on the organisation's core purpose. There is no evidence here of identity transformation. Instead, deliberative processes appear to be concerned with how to manage change in a way that does not impact negatively on the organisation's collective identity in respect of its mission.

MENTHEAL is aware that the expansion of capacity to provide services will have a significant impact on relationships with service users and beneficiaries. In this regard, the organisation recognises the need to transform its collective identity. The discussion with SD showed that attention is being given to the understanding of these relationships; the organisation acknowledges that there will be a change in the relationships, and also seeks to influence that change. This recognition of the possibility of varying the 'representation' of the relationship with beneficiaries and service users might indicate the dimension of '*reflectability*' (the first operation in transforming collective identity, as discussed by Lenoble and Maesschalck (Lenoble and Maesschalck 2010 : part II chapter 6 section 2 and chapter one of this volume part III C)). However, from the findings so far, it is not certain *how* these relationships have changed, and furthermore, it is not clear whether the organisation has adapted to its expansion by altering the representation of the relationship with service users and beneficiaries. Consequently, it is not apparent from the findings that the organisation's identity for action is transformed through the expansion of its capacity to provide services.

By contrast, the adoption of the civil rights approach does appear to indicate transformation of collective identity, although in a different sense to that just discussed. First, the decision to frame its campaigning in terms of anti-discrimination might tentatively be suggested to be a reframing of MENTHEAL's representation of the public interest it is aiming to promote; in other words, reframing its reason for action, and hence its collective identity for action. In explaining its campaign against discrimination, the organisation explicitly draws upon, and sets itself as part of, a history of campaigns against discrimination in differing forms. As noted earlier, this approach is in keeping with the organisation's established identity as existing in the interests of service users and carers. The approach involves reflection on the organisation's established identity, yet it consciously represents this identity in a particular way in terms of tackling discrimination and promoting civil rights. In doing this, MENTHEAL shows awareness that it can alter its representation of its purpose, and that it has considered the identity for action that it is constructing (thus indicating a 'dimension of "*destinability*"' (Lenoble and Maesschalck 2010 part II chapter 6 and chapter one of this volume)). One question that has not been answered by these initial findings is whether this appeal to anti-discrimination enables the organisation more effectively to make its case in seeking to influence policy and public attitudes (that is, whether anti-discrimination campaigning is effective in satisfying normative expectations of beneficiaries with respect to influencing policy and public attitudes).

Collective identity for action also appears to be altered by the adoption of the aspect of the civil rights approach involving training to enhance service users' ability to engage with politicians and the media. It could be suggested that such training should be understood solely at the collaborative/relational level, as developing the capacity of actors to engage in deliberation, given the organisation's emphasis on service user and carer involvement in campaigns and debate on policy. However, to focus just on this collaborative/relational dimension would be to miss significant features of the civil rights approach. The approach aims to enhance service users' ability to explain their experiences and present their arguments directly to politicians and policy-makers. Therefore it appears to seek to increase emphasis on the autonomy, or individual voice, of service users, and this indicates a development in the organisation's understanding of its relationship with service users and beneficiaries. As with the move to campaigning on anti-discrimination, therefore, the adoption of this aspect of the civil rights approach can be understood as involving both awareness that there can occur development of the organisation's identity as user and carer led, and deliberate adaptation of this identity suggesting a conception of destinability. As noted above, the civil rights approach is held to provide an effective means of engaging with politicians, and it may also help the recovery of people suffering mental health illness. In these respects, it has potential to increase satisfaction of normative expectations. However, a number of questions need further consideration before a full account of any transformation in identity for action can be presented, for example concerning how MENTHEAL reached the decision to adopt the civil rights approach, and its experiences in developing the approach in practice.

V.   IMPLICATIONS FOR REGULATION

There already exists in England a system of semi-independent regulation that might help facilitate the development of basic conditions of more reflexive social learning in the governance of healthcare. Local authority Oversight and Scrutiny Committees, Monitor, and the CQC might all have a part to play. These bodies might include in their conception of the regulatory function the need to overcome obstacles to social learning in the collaborative/relational, experimentalist and Schönian pragmatist senses. Of course this implies a significant challenge to the currently dominant conception of regulation. Indeed, the regulators themselves may be viewed as collective actors engaged in social learning, addressing the problem of how to interpret their roles and approach the tasks of monitoring, evaluation and enforcement in the evolving healthcare environment.

The role of regulation in promoting patient and public involvement has been explicitly recognised in recent government policy. The report of the Expert Panel set up to review PPI in 2006 recommended that:

> assessment criteria are established to enable regulators to assess the performance of commissioners ... including an assessment of how local arrangements for involving service users and the public, in particular the LINks, are supported and utilised, and how well commissioners have sought and responded to the views and needs of communities and needs within their populations (DH 2006a: paragraph 11.6).

The Government's White Paper issued soon afterwards accepted this recommendation:

> The regulators will seek to develop assessment criteria to measure performance against national standards ... Current core standards for the NHS include the need to seek out and take account of the views of patients, carers and others in designing, planning, delivering, and improving healthcare services. LINks and OSCs will help commissioners be more accountable to local people (DH 1996b: 20).

The ensuing 2008 Act provided that the Secretary of State may direct the CQC to devise indicators which will be used to assess PCTs, NHS providers and local authorities across all aspects of their performance, including in relation to PPI.

It is suggested that, in devising such indicators, the CQC might have regard to the need to help facilitate and reinforce the collaborative and relational foundations of social learning, as set out above (section III A). If patients, the public and other stakeholders are unable for whatever reason to contribute ideas and challenges, and if decision-makers are not sufficiently receptive to such inputs in a manner that allows genuine dialogue, deliberation and revision, then the most basic conditions of reflexive governance (in the sense of collaborative social learning that maximises the satisfaction of members of the collective action to the extent possible) will not be secured. Whereas in the energy sector a special body might need to be created and tasked with monitoring participation (see the discussion of proposals for a Council for Participatory Governance in chapter four by Prosser et al, in this volume), in the healthcare sector this function is already part of the remit of the CQC. Again, the PPI framework already includes processes encouraging self-assessment by key actors in healthcare networks of their own performance on PPI criteria that in the energy sector might require a new form of 'participation impact assessment' (see in this volume chapter four by Prosser et al, and chapter three by Scott on the established role of Regulatory Impact Assessments in combating regulatory overload).

The CQC might have a further regulatory role in encouraging and monitoring experimentalist practices on the part of healthcare bodies, for example through support for the grass roots development of benchmarking schemes within and between different sectors and functions. There is already some evidence that Secondary Care Trusts voluntarily exchange benchmarking information (North-cott and Llewellyn 2005: 429). Under the auspices of the NHS Confederation, the Foundation Trust Network (FTN) has developed its own benchmarking scheme in collaboration with management consultants focusing on quality (clinical outcomes and patient experience), cost effectiveness, and operational manage-ment. As has been seen, iterative codesign as a feature of democratic experimen-talism implies a collaborative relationship between those responsible for policy and implementation. This relational quality might be easier to create and maintain between regulated bodies and the semi-independent CQC than with central government directly. Having determined the indicators by which to evaluate social learning processes, the CQC might then monitor progress in relation to them.

It may be objected that this vision is unrealistic in the current climate, given competing claims on the time and resources of regulators and the priority likely to be accorded basic quality standards and pressing issues such as hygiene control, survival rates, and waiting times for hospital operations. There may be difficulties also in encouraging regulators to conceive of their role in such social learning terms. Certainly mainstream policy discourse, even in its more sophisti-cated variants, tends to over-simplify the task of regulation. Consider, for example, the three stages in an effective regulatory process advocated in the Kennedy report:

(1)   It is necessary to establish the views of patients, public, professionals and other bodies in healthcare networks as to what is important in various domains.

(2)   The views of stakeholders should be sought as to what would promote improve-ment in regard to the particular matter identified as important.

(3)   Finally, it is necessary to decide how best to measure progress in the achievement of improvement, through the development of indicators and data on performance in relation to those indicators (Kennedy 2006: 67).[11]

---

[11]   Indicators and measures of improvement are necessary since the cultural changes within and between healthcare organisations that are preconditions of effective social learning can only occur gradually. 'Any new organisation, created to carry out a range of complex tasks, will need time to learn and develop . . . and will need subtle measurement' (Kennedy 2006: 67). 'The indicators of success may take a myriad of forms and be hard to discern . . . the tools have to be designed.'

A first assumption here is that the views of patients, the public and other stakeholders, as to both what is important and what would promote improvement, can easily be ascertained and made known to the regulatory agency. These views are presumed to be fixed and there is no space for dialogue or deliberation, either with the regulator or other bodies such as commissioners and service providers. Secondly, it is assumed that objective indicators can be devised that are capable of measuring progress towards the substantive attainment of the improvements specified by stakeholders. The third assumption is that there is a causal link between the activity of regulators in publishing indicators and standards on the one hand, and the behaviour of regulated entities on the other hand: 'Once it was *known* what the regulator was seeking to measure, because it was regarded as constituting good performance ... organisations would *direct their efforts so as to comply with what was called for*' (Kennedy 2006: 63, emphasis supplied). In this way it is presumed that 'the regulatory system creates a virtuous circle, listening to what promotes improvement, reflecting it in what is asked of organisations, measuring compliance, and thereby entrenching improvement' (Kennedy 2006: 63).

This model of the regulatory process appears responsive in the limited sense that what is measured is not imposed from above, but rather 'owned by those within the system ... grown from the bottom up.' However, the analysis is naïve as to the complexity of the governance issues involved in deciding what constitutes 'improvement', and as to the nature of the relationship between key actors and patients and the public necessary to negotiate and achieve this. As has been seen, fully reflexive governance is dependent on deliberation and openness to alternative possibilities in the framing of problems and the suggestion of solutions, and on other conditions of capacitation as suggested by the pragmatic and genetic approaches to social learning. Regulators may help facilitate such conditions, but healthcare governance problems can only be resolved ultimately by the key actors and stakeholders themselves.

VI.   CONCLUSION

The economic and democratic elements in the Government's current strategy for healthcare modernisation co-exist in uneasy tension. In England at least, the subordination of voice to choice in PPI policy both reflects and reinforces the Government's wider strategy for public service reform (DH 2006c: Foreword). As competition intensifies and the form of organisation of healthcare approximates increasingly to the regulatory model found in the public utilities sectors, the neo-institutional economic approach to governance is becoming more important. At the same time, other pressures at national and supra-national levels are reinforcing the general trend in western societies towards more rather than less democratic forms of governance.

Against this background, three main lessons may be drawn from the analysis provided in this chapter. First, government policy should pay specific attention to the *social learning* dimension of governance in public service sectors such as healthcare, as distinct from more familiar issues of efficiency, legitimacy and accountability. Such recognition might lead to a better understanding of the relationship between the economic and democratic strategies for healthcare modernisation, and of the need to avoid undermining the basic collaborative and relational conditions of effective social learning. Secondly, the fundamental problem for government remains how to secure these collaborative and relational foundations and how to build on them the further experimentalist and pragmatist elements necessary for fully reflexive governance. While the continuing highly centralised nature of NHS administration may make such qualities difficult to create and sustain, it has been suggested that the CQC has a central role to play in helping develop these capacities. In performing this regulatory function, the CQC might draw on new resources for innovation and experimentation accompanying the increased involvement of independent sector bodies in the provision of health and social care services.

Finally, the limits of what can be achieved through regulation and other forms of government intervention must be properly acknowledged. Combined with appropriate economic and social policy initiatives on the part of government, regulation can help secure the conditions of more effective social learning, but it cannot compel the resolution of the most complex and intractable governance problems. Such resolution is likely to require a kind of radical transformation in the identity and role of key actors in healthcare networks that cannot be externally imposed. The genetic approach to governance, with its emphasis on self-capacitation, implies a more subtle and indirect form of institutional 'supervision of the learning process', and the need to 'act on *actors' capacities*' (Lenoble and Maesschalck 2010: part II chapter 6 section 2). The preliminary conclusions drawn from the NGO case study show how the increasingly important role of voluntary organisations in health and social care networks may be understood from this perspective.

ANNEX A: HEALTH AND SOCIAL CARE NETWORK (ENGLAND)

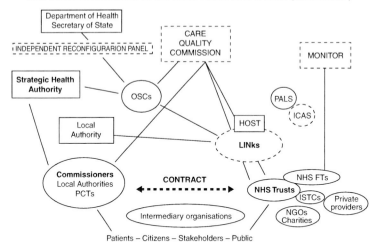

Patients – Citizens – Stakeholders – Public

Key

FTs	Foundation Trusts
ICAS	Independent Complaints Advisory Services
ISTCs	Independent Sector Treatment Centres
LINks	Local Involvement Networks
NGOs	Non-Governmental Organisations
OSCs	Oversight and Scrutiny Committees
PALS	Patient Advice and Liaison Services

ANNEX B: ECONOMIC RESTRUCTURING OF HEALTHCARE (ENGLAND)

The New Labour Government elected in 1997 continued the Conservative economic reform agenda based on increasing competition and market incentives. By 2003, a package of inter-related measures was introduced with the aim of encouraging the development of a quasi-market for healthcare services. While PCTs retained the principal purchasing function, the main focus was on increasing supply-side competition. The key elements in the restructuring of decentralised interaction from this period are as follows:

- NHS foundation trusts began to be established in April 2004 as semi-independent corporate entities, able to compete with one another and other providers in the private and voluntary sectors. By April 2009, 117 foundation hospital trusts had been created. These hospitals are not bound by the hierarchical constraints that continue to apply to ordinary NHS trusts. They enjoy increased powers to borrow for capital developments, set up subsidiary companies, and retain the proceeds of asset sales. They are free to sell services to NHS purchasers on the basis of legally-binding contracts, rather than the non-litigable contracts previously used for transactions between NHS bodies. They are accountable to a new regulatory agency ('Monitor'), rather than the NHS line-of-command, and must comply with the requirements of another regulatory body, the CQC, in respect of national standards and inspection.

- The role of the private sector in NHS provision was expanded through introduction of a new category of ISTCs, dedicated largely to NHS work. The first wave of ISTCs was commissioned by the Department of Health in late 2002. By late 2007, 24 first-wave ISTCs were operating, owned by a range of home and overseas enterprises. Contracts have recently been let for a second wave of about 20 additional ISTCs, and this is being supplemented by the creation of an 'extended choice network' of independent providers, providing NHS treatments on an ad hoc basis. ISTCs were set to undertake half a million procedures per year by the end of 2008.
- A new system of standard tariffs was introduced to remunerate public and private sector providers, known as 'payment-by-results' (PbR). Providers are reimbursed according to fixed tariffs for procedures based on health resource groups, a simpler costing system with fewer categories than US diagnosis-related groups. This ends negotiation over price, and shifts the emphasis to competition based on quality or access times. However, it also helps build a supplier market for NHS work, because any accredited provider offering care at national tariffs can tender for NHS activity. Foundation trusts began using PbR in 2004 and, from 2005, all NHS trusts utilised it for elective care, representing about 30 per cent of activity. PbR is expected to cover about 90 per cent of English inpatient, day-case and outpatient work by 2008/09. Under the 'Choose and Book' system introduced in 2006, NHS patients awaiting referral to hospital could select from four or more locations. Since then the scope of choice has been increased to the point that, in addition to local options, patients may select from a 'national menu' of NHS Foundation trusts and ISTCs. The incoming Brown Government announced its intention to widen this to a 'free choice' system, in which patients referred for most kinds of planned treatments can select any foundation trust hospital, ISTC, or independent hospital in the 'extended choice network'. The rules permit both public and private hospitals to market and advertise their services. Choice supports the growth of the NHS market, both because of the possibility that many prospective patients will select the independent sector options, and because real choice will require over-supply and an expansion of provider capacity.
- In place of hierarchical command and control, oversight of the new quasi-market in healthcare has been entrusted to a number of arms-length regulatory agencies. In 2003 the existing NHS body concerned with standards and inspections, the Commission for Healthcare Improvement, was re-configured and given an expanded remit. The new agency, the Healthcare Commission, stood outside the central Department of Health bureaucracy and was subject to wide-ranging responsibilities for promoting improvement in the quality of health and healthcare across both public and private sectors. The Health and Social Care Act 2008 merged the Healthcare Commission, Commission for Social Care Inspection, and Mental Health Act Commission to create the CQC. While this body is now the 'super-regulator' for health and social care, Monitor retains its separate function as the regulator of NHS foundation trusts.

The Contribution of Network Governance in Overcoming Frame Conflicts: Enabling Social Learning and Building Reflexive Abilities in Biodiversity Governance[1]

TOM DEDEURWAERDERE

I. INTRODUCTION

T HE EMERGING NETWORKS of state and non-state actors aim to offer innovative answers to the present difficulties of the multi-lateral environmental governance system (Kanie and Haas 2004; Delmas and Young 2009). These new forms of governance can be characterised by an attempt to take into account the increasing importance of non-hierarchical forms of governance based on the negotiated interaction between a plurality of public, semi-public and private actors (Sørensen and Torfing 2007). Prominent examples of networks that have been instrumental in forging successful working arrangements are the World Commission on Dams, the Global Environment Facility and the flexible mechanisms of the Kyoto Protocol (Streck 2002). Another ongoing effort is the United Nations Global Compact which combines multiple stakeholders in a trilateral construction, composed of representatives from governments, private sector and non-governmental organisations (Haas 2004: 6).

This chapter addresses the dynamics, the successes and the failures of governance networks in the particular field of global environmental governance. One of the main advantages of network governance, both over traditional command and control regulation and incentive politics, is its capacity to deal with situations of intrinsic uncertainty and decision-making under strong bounded rationality

[1] The research presented in this chapter has been supported both by the 6th EC Framework Programme on Research and Development (REFGOV) and the Interuniversity Attraction Pole Programme (IAP) – Belgian State – Belgian Science Policy (BELSPO).

(Ostrom 2001, Brousseau and Curien 2001). In these situations, network institutions can create a synergy between different competences and sources of knowledge. Because of their capacity to deal with complex dynamic and global interrelated problems, it is expected that governance networks can make an important contribution to global environmental governance (Haas 2004).

From a theoretical point of view, however, the notion of network governance is characterised by a profound ambiguity. According to the analysis of network governance by Schout and Jordan, there are two very different approaches to network governance: one that focuses on networks as self-organising systems, and one involving active steering and support to the network dynamics (Schout and Jordan 2005).

The first approach, based on self-organisation, aims to reform our modes of governance by delegating a number of tasks to networks of self-regulated actors who negotiate their own collective coordination agreements. The main shortcoming of this model is that it presupposes the existence of a set of actors who share a commitment to a cooperative inquiry into decentralised solutions to their coordination problems (Koppenjan 2007). In the specific case of European governance, for example, the absence of such conditions for the emergence of collective action by self-organisation has condemned the policy of environmental policy integration through network governance to go unheeded. For instance, in spite of the high-level support for environmental policy integration through self-regulation, no supplementary capacity has been created for building a common information base, or for common agenda-setting between different sectoral officials (Schout and Jordan 2005: 12–14). As a consequence, very little horizontal articulation has been created between sectoral Directorates General of the Commission or between national experts. Ultimately, the policy of integration through self-regulation has remained limited to some temporary bursts of coordination activity by the Council of Ministers, driven by short-term crises or intense lobbying by pressure groups (Lenschow 1999).

As Schout and Jordan demonstrate, a second approach is possible, which is not based on the assumption of an automatic institutionalisation of self-regulated networks of activity, but which explicitly addresses the question of the appropriate institutional framework for network operation. Accordingly, in their analysis, Schout and Jordan propose that networks should be supplemented with institutions that help to steer the network design, carry out audits, adopt a critical stance and formulate management alternatives (Schout and Jordan 2005: 9). Such institutions could also accompany processes of social learning in the networks, which aim to integrate common objectives into the network as a whole (Schout and Jordan 2005: 14–15). Several questions are raised by this second approach. Under what conditions can the processes of institution-building lead to effective governance systems? When, and to what extent, is there a need for steering the networks or for accompanying the social learning processes? Under what conditions do governance networks contribute to issues of general interest, and, if they do, how is the learning process organised that allows defining a notion of general interest amongst the network participants?

The hypothesis of this chapter is that the debate on the contribution of steering and accompanying social learning processes in the governance networks could benefit from its confrontation with the debate on the use of reflexivity in the theory of governance (Lenoble and Maesschalck 2010: part II chapter 6). Such a broadening of the debate allows the identification of a double insufficiency that characterises the conception of reflexivity that guides the actual propositions for overseeing the governance networks. The alternative position we would like to elaborate is based on a reorientation towards an incentive politics that is better adapted to the reflexive resources of the context.

Indeed, both the approaches of network oversight in terms of external regulation of self-regulation (Ogus 2000) and the approaches in terms of joint regulation or co-regulation by state and non-state actors (Grabosky and Braithwaite 1986) mobilise a certain form of reflexivity in order to reform the conventional structures of command and control governance of the Welfare State. The defenders of regulated self-regulation, on the one hand, tend to privilege a first order reflexivity of automatic adjustment of the actor strategies in various sub-networks, through appropriate external institutional design of the network dynamics. Regulation of self-regulation occurs, for example, in forms of market self-regulation, such as in eco-labelling or the adoption of codes of conduct (Neale 1997), in instances of technical standard setting at the science-policy interface (Lessig 2000), or between the different levels of management of local common pool resources in polycentric arrangements (Ostrom 2001). Defenders of co-regulation, on the other hand, point to the necessity of second order procedures of social learning on the overall normative orientation of the network interaction. Examples of co-regulation are the social learning processes in stakeholder forums (Kanie and Haas 2004) and collaborative policy networks for natural resource management (Innes and Booher 2003). A well studied example of the latter is the Water Sacramento forum in California, where various stakeholders were able to enhance their knowledge and to reach a strategic consensus on the goals for regional water management, without the involvement of a centralised water regulation agency (Innes and Booher 2003).

On both sides of the debate, one can observe recourse to reflexive capacities, either of adjustment or of social learning, that are likely to ameliorate the structures of regulation. However, the use of reflexivity differs considerably from one case to another. In the first case, one only looks for a functional adjustment of the actors taking part in the game, while in the second case the organisational context itself is mobilised directly in order to favour a social learning process oriented towards the emergence of norms of reciprocity in behaviour, relying on existing resources of reciprocity in a retrospective manner.

Whether it occurs through a functional or a retrospective mechanism, in both cases the use of reflexivity is not elaborated for itself. Reflexivity is presupposed given as a resource that can be mobilised in the support to the network dynamics.

A closer analysis of the governance networks should allow, first, to point to this deficiency of the mechanisms of network oversight and, secondly, to propose an orientation based on a different use of reflexivity which explicitly constructs the conditions of success of the reflexive learning operation, leading to the satisfaction of the normative expectations of the network participants.

In order to study these questions, we first discuss the situations where governance networks were mobilised to perform various functions of governance in the field of global environmental governance. Then we introduce our theoretical framework for analysing regulation of self-regulation and social learning in the governance networks. In the third and fourth section, we present two in-depth case studies of network governance and analyse the conditions under which the normative expectations of the participants in the networks can be addressed. A final section draws some conclusions of the analysis.

II.   EMERGING MODES OF MULTI-LEVEL ENVIRONMENTAL GOVERNANCE

In this chapter, we explore the character of two major responses to the shifting demand for governance — decentralised network governance (Ostrom 2001) and earth system governance (Biermann 2007) — and ask a series of questions about the capacity of these forms of governance to handle a range of concerns relating to complexity of rule-making on environmental issues of global concern.

Decentralised network governance and earth system governance emerged as innovative responses to the collective action problems raised by environmental goods and the need to address them by the creation of a global order. Earth system governance plays an important role in addressing systemic problems such as climate change, in which actions occurring anywhere affect the entire earth system, while decentralised network governance has been developed to deal with cumulative problems, such as the loss of biological diversity, in which actions whose initial effects are local or regional add up to consequences that are significant at the global level (Turner et al 1990). Two important features are common to these two emerging modes of global governance: the recognition of the role of hybrid networks composed of state and non-state actors in the provision of various types of collective goods, and the attribution of a new role to the Government (Delmas and Young 2009).

In decentralised network governance, governance is accomplished through networks of public, semi-public, and private actors associated with international, national and regional institutions. In the past, the role of the Government in the regulation of the networks was mainly restricted to the management of negative externalities, generated by the capture of rents in network industries, for example. The rents and the externalities are still there, but the activities of networks have to be situated increasingly in a complex web of interdependencies with both positive and negative impacts. In this new context, governments have to manage both negative externalities and to facilitate the generation of positive network effects which contribute to the provision of global collective goods which are cumulative, such as the conservation of biological diversity. As a consequence, governments have been increasingly involved in activities such as the building of adaptive capacities in the governance networks, the stimulation of social learning, support for research into standardisation, and other activities that contribute to the network dynamics.

However, such a mode of governance is clearly insufficient in the case of systemic change. Here, individual networks may take actions that go against the actions of others, because of the direct global interdependencies. For example, in the Montreal Protocol, China would start producing ozone depleting substances such as Chlorofluorocarbons (CFCs) while cooperators try to restrict it. Earth system governance is an answer to the problems raised by functional interdependencies on the global scale (Biermann 2007).

In 2001, four global change programmes — DIVERSITAS, the International Geosphere-Biosphere Programme, the World Climate Research Programme, and the International Human Dimensions Programme on Global Environmental Change — joined forces to intensify cooperation through the establishment of an overarching Earth System Science Partnership. The research communities represented in this partnership contend that the earth system now operates 'well outside the normal state exhibited over the past 500,000 years' and that 'human activity is generating change that extends well beyond natural variability — in some cases, alarmingly so — and at rates that continue to accelerate' (Steffen et al 2004). To cope with this challenge, the four global change research programmes have called 'urgently' for 'an ethical framework for global stewardship and strategies for Earth System management' (Steffen et al 2004).

In the case of earth system governance, global governance arrangements are created which put new constraints on Member States. These can take the form of new independent authorities of last resort, such as intergovernmental organisations or independent dispute resolution authorities. In this context, states become intermediary players between demands and constraints from lower level constituencies on the one hand and constraints from the global order on the other. This leads to a more differentiated global governance system, where collective preferences of states play an increasing role in different forms of common but differentiated responsibilities, as we can see, for example, in the global precautionary regime and the debate over the governance of genetically modified crops.

Global network governance emerged within earth system governance as an important complement to conventional rule-making through intergovernmental arrangements. It shares many of the features of decentralised network governance, such as the hybrid actor networks and the flexible rule-making. It is characterised by the involvement both of intergovernmental entities and international non-state actors and has recourse to interactive rule-making for dealing with highly fragmented communities on the global scale. The main difference with decentralised network governance is the absence of a strong overarching authority for steering or supporting the network dynamics, such as the national governments or the European Union. The role of accompanying the operation of global networks is typically attributed to international non-governmental organisations, or to commissions and executive agencies of the intergovernmental organisations. A good illustration of this situation is the Forest Stewardship Council, which was established by concerned business groups, social groups and environmental organisations to oversee the operation of a worldwide network of national and regional forest certification bodies. Another example, to which we will turn later in this chapter, is the Commission on Genetic Resources for Food and Agriculture (CGRFA), which is an intergovernmental forum at the Food and Agriculture Organisation that provides policy guidance to the members of the international seed network of the Consultative Group on International Agricultural Research (CGIAR).

Several features of the environmental problems arising today have contributed to the emergence of this new role of networks of non-state actors and governments in the field of environmental governance. In this chapter, we explore:

(1) the roles of ecological entities whose boundaries do not overlap exactly with federated or global entities;
(2) the presence of heterogeneous and ill-defined collective preferences regarding abstract goods such as the global gene pool or value laden constitutional principles such as sustainable development; and
(3) the contribution of institutional diversity to robustness (stability) and resilience (adaptability) of complex socio-ecological systems in face of change.

To assess the potential of decentralised and global network governance to address these problems of environmental governance, we focus in the remainder of this chapter on two challenges: first, the challenge to overcome collective action failures in the context of highly fragmented global communities and dynamic ecological systems and, secondly, the need to foster social learning on the overall normative orientation of the governance networks.

III.   THEORETICAL MODELS FOR NETWORK GOVERNANCE AND THE HYPOTHESIS OF REFLEXIVE GOVERNANCE

For the purpose of the analysis of network governance, a more detailed framework is needed that helps to generate hypotheses about possible influences of governance on collective action failures and social learning. In the various models of network governance, a number of approaches to institutions have been distinguished. One of the most important distinctions is that between rational choice institutionalism and social constructivist or sociological institutionalism (Sørensen and Torfing 2007: 30). Drawing on the research findings of these two approaches, the analysis in this chapter distinguishes between two basic types of network governance, based on external institutional design and disruptive learning respectively, and discusses some mechanisms of disruptive learning as they have been developed in the context of contemporary pragmatism in the work of Charles Sabel on democratic experimentalism (Dorf and Sabel 1998) and the work of Jacques Lenoble and Marc Maesschalck on the genetic approach to governance (Lenoble and Maesschalck 2010: part II chapter 6).

Networks are not a panacea. They are prone to a set of collective action failures (Hertting 2007). Rational choice institutionalism has developed as a set of tools for remediating collective action failures by analysing the network dynamics from the point of view of methodological individualism. A common network failure occurs when network participants free-ride upon the trust of other participants and attempt to improve their own position by providing misleading information on their preferences or by extracting rents from information asymmetries. In some cases, institutional regulation from outside the network will be required to correct such behaviour and produce a form of cooperation under the shadow of hierarchy (Scharpf 1994). In other cases, an appropriate transformation of the game structure, for example by a system of graduated sanctions (Ostrom 1990) or by monetary incentives, might be sufficient to deter free-riding behaviour. In both cases, deliberate institutional design is used to turn the non-cooperative equilibrium into a cooperative outcome.

A second set of network governance failures are due to coordination problems. For example, an agreement for building a common infrastructure with benefits to all, or for removing common barriers, might be hampered by a lack of assurances that all will effectively take part in the implementation of the agreement. Here, the uncertainty on the intention of the other players is a rationale for non-cooperation. A similar problem arises in situations where the generosity of one of the participants is required to select an outcome, among a set of outcomes that all improve upon the current situation, even if it is a less preferred option for his or herself. Solutions to these situations are to be found in devices for providing information on the intentions of the participants, for binding the participants to agreements and in leadership. These and other solutions to the coordination problems have lead to a rich literature on establishing cooperative practices through the diffusion of models of innovative practices (Braithwaite and Drahos 2000) and on the building of credible commitment in network cooperation such as in the case of open source biotechnology to which we will turn below (Hope 2008).

Within the rational choice perspective, the potential of governance networks is mainly realised through appropriate institutional design aimed at increasing the stability of the cooperative outcomes and the ability to coordinate action (Mayntz 1993: 15, Scharpf 1994: 41). An important aspect of this game structuring is the deliberate design of institutional conditions which visualise and increase the interdependency structures between specific actors (Kooiman 1993: 251). We find some features of this approach in the case of recourse to governance networks in the field of natural resources management, through examples such as the recourse to sustainability indicators, common information management tools, and conditional delegation of decision-making to the networks participants 'under the shadow of hierarchy'.

The rational choice perspective mainly focuses on institutions as external constraints on the action of the individuals and organisations in the networks. The influence of the external constraints on the dynamics of the governance networks does not mean, however, that the actors are structurally determined by the institutional context. On the contrary, a set of other factors, such as the development of social identities, adaptive capacities, and the building of reflexive abilities also affect the success of the social learning process in the governance networks. Sociological institutionalism addresses these social and cognitive conditions of the learning processes. Its emphasis is on the actors as normative creatures, whose identity, capacity and aspirations are shaped by the political and social communities to which they belong. From this perspective, actors match the institutionally embedded rules, norms and cognitive paradigms with their own identity and the situation in which they are placed, and they are acting appropriately on the basis of their own constitutive interpretation of the institutionally defined rules (March and Olsen 1995).

Several mechanisms for explaining the success and the failures of the social learning processes have been advanced from a sociological institutionalist perspective. A first mechanism, which is closest to the original intention of the sociological institutionalist position, focuses on the important role of democratic identities and capacities. These can be built in the networks through story-telling, to discourses referring to the network actors as 'responsible citizens' or 'responsive administrators', through the mobilisation and the enhancement of their ability to act individually and collectively, and through ensuring a level of equality in the distribution of the political competences (Sørensen and Torfing 2007: 176–77). The aim of these mechanisms is the formation of a strong sense of communality among the involved actors, and the creation of shared meaning and common visions that facilitate consensus (Sørensen and Torfing 2007: 176).

A second mechanism deepens this first perspective, by focusing on the conditions for changes in beliefs that lead to effective change in behaviour. The need for this deepening is related to the fact that the normative integration of the actors envisioned by the first mechanism does not necessarily lead to new beliefs and strategies that fall outside the existing repertoire of beliefs and strategies of the actors. However, such social learning is required for the transition towards sustainable development, which implies a process leading to long-lasting change in behaviour founded on the changes in knowledge (Siebenhüner 2002: 421). The conditions for reframing beliefs in open-ended situations have been studied in more detail by Charles Sabel (1994), both in the context of firm behaviour and in the context of public policy. In his work, Sabel showed the important role of two specific conditions that are crucial to effective open-ended learning: first, the role of practical incentives for promoting the exploration of disruptive possibilities (Dorf and Sabel 1998: 286), and, secondly, a set of institutional rules that define the engagement in the cooperative enterprise. An example of a process illustrating the first condition is the recourse to benchmarking. Benchmarking consists in a survey of current or promising products and processes, which identify the products and processes superior to those which a firm presently uses, yet are within its capacity to emulate and eventually surpass. Benchmarking thus allows a comparative evaluation between different groups with possible improvements, and hence provides an incentive to disrupt the current routines and representations of possible outcomes. A second example is the simultaneous engineering by teams in the firm based on the initial benchmarking and on the correction of errors revealed by comparing the results amongst the teams. The second condition points to the importance of defining a set of rules of engagement of the actors in the joint enterprise. Examples of such rules are mutual monitoring of each participant's contribution, information-sharing and the mutual assessment of each participant's reliability in relation to the joint activity.

A second deepening of the understanding of the conditions of possibility of successful social learning is based on the genetic approach to governance, which focuses on the generation of the reflexive abilities which condition the success of the learning operation. Its starting point is the observation that social learning on new beliefs and action strategies can still experience blocking in spite of the building of the democratic identities envisioned in the first mechanism, and the action on the adaptive capacities envisioned in the second mechanism. According to Argyris and Schön, this blocking is due to a deeper level of representations which remain implicit in the learning process and which do not appear through the official story-telling or the explicitly organised experimental process (Argyris and Schön 1996). Their analysis shows the presence of unconscious repetitions of the current position of the actors and the engagement in defensive actor strategies as a tangible effect of these repetitions. This observation points to the need to explicitly build the ability for the actors to critically reflect on their own identities and representations, and to build the ability for the actors to engage with other actors in productive action strategies, without subordinating this joint inquiry to the reproduction of their existing frames or identities. In the genetic perspective, the focus therefore will be on the explicit generation of the reflexive abilities which condition the success of the learning process. Two mechanisms can be identified that play a role in this process (Lenoble and Maesschalck 2010: part II chapter 6). The first mechanism is based on the telling of 'deep stories', in which the implicit representations and identities are made explicit, in order to open the way for further redescription of identities in the process of social learning. The second has recourse to a mechanism of 'terceisation', which refers to the need to be confronted, through a critical experience, to a 'third perspective' on the situation of blocking, as a condition for the destabilisation of the current meanings and identities. For instance, reflexive abilities for social learning can be generated through the explicit confrontation with new user groups, which are not part of the current social learning process and by an engagement in a common process of redefinition of the learning as a result of this destabilisation.

Based on these three mechanisms, geared respectively to normative integration of the actors by building democratic identities, to the social learning of disruptive beliefs and to the generation of the reflexive abilities that condition the success of the learning process, increased productive learning in the governance networks can be expected to occur when the learning process generates both a horizon of reflection on common beliefs and identities, and a destabilisation of the current beliefs and identities through the confrontation to a 'third perspective'.

IV.   TWO CASE STUDIES ON GOVERNING SOCIAL LEARNING IN LOCAL AND GLOBAL ENVIRONMENTAL INSTITUTIONS

This section discusses two in-depth case studies which analyse the dynamics of governance networks in a rational choice and a sociological institutionalist perspective. The first is the case of the provision of forest related services in fragmented forest landscapes in Flanders, and the second is the case of global cooperation in the exchange of genetic resources in the seed bank network of the CGIAR. These two case studies are part of a broader set of cases that were analysed in two research networks, the Global Public Services sub-network of the REFGOV integrated project (RTD FP6 CIT3–513420) and the Biodiversity sub-network of the DEMOGOV Interuniversity Attraction Pole (IUAP VI-06).

A.   Research Methodology

Two considerations guided the selection and the methodology of analysis of these case studies. First, they were selected on the basis of evidence that showed clearly established limits both of incentive policies and direct regulation, and which established the role of social learning in overcoming these limits in the particular fields. The second consideration is related to the analysis of the conditions of social learning in the genetic approach. Because the focus of the genetic approach is on the way through which the actors explicitly build their ability to critically reflect on their own identities and representations, a methodology of joint inquiry/joint case study design was adopted (Reason and Bradburg 2001). Indeed, what seemed most relevant for this research is the identification of a viewpoint that could act as a mechanism of terceisation from the perspective of the collective actors themselves. Therefore, the collective actors were involved from the outset in the building of the survey methodology, the evaluation of its objectives, and the validation of the results.

In the case of the governance of international seed bank networks, original surveys were conducted in close collaboration with the Policy Research and Support Unit of Bioversity International and the Commission on Genetic Resources for Food and Agriculture of the Food and Agriculture Organisation. In the case of the study of the forest groups in Flanders, the research was based on general published survey data on the forest groups (Serbruyns and Luysseart

2006; Van Gossum and De Maeyer 2006; Verheyen et al 2006), unpublished survey data on the social learning processes within one forest group, and complementary interviews to deepen the understanding of the blocking of the learning process. In both cases, the findings were combined with information coming from internal meeting notes and official reports, and confronted to results from previous studies published in the literature.

B.   The Case of the International Seedbank Network of the CGIAR

There are few clear examples of truly global international regimes in the field of environmental governance that have global funding mechanisms and global independent dispute resolution mechanisms. Some illustrative cases of possible global governance systems are the Convention on the Law of the Seas (Wouters 2003) and the ozone regime (Young 2008: 14). Nevertheless, some interesting second-best solutions have been adopted. For instance, some multilateral environmental agreements have created global funding mechanisms to offset the incremental costs that contracting parties incur when implementing a treaty. A clear case is the Global Environment Facility, which operates as a complementary funding mechanism in the implementation of a number of multilateral environmental agreements. Another interesting second-best global governance model, which provides a good illustration of the dynamics of network governance on the international level, is the contribution of the CGIAR network to the international regime for crop genetic resources.

Over the last 40 years, the CGIAR centres have played a leading role in promoting open access to biological resources through the organisation of a network of specialised ex situ conservation facilities throughout the world. The open access policy is clearly reflected in the 2003 CGIAR policy guidelines:

> The germplasm [that is the seeds or the parts of a plant that allow reproduction] designated by the Centres is held in trust for the world community in accordance with the agreements signed with the FAO [...]. Based on the conviction that their research will continue to be supported by public funds, the Centres regard the results of their work as international public goods. Hence full disclosure of research results and products in the public domain is the preferred strategy for preventing misappropriation by others (CGIAR 2003).

Being part of the open access network for germplasm produces a network externality: researchers provide access to their own limited resources and information and in turn they gain access to resources and information from all other member organisations. For instance, a quantitative analysis of 15 years of exchange of maize germplasm between the International Maize and Wheat Improvement Centre (CIMMYT) in Mexico and 15 other developing countries shows that the recipient countries received four times as many specimens as they contributed to the international CGIAR repository (Fowler, Smale and Gaiji 2001). However, in spite of these obvious benefits, the collective action failures of networks that we discussed above could undermine the long-term sustainability of the CGIAR networks. Individual centres can free-ride upon the efforts of the others and extract rents by keeping some of their own materials under conditions of relative secrecy. Alternatively, lack of trust between the network members might deter some participants from engaging in the exchange of materials.

The conservation and sustainable use of plant genetic resources for food and agriculture is regulated by the International Treaty on Plant Genetic Resources for Food and Agriculture (ITPGRFA), which entered into force on 29 June 2004. The ITPGRFA is an innovative agreement, with a global funding scheme (the multilateral fund) and an independent dispute resolution mechanism (the third party) (Halewood and Nnadozie 2008). The objective of the Treaty is to establish a global commons for a selected list of plant genetic resources that are considered to be essential in the long-term protection of food security. The success of the intergovernmental negotiation processes that lead to the Treaty was achieved in part thanks to the knowledge about an already well functioning commons that had been built up in the context of the CGIAR network. The collective learning organised in this network paved the way for the formal legal arrangement in the context of the Treaty. For instance, the CGIAR centres already had a standard Material Transfer Agreement that was used since 1998. The Treaty could further build on this agreement in the development of its own transfer agreements (Halewood 2009). Moreover, the strong normative community built around the CGIAR network continues to play an important role in the implementation of the Treaty, through the elaboration of and experimentation with possible solutions for current implementation problems. For instance, in the field of material transfer agreements, the CGIAR centres have adopted agreements that apply also for materials that are not listed in Annex 1 of the Treaty but that are held by the CGIAR centres. These could possibly serve as a starting point for drafting agreements that go beyond the current Treaty obligations.

A set of design rules, which provide some of the incentives to alleviate the collective action failures, have been identified that play a role in successful 'open source' collaboration in biotechnology (Hope 2008: 183–86). The most important are:

(1) freedom for recipients of materials to fully exploit the material and distribute it to others;
(2) the full disclosure of information that is required to use the research material;
(3) non-discrimination in participation; and
(4) the demonstration of credible commitment by the provider of the material that he or she can guarantee the protection of the rights of the recipients.

These three design principles go a long way in explaining, from a rational choice perspective, the cooperative dynamics within the CGIAR networks. Credible commitment is provided by the clarification of the ownership rights in various declarations, such as the 1994 In Trust Agreement (Halewood 2009), and has been strengthened by the adoption in 1998 of the standard material transfer agreement. Full information disclosure is enabled by the common information infrastructure which can be accessed online through the System-wide Information Network for Genetic Resources (SINGER). Finally, the material is available for all recipients in the North and in the South and can be freely distributed as an international public good.

However, this first perspective does not highlight how the learning within the CGIAR network influenced the basic frame conflicts within this policy arena. A major external incentive for triggering the learning process within the CGIAR network was the adoption of the Convention on Biological Diversity in 1993. The Convention reasserted the principle of national sovereignty over biological resources. As a result the ownership status of the centres became highly uncertain. At that time some feared that the World Bank would take control over the centres holdings (as a major donor to the CGIAR) or that countries would make demands for the return of the materials that were originally acquired from them (Halewood 2009). The drafting of the various guidelines and agreements within the CGIAR can be understood as a direct reaction to this external shock, but it did not lead to a major shift in the basic representations within the CGIAR.

A good illustration of the persistence of a basic frame conflict in this policy field is the failed attempt, in 1989, to agree upon the International Undertaking for plant genetic resources, which proclaimed the 'universally accepted principle that plant genetic resources are a heritage of mankind and consequently should be available without restriction' (article 7). Eight countries abstained from adopting the agreement, on the basis that, among other things, it did not provide sufficient guarantees for the intellectual property rights on plant varieties as embodied in plant breeders' rights (Mekouar 2002).[2] This conflict between the protection of breeders' rights and farmers' rights is part of larger disagreement over the framing of biodiversity resources. On the one hand, biological resources are constructed as a public good, such as reflected in the failed attempt of the International Undertaking, the ITPGRFA Treaty and in the concept of farmers' rights embodied in national legislation such as in India. On the other hand, in international treaties such as the Agreement on Trade-Related Intellectual Property Rights or the Budapest Treaty, biological resource are framed as proprietary resources, to be protected by exclusive use rights such as patents on the intangible components of the biological resources. As a result of this frame conflict, many developing countries abstained from joining some of these Treaties, which is for example the case of the Budapest Treaty which regulates the patenting of microbial genetic resources.

The learning in the CGIAR did not produce any disruptive beliefs or a new strategic consensus among the centres that would allow overcoming the basic frame conflict. The main result of the learning in the CGIAR centres was an

---

[2] www.fao.org/Legal/default.html.

adjustment of their rules for exchanging materials and dealing with ownership issues, in order to maintain the self-governance of the network. In this process, the centres maintained a conception that is close to the common heritage doctrine that was already envisioned in the 1989 International Undertaking. Moreover, in spite of some decentralised experimentation by individual CGIAR centres with more specific license agreements with private partners, no systematic benchmarking or mutual monitoring was organised as it would be the case in the recourse to a democratic experimentalist model to the learning process.

In sum, the learning process in the CGIAR can be best characterised as an incremental learning process where the actor strategies were adjusted, as a reaction to the realities of a new policy environment. This incremental learning within the CGIAR has been facilitated by the Commission on Genetic Resources on Food and Agriculture (CGRFA), which provides overall policy guidance to the CGIAR centres. The CGRFA formulated in 1993 four model agreements that could be used for clarifying the ownership issues, which directly inspired the 1994 In Trust agreements between the centres and the FAO (Halewood 2009). This role of the CGRFA appropriately reflects the role of external institutions in the steering of networks, as external facilitators of the network dynamics, which is also recognised as an important aspect of network steering in the rational actor perspective. However, such external steering does not address the deeper laying frame conflicts in this policy field. This latter aspect will be addressed when discussing the genetic approach to social learning in section V.

C.   The Case of Small-Scale Forestry in Flanders

Decentralised network governance addresses multilevel governance issues in situations involving cumulative and/or disjointed environmental problems. In the case of environmental goods with low global interdependencies, multilevel governance takes the form of a decentralised network of organisations and communities linked to regional, national, and international institutions. The role of the higher level institutions is to handle coordination functions, to exploit possible economies of scale, and to reduce information asymmetries among actors in the network.

A recent innovation in this field has become known as the 'new environmental governance' (Gunningham 2009). This enterprise recognises the shift taking place in the role of the state and highlights the benefits of a more decentralised and consensual approach, which seeks to coordinate at multiple levels and which is distinctively polycentric (Gunningham 2009: 27). This approach in turn provides greater scope for non-state actors to assume administrative, regulatory, managerial and mediating functions previously handled by the state. Examples of this approach in the United States include the Habitat Conservation Plans developed under the Endangered Species Act, and the Chesapeake Bay and San Francisco Bay Delta Programmes. Within the European Union, the Water Framework

Directive[3], an example of the Open Method of Coordination, is sometimes treated as an example of this approach. Other examples are the Resource Management Act in New Zealand, the Flemish Forest Decree in Belgium and Natural Resource Management in Australia.

The new regional emphasis in forest management in Flanders, Belgium, provides a useful example for thinking about the distinctive features of this approach (Dedeurwaerdere 2009). In this ambitious experiment, 19 regional forest groups have been created (*cf* www.bosgroepen.be). These bodies have formal office holders and responsibility for undertaking consultation, planning and priority setting. Provision is made to enable each region to develop its own regional plan and regional investment strategy for addressing management challenges within parameters set nationally.

Why is this innovative scheme successful, in a policy field where the command and control and economic incentive policies that were already in place from 1990 to 1996 were not able to produce the desired outcomes? First, the failure of the transition to sustainable forest management in the past cannot be explained by an insufficient level of economic incentives, such as cost share policies (Serbruyns and Luyssaert 2006). Secondly, from an ecological point of view, the 1990 Forest Decree was already based on a detailed set of criteria and indicators for multi-functional forest use and management, which have been agreed upon in the Pan European Forestry process, where both forest interests and nature movements are represented. It seems therefore that the issue at stake here is not the lack of appropriate legal concepts, which do not integrate the ecological point of view.

The main innovation introduced from 1996 on, through the progressive creation of the forest groups, is the explicit organisation of processes of collective learning amongst the forest owners and stakeholders. The task of the forest group is to assist individual forest owners with the drafting of their individual forest management plans, to organise their approval as part of an overall management plan of the forest group, and to deliver a set of forest management related services to help with the implementation of these management plans.

The learning process within the forest groups has been conceived as a gradual process where (1) management objectives are defined based on the perceptions of opportunities by forest owners, and where (2) the information generated is used to adapt the operational objectives of the forest group. The progress and gaps in the learning process can be analysed by using the available data of the Bosgroep Zuiderkempen (BZK), which is considered a reference case by the Flemish Government. The main sustainability indicators and targets that have been adopted by the BZK forest group concern the social and cultural functions of the forests, and the protection of forest borders and of heath landscapes. Forest management measures for fragile habitats have been planned, and further action

---

[3] Directive 2000/60/EC of the European Parliament and of the Council of 23 October 2000 establishing a framework for Community action in the field of water policy [2000] OJ L 327 (22/12 2000)

for combating invasive species (especially American bird cherry, *Prunus serotina*) will be pursued in the priority working area. These targets have been set by the forest owners in the general assembly of the forest groups and are the result of building awareness, discussion and negotiation amongst the forest owners.

However, important aspects of sustainable forestry, such as access to private forests in Flanders and biodiversity conservation, still remain under-represented in this learning process and have not been adopted by the forest group. A second mechanism of social learning in the forest groups, based on learning by mutual monitoring between subgroups within the organisation, aims at fostering learning on these issues that still encounter a lot of resistance from the forest owners. The main difference with the previous mechanism is that learning by mutual monitoring is especially appropriate for more experimental forms of learning — the so-called disruptive forms of learning (Sabel 1994). Disruptive learning processes lead to actions that cannot be framed within the current representations of the forest groups. If these experiments lead to successful outcomes, then they provide in turn an incentive for the revision of the current representations.

For example, in 2006, an experiment was organised with the larger forest owners of the forest group. The drafting of the management plan was outsourced to an independent consultant, with the explicit aim to evaluate the contribution of the forest groups to learning on sustainable forestry. This experiment produced a double result. First, a partnership with independent consultants for dealing with large private forest owners was initiated. Secondly, and more importantly, the experiment led to a realisation of the need to have two different approaches to sustainable forest products: the first based on the current standards for certified wood products, which mainly targets the ecological extraction of the timber value of large forest plots, and, the second, based on a new standard to be developed with the small-scale forest owners and which put a greater accent on the social and landscape values of the forests.

A new pilot project will commence in 2009, again with some specific subgroups, in order to develop a specific methodology for integrating forest biodiversity in the management plans of small forest owners (Bosgroep Zuiderkempen 2006). The explicit goal of the pilot project is to reconsider the basic concepts of the management plans with the forest owners and to foster the development of new initiatives that do not directly fall under the current conceptions of sustainable forest management (personal communication, BZK coordinator). These and other experiments illustrate the organisation of open-ended initiatives in subgroups, and attempt to go beyond the insufficiencies of the incremental learning. They question the legitimacy of the current conceptions of sustainable forestry by putting opposing beliefs in practice within the forest groups.

V.   BROADENING THE NORMATIVE ORIENTATION OF THE GOVERNANCE NETWORKS

The foregoing section discussed a double improvement of network governance, based on regulated self-regulation and on social learning respectively. The analyses of the case studies showed the contribution of network governance in decentralised and global orders to the provision of collective goods and allowed some hypotheses on the conditions of success and failure of the governance networks to be generated. However, each improvement emphasises only one part of the network dynamics, either the stabilisation of the cooperative outcomes resulting from the mutual adjustments of the various actor strategies, or the social learning on the content of the overall normative orientation of the interaction within the governance networks. Missing from both is a reflection on the articulation between the strategic and normative level of the analysis.

In order to construct a more complete approach, which takes into account both the strategic interactions and the normative orientation of the governance networks, the proposition in this section is to build upon the genetic approach and to consider a different, reflexive articulation between the social learning processes and the adjustment of the actor strategies in the networks. In the genetic approach, the stake is not so much to rely on existing reflexive abilities, whether they are capacities of self-adjustment or of cooperative learning, but to act on the conditions of emergence of reflexive abilities through the mechanism of terceisation. If we take into account this new order of conditionality, we must combine the double improvement proposed in the theories of network governance in a different way.

First, the confrontation, through a critical experience, to a 'third perspective' on the situation of blocking, shifts the attention from the adjustment between various actor strategies to their confrontation with the perspective of other potential beneficiaries of the collective goods. Secondly, the destabilisation of the social learning process, as a result of this confrontation, shifts the attention from learning within the existing networks to the association of new user groups in a process of redefinition of the collective identity. In sum, instead of considering an independent action on either the social learning within a given environment or on the design principles governing the interaction between various communities, a reflexive understanding of this process develops a joint action on the processes of social learning and the association of new actors to the development of the strategies in order to create the conditions for their common transformation.

A.   The Building of Reflexive Abilities in the International Seedbank Network

The case of the network of the CGIAR centres is a clear case where common norms and institutional policy in cooperative networks have played a role in

creating a de facto open access regime in genetic resources. A historical reconstruction by key actors that were involved in the building of the open source
collaboration shows the importance of strong bonds amongst the scientists and
common goals amongst the various organisations and individuals (Byerlee and
Dubin 2009). Field training of young scientists in the nurseries of the network
and workshops amongst senior scientists played an important role in this.
Another key element was the involvement of the recipients in the further use and
distribution of the germplasm. Indeed, improved germplasm produced within
the CGIAR network is distributed as an international public good, but the
strategic decisions on the choice of the plant varieties to be developed as
commodities based on this germplasm and distribution to the farmers is organised by the participating countries and organisations.

The in-depth reconstruction of the history of the CGIAR network shows that
the main focus of learning process in the development of CGIAR has been on
social integration of the plant breeders' community on the global scale. Recently,
new challenges, however, showed some of the limits of this social learning process
and the need to open up the network to new issues and participants. Examples of
these challenges are global infectious diseases affecting food crops, animals and
sometimes humans, and the development of crop and non-crop biofuels. These
challenges were present in the early stages of the green revolution, but have
gained in importance due to the increasing pace of climate change and the recent
outbreaks of new variants of bird and pork influenza. As a response to these new
challenges, officers at the ITPGRFA attempted to initiate a common workshop
with other United Nations agencies on the access to genetic resources related to
global infectious diseases, but this attempt failed until today (personal communication, ITPGRFA Treaty Officer).

A more successful attempt to broaden the learning process was undertaken by
the CGRFA. The CGRFA is a permanent forum within the Food and Agriculture
Organisation where governments discuss and negotiate matters relevant to
biodiversity for food and agriculture. At its 11th regular session in 2007, the
Commission recommended that FAO and CGRFA contribute to 'further work on
access and benefit sharing for genetic resources for food and agriculture in an
integrated and interdisciplinary manner', 'in relation to all components of
biodiversity for food and agriculture' (CGRFA-11/07/REP). In this context a set
of workshops and studies were organised in the field of microorganisms and
invertebrates, animal genetic resources, aquatic genetic resources and forest
genetic resources. In the field of microorganisms in particular, it appeared that an
important goal of ex situ conservation of biological materials is the development
and conservation of scientific reference materials for use in cumulative follow-on
research or as research and diagnostic tools. The need to develop such 'man-
made' reference materials does not appear in the realm of the plant breeders'
world and is specifically related to the high level of mutations of microorganisms
in situ settings. As a consequence of this broader understanding of the contribution of ex situ biodiversity, new needs were identified, such as the promotion of

global food security through increasing access to microbial research tools, and a process started to develop solutions for collaboration in this new area.

By addressing the broader issues of the contribution of biodiversity to food and agriculture, the CGRFA initiated a process that will require participants in the CGIAR network to look beyond their plant breeding identity. Based on this broader identity, new actors have been associated to the networks, such as in the project to link up microbial holdings of the CGIAR with the international research infrastructure of the World Federation of Culture Collections, in a framework that would guarantee continued access to microbial materials for developing countries. However, for this broadening to succeed, further work on social learning within the extended community will be needed. In particular, there is no agreement yet on the way in which an open source model, based on the CGIAR model, could be developed for the microbial world, and how to overcome the differences in position between governmentally funded collections and private non-profit collections (Dedeurwaerdere et al 2009). Nevertheless, it can be said that, as a result of the confrontation with the new challenges through the initiative of the CGRFA Commission, a reflexive process of redefinition of the identity was initiated. Both the CGRFA and the newly created Bioversity International (1 December 2006) contributed to opening up the learning process in the plant breeding community beyond the current blocking. They also initiated a critical process of evaluation of the existing identity by its confrontation to the broader reality and problems of biodiversity as it contributes to food and agricultural production.

B.   The Building of Reflexive Abilities in the Forest Groups

The contribution of the forest groups to forest governance can be modelled as a situation where cooperation is built through a combination of instrumental trust, based on reciprocity and enforced by increased transparency and means of verification, and social trust, based on signs of respect and esteem (Tyler 1998). To build trust with the Government and amongst the forest owners, the forest groups have focused both on instrumental and social trust. Instrumental trust has been built by enhancing verification of reciprocity through the gradual learning on common criteria and indicators. Social identities of the forest owners have been enforced, through generating respect for the owners' ideas and interests, by bringing owners back to their forest and by stimulating a sense of forest stewardship (Bosgroepen 2005).

Within forest groups, the actors are considered and treated from the perspective of forest owners and forest managers. Indeed, that is the common thread in the way in which nature associations and private owners are brought together and the way cooperation is built between active forest managers and passive forest owners. However, in this manner, no new identity is built in the forest groups around the concept of multifunctional management. Instead, the old identities are simply reproduced within this new framework. Hence, the social learning method based on the criteria and indicators is incapable of achieving a more profound transformation of the identity of the forest groups, which is however needed to address the issues raised by the users of the forest related ecosystems services (such as for recreation and landscape values) and for the building of cooperation with the local communities.

Within the forest groups, there is also a second approach, which takes into account the limits of this first approach and attempts to address the challenge of broadening cooperative learning with the users as a 'third party', without subordinating this cooperation to the current identity of the forest groups. Indications for such a second approach are clearly present in initiatives such as the experiment with the access negotiations in the Bosgroep Zuiderkempen and the integration of the complaints of the local population in the working of the forest groups (Bosgroepen Zuiderkempen 2006). This is also reflected in some position statements by the forest groups, on the cultural and social values of the forests, and the concern frequently expressed about the remaining gap between the interests of the nature associations on the one hand and the inhabitants on the other (Bosgroep Zuiderkempen 2005, Bosgroepen 2006). Hence, instead of the reproduction of the old social identities, within the context of a new cognitive frame, as is the case in the first approach, this second approach points to a more profound transformation that is going on at the same time, which is a more fundamental transformation of the identity of the forest group.

By addressing the reconstruction of the collective identity of the forest groups, through experimenting with the association of forest user groups to their activities, the initiative of BZK attempts to address this failure of the experimentalist approach to social learning. The forest group coordinator has played a key role in opening up the learning process, by confronting the viewpoints and practices of the forest owners to the viewpoint and practices of the various forest user communities. As a result of this broadening of the learning process on sustainable forestry, new initiatives were developed with the user communities. For example, through the negotiation of access plans between the forest group, user representatives and the local authorities, a total area of 342 ha of private forest has been opened up to the various user groups (30 per cent of the working area). If similar results could be accomplished in the other forest groups in Flanders, then an expected total area of around 5000 ha could be opened up for forest users in the near future, which is more than the total area of the largest remaining public forest in Flanders.

However, in many situations of private forest ownership, the learning process is still blocked by the frame conflicts that persist between forest owners and forest users. Further progress would require developing similar initiatives for building reflexive abilities in the other governance networks. Such initiatives would allow sustaining the broadening of the normative orientation of the social learning process, in a way which is open to its own destabilisation, by a confrontation to the perspectives of various user communities which can benefit from the forest related ecosystem services.

VI. CONCLUSION

The development of global and decentralised network governance has produced a range of innovations regarding governance mechanisms. These innovations are reflected in major evolutions in environmental policy. Examples of these evolutions discussed in this chapter are new environmental governance in Australia, democratic experimentalism in the European Union, and the global crop commons for food security established through the Consultative Group on International Agricultural Research.

This chapter has analysed the epistemological foundations and the practical implications of the models of network governance, by focusing on the question of the role of inferential reflexivity in generating cooperative outcomes on global environmental issues. The chapter defines reflexive governance as a normative process geared to the building of reflexive abilities in the governance networks. The building of reflexive abilities shifts the attention to the development of a joint action on the processes of social learning and the strategic interactions between the actors in order to create the conditions for their common transformation.

Two important examples of experiences with reflexive governance in the field of environmental governance have been studied as an illustration of the theoretical arguments, one in the context of global centralised orders — the international network of seedbanks of the CGIAR — and one in the context of global decentralised orders — the decentralised learning on sustainable management of forest ecosystems. An important lesson to be drawn from this analysis is the complementary role of reflexive governance in non-state organisations and communities on the one hand, and more conventional rule-making in intergovernmental organisations based on the consultation of transnational and national civil society organisations on the other. In particular, global problems need not always be addressed through reflexive learning processes on a global scale. For instance, the analysis showed that sub-politics in intermediary organisations, such as the forest groups, are often more appropriate for building social learning on issues of global concern, in contexts where highly specialised communities use and produce the collective goods.

Ultimately, much of our knowledge about the interaction between decentralised network governance, global network governance, and earth system governance remains highly tentative, contingent and uncertain. However, we hope that this chapter has shown that the epistemological approach of social learning in the networks based on a double conditionality, strategic and normative, while recognising the presence of multiple explanations and the interaction of different factors, is able to make the problem of multilevel environmental governance more tractable, and provide guidance for evaluating the conditions for organising effective social learning in other specific situations.

List of References

Abbott, K and Snidal, D (2009) 'The Governance Triangle: Regulatory Standards Institutions and the Shadow of the State' in W Mattli and N Woods (eds), *The Politics of Global Regulation* (Princeton, Princeton University Press).

Aglietta, M and Scialom, L (2011) 'For a Renewal of Financial Regulation' in E Brousseau and JM Glachant (eds), *Manufacturing Markets: Legal, Political and Economic Dynamics* (Cambridge, Cambridge University Press) (forthcoming).

Aoki, M (2010) *Corporations in Evolving Diversity: Cognition, Governance, and Institutions* (Oxford, Oxford University Press).

Argyris, C (1974) 'Single-Loop and Double-Loop Models in Research on Decision Making' 21 (3) *Administrative Science Quarterly* 363–75.

——(1982) *Reasoning, Learning and Action: Individual and Organisational* (San Francisco, Jossey-Bass Publishers).

——(1993) *Knowledge for Action. A Guide to Overcoming Barriers to Organizational Change* (San Francisco, Jossey Bass).

Argyris, C and Schön, D (1974) *Theory in Practice. Increasing Professional Effectiveness* (San Francisco, Jossey-Bass).

——(1978) *Organizational Learning: A Theory of Action Perspective* (Reading, Mass, Addison Wesley).

——(1996) *Organizational Learning II: Theory, Method and Practice* (Reading, MA, Addison Wesley Publishing Company).

Armour, J, Deakin, S and Konzelmann, S (2003) 'Shareholder Primacy and the Trajectory of UK Corporate Governance' 41 *British Journal of Industrial Relations* 531–55.

Armstrong, B, Eberlein, B et al (2007) '"The Electricity Reforms Market and Governance Models" – Canada Energy Case Study' REFGOV Working Paper Series SGI – 4 (Louvain-la-Neuve, Centre for Philosophy of Law, Université catholique de Louvain).

Arnstein, SR (1969) 'A Ladder of Citizen Participation' 35 *Journal of the American Institute of Planners* 216–24.

Axelrod, R (1990) *The Evolution of Cooperation* (Harmondsworth, Penguin).

Ayres, I and Braithwaite, J (1992) *Responsive Regulation: Transcending the Deregulation Debate* (Oxford, Oxford University Press).

Bachmann, R (2003) 'The Coordination of Relations across Organizational Boundaries' 33 (2) *International Studies of Management and Organisations* 7–21.

Baggott, R and Harrison, L (1986) 'The Politics of Self Regulation: The Case For Advertising Control' 14(2) *Policy and Politics* 145–59.

Baker Mallett (2005) *Baker Mallett Study on the Implementation of the Major Projects Agreement on the BAA Terminal 5 Programme* (Stockton-on-Tees, Baker Mallett).

——(2008) *BAA Terminal 5 Programme The Major Projects Agreement – End of Programme Audit Report* (Stockton-on-Tees, Baker Mallett).

Baldwin, R and Black, J (2008) 'Really Responsive Regulation' 71 *Modern Law Review* 59–94.

Bardach, E and Kagan, R (1982) *Going By the Book: The Problem of Regulatory Unreasonableness* (Philadelphia, Temple University Press).

Barnard, C (2000) 'Social Dumping and the Race to the Bottom: Some Lessons for the European Union from Delaware?' 25 *Eur L Rev* 57–78.

Bevan, G and Hood, C (2006) 'What's Measured is What Matters: Targets and Gaming in Healthcare in England' 84 *Public Administration* 517–38.

Bhatia, AV (2007) 'New Landscape, New Challenges: Structural Change and Regulation in the U.S. Financial Sector' *International Monetary Fund*, WP/07/195.

Biermann, F (2007) '"Earth System Governance" as a Crosscutting Theme of Global Research' 17(3–4) *Global Environmental Change* 326–37.

Black, J (1997) 'New Institutionalism and Naturalism in Socio-Legal Analysis: Institutionalist Approaches to Regulatory Decision Making' 19(1) *Law and Policy* 59–93.

——(2000) 'Proceduralizing Regulation: Part I' 20(4) *Oxford Journal of Legal Studies* 597–614.

——(2001) 'Proceduralizing Regulation: Part II' 21(1) *Oxford Journal of Legal Studies* 33–58.

——(2002) 'Critical Reflections on Regulation' 27 *Australian Journal of Legal Philosophy* 1–37 and CARR Discussion paper 17 (London, London School of Economics, 2003).

——(2003) 'Enrolling Actors in Regulatory Systems: Examples from UK Financial Services Regulation' *Public Law* 63–91.

Blair, M and Stout, L (1999) 'A Team Production Theory of Corporate Law' 85 *Virginia Law Review* 247–328.

Blanpain, R (dir) (2006) *Freedom of Services in the European Union – Labour and Social Security Law: The Bolkestein Initiative* (The Hague, Kluwer Law International) 386.

Borenstein (2002) 'The Troubles with Electricity Markets: Understanding the California's Restructuring Disaster' 16 *Journal of Economic Perspectives* 191–212.

Borenstein and Bushnell (1999) 'An Empirical Analysis of the Potential for Market Power in California's Energy Industry' 47(3) *Journal of Industrial Economics* 285–323.

Bosgroepen (2005) Bosgroepen, missie en visie, unpublished manuscript (Brussels).

Bosgroep Zuiderkempen (2006) Werkplan v.z.w. Bosgroep Zuiderkempen (1 Januari 2007–31 December 2012) unpublished manuscript (Westerlo).

Brady, T, Davies, A, Gann, D and Rush, H (2008) 'Learning to Manage Mega Projects: The Case of BAA and Heathrow Terminal 5, Programme Project and Risk Management' xxix *Project Perspectives*, 32–9.

Braithwaite, J (2008) *Regulatory Capitalism: How it Works, Ideas for Making it Work Better* (Cheltenham, Edward Elgar).

Braithwaite, J and Drahos, P (2000) *Global Business Regulation* (Cambridge, MA, Cambridge University Press).

Braithwaite, V (2009) *Defiance in Taxation and Governance: Resisting and Dismissing Authority in a Democracy* (Cheltenham, Edward Elgar).

Bratspies, R (2009) 'Regulatory Trust' 51 *Arizona Law Review* 575–631.

British Airways (BA) (2008) Summary of BA Presentation that was presented at the Department for Transport Review of Regulatory Framework for Airports meeting held on 16 July 2008 *Economic Regulatory Review Seminar*.

Britz, G and Herzmann, K (2008) *From Deliberation to Hierarchy? Changes in Energy Network Access in Germany,* Working Paper series: REFGOV-SGI-3, (Louvain-la-Neuve, Centre for Philosophy of Law, Université catholique de Louvain).

Broscheid, A and Coen, D (2007) 'Lobbying Activity and Fora Creation in the EU: Empirically Exploring the Nature of the Policy Good' 14(3) *Journal of European Public Policy* 346–65.

Brousseau, E (1999) 'Néo-Institutionnalisme et Evolutionnisme: Quelles Convergences?' 35 (1) *Economies et Sociétés* 189–215.

——(2004) 'Property Rights on the Internet: Is a Specific Institutional Frame Needed?' 13(5) *Economics of Innovation and New Technology* 489–507.

Brousseau, E and Curien, N (2001) 'Economie d'Internet, économie du numérique' 52 *Revue Economique* 7–36.

Brousseau, E and Glachant, JM (2010) 'Regulating Networks in the 'New Economy': Organizing Competition to Share Information and Knowledge' in E Brousseau, M Marzouki and C Méadel (eds), *Governance, Regulations, Powers on the Internet* (Cambridge, Cambridge University Press) (forthcoming).

——(2011) *Manufacturing Markets: Legal, Political and Economic Dynamics* (Cambridge, Cambridge University Press) (forthcoming).

Brousseau, E and Nicita, A (2009) 'Markets as Institutional Frames: New Institutional Economics Meets Industrial Organizations' *Revue d'Economie Industrielle* (forthcoming).

Brousseau, E and Pénard, T (2009) 'Assembling Platforms: Strategy and Competition, in G Madden and R Cooper (eds), *The Economics of Digital Markets* (Cheltenham (UK) and Northampton (USA, MA) Edward Elgar Publishing) 13–27

Brousseau, E and Raynaud, E (2009) 'Centralizing/Decentralizing Governance: What Are the Trade-offs?' Working Paper (Paris, EconomiX, University of Paris Ouest).

Brousseau, E, Dedeurwaerdere, T and Siebenhüner B (2010) 'Knowledge Matters: Institutional Frameworks to Govern the Provision of Global Public Goods' in E Brousseau, T Dedeurwaerdere and B Siebenhüner B (eds), *Reflexive Governance and Global Public Goods* (Cambridge, Mass, MIT Press) (forthcoming).

Brown, C and Scott, C (2009) 'Reflexive Governance in Better Regulation: Evidence from Three Countries' REFGOV Working Paper series SGI – 9 (Louvain-la-Neuve, Centre for Philosophy of Law, Université catholique de Louvain).

Burris, S, Drahos, P and Shearing, C (2005) 'Nodal Governance' *30 Austl J Leg Phil.*

Bushnell (2007) 'Oligopoly Equilibria in Electricity Contract Markets' 32 *Journal of Regulatory Economics* 225–45.

Byerlee, D and Dubin, HJ (2009) 'Crop Improvement in the CGIAR as a Global Success Story of Open Access and International Collaboration' *International Journal of the Commons* (forthcoming).

Calame, P (2001) 'Active Subsidiarity: Reconciling Unity and Diversity' in O De Schutter, N Lebessis and J Paterson (eds), *Governance in the European Union,* ('Cahiers' of the Forward Studies Unit, European Union, Office for Official Publications of the European Communities) 227–40.

Calliess, GP and Zumbansen, P (2010) *Rough Consensus & Running Code: A Theory of Transnational Private Law* (Oxford, Hart Publishing).

Carmel, E and Harlock, J (2008) 'Instituting the "third sector" as a governable terrain: Partnership, Performance and Procurement in the UK' 36(2) *Policy and Politics* 155–171.

Cary, WL (1974) 'Federalism and Corporate Law: Reflections upon Delaware' 83 *Yale LJ* 663.

Cashore, B (2002) 'Legitimacy and the Privatization of Environmental Governance: How Non-State Market-Driven (NSMD) Governance Systems Gain Rule Making Authority' 15 *Governance* 503–29.

Casson, M (1991) *The Economics of Business Culture: Game Theory, Transaction Costs, and Economic Performance* (Oxford, Oxford University Press).

CGIAR (2003) Booklet of CGIAR Centre Policy Instruments, Guidelines and Statements on Genetic Resources, Biotechnology and Intellectual Property Rights, Version II. Booklet produced by the System-wide Genetic Resources Programme (SGRP) with the CGIAR Genetic Resources Policy Committee (Rome).

Charny, D (1991) 'Competition Among Jurisdictions in Formulating Corporate Rules: An American Perspective on the "Race to the Bottom" in the European Communities' 32 *Harvard International Law Journal* 423.

Choi, SC, Gulati, MG (2004) 'Choosing the Next Supreme Court Justice: An Empirical Ranking of Judge Performance' *S CAL L REV* 78–23.

Civil Aviation Authority (CAA) (2008) *Economic Regulation of Heathrow and Gatwick Airports 2008–2013* (CAA decision, 11 March 2008 (London, CAA)).

Coen, D and Thatcher, M (2008-a) 'Network Governance and Multi-level Delegation: European Networks of Regulatory Agencies' 28(1) *Journal of Public Policy* 49–71.

——(2008-b) 'Reshaping European Regulatory Space: An Evolutionary Analysis' 31(5) *West European Politics.*

Cohen, M, March, J and Olsen, J (1972) 'A Garbage Can Model of Organizational Choice' 17 *Administrative Science Quarterly* 1–25.

Committee of Public Accounts (2005–06) *Energywatch and Postwatch* HC 654.

Committee on Public Participation in Planning (1969) *People and Planning.* (London, HMSO).

Competition Commission (CC) (2008) *BAA Airports Market Investigation – Provisional Findings Report* (20 August 2008 (London, CC)).

Construction Task Force, (1998) *Rethinking Construction: The Report of the Construction Task Force* (London, Department of the Environment, Transport and the Regions).

Council of Europe (2000) 'The Development of Structures for Citizen and Patient Participation in the Decision Making Process Affecting Healthcare' (Council of Europe).

Crabit, E (2000) 'La directive sur le commerce électronique' *Revue du marché unique et de l'Union européenne* 749–834.

Craig, G, Taylor, M and Parkes, T (2004) 'Protest or Partnership? The Voluntary and Community Sectors in the Policy Process' 38(3) *Social Policy & Administration* 221–39.

Cranston, R (1979) *Regulating Business: Law and Consumer Agencies.* (London, Macmillan).

Da Cunha, PV and Junho Pena, MV (1997) *The Limits and Merits of Participation* (Washington DC, World Bank).

De Schutter, O (2005) 'The Implementation of Fundamental Rights through the Open Method of Coordination' in O De Schutter and S Deakin (eds), *Social Rights and Market Forces: Is the Open Method of Coordination of Employment and Social Policies the Future of Social Europe?* (Bruxelles, Bruylant) 279–343.

——(2007) 'Fundamental Rights and the Transformation of Governance in the European Union' *Cambridge Yearbook on European Legal Studies* 133–75.

De Schutter, O and Francq, S (2005) 'La proposition de directive sur les services dans le marché intérieur: reconnaissance mutuelle, harmonisation et conflits de lois dans l'Europe élargie' *Cahiers de droit européen* 603–60.

Deakin, S (1999) 'Two Types of Regulatory Competition: Competitive Federalism Versus Reflexive Harmonisation. A Law and Economics Perspective on Centros' 1 *Cambridge Yearbook of European Legal Studies* 231–60.

——(2007) Reflexive Governance and European Company Law, CLPE Research Paper 20/2007, 3, 4, 26–27 Special Issue: EU Governance.

——(2009) 'Regulatory Competition after *Laval*' 10 *Cambridge Yearbook of European Legal Studies* 581–609.

Deakin, S and Carvalho, F (2010) 'System and Evolution in Corporate Governance' in GP Calliess and P Zumbansen (eds), *Law, Economics and Evolutionary Theory: Interdisciplinary Perspectives* (Cheltenham, Edward Elgar) (forthcoming).

Deakin, S and Koukiadaki, A (2009) 'Governance Processes, Labour Management Partnership and Employee Voice in the Construction of Heathrow Terminal 5' 38(4) *Industrial Law Journal* 365–89.

Deakin, S, Hobbs, R, Konzelmann, SJ and Wilkinson, F (2006) 'Anglo-American Corporate Governance and the Employment Relationship: A Case to Answer?' 4 (1) *Socio-Economic Review* 155–74.

Deakin, S, Hobbs, R, Nash, D and Slinger, G (2004) 'Implicit Contracts, Takeovers and Corporate Governance: in the Shadow of the City Code' in D Campbell, H Collins and J Wightman (eds), *Implicit Dimensions of Contract* (Oxford, Hart Publishing).

Dedeurwaerdere, T (2009) 'Social Learning as a Basis for Cooperative Small-Scale Forest Management' 8 *Small-Scale Forestry* 193–209.

Dedeurwaerdere, T, Iglesias, M, Weiland, S and Halewood, M (2009) 'Use and Exchange of Microbial Genetic Resources Relevant for Food and Agriculture' Report submitted to the Twelfth Regular Session of the Commission on Genetic Resources for Food and Agriculture, 19–23 October 2009 (forthcoming).

Defra (2006) *Managing Radioactive Waste Safely – A Framework for Implementing Geological Disposal* (London: Department for Environment, Food and Rural Affairs).

Delmas, MA and Young, O (2009) *Governance for the Environment: New Perspectives* (Cambridge, MA, Cambridge University Press).

Dent, M (2006) 'Patient Choice and Medicine in Health Care: Responsibilization, Governance and Proto-Professionalization' 8 *Public Management Review* 449–62.

Department for Business Industry and Skills (nd) 'Impact Assessment Toolkit' (London, Department for Business, Industry and Skills).

Department for Communities and Local Government et al (2007) *Planning for a Sustainable Future* Cm 7120.

Department of Commerce and Treasury (1995) Regulation of Access to Vertically-Integrated Natural Monopolies. (Wellington, New Zealand Government).

Department of Health (DH) (2000) 'The NHS Plan' (Cm 4818-I).

——(2006a) 'Concluding the Review of Patient and Public Involvement: Recommendations to Ministers from the Expert Panel' (May 2006).

——(2006b) 'A Stronger Local Voice: A Framework for Creating a Stronger Local Voice in the Development of Health and Social Care Services' (July 2006).

——(2006c) 'The Future Regulation of Health and Adult Social Care in England' (Consultation Paper, November 2006).

Department of Trade and Industry (2003) 'Our Energy Future: Creating a Low Carbon Economy' (Cm 5761).

——(2006) 'The Energy Challenge: Energy Review Report 2006' (Cm 6887).

——(2007) 'Meeting the Energy Challenge: A White Paper on Energy' (Cm 7124).

Doherty, S (2008) *Heathrow's T5: History in the Making* (Chichester, Wiley).

Dorf, M and Sabel, C (1998) 'A Constitution of Democratic Experimentalism' 98(2) *Columbia Law Review* 267–473.

Drèze, J and Sen AK (1995) *India: Economic Development and Social Opportunity* (New Delhi, Oxford University Press).

Dubois (2009) 'Adaptability of Competitive Electricity Reforms: a Modular Analysis' *Energy Policy* (forthcoming).

Dunsire, A (1993) 'Manipulating Tensions: Collibration as an Alternative Mode of Government Intervention' MPIFG Discussion Paper 93/7 (Köln Max Planck Institut).

Eberlein, B (2005) 'Regulation by Co-operation: The Third Way in Making Rules for the Internal Energy Market' in PD Cameron (ed), *Legal Aspects of EU Energy Regulation* (Oxford, Oxford University Press) 59–88.

Eberlein, B and Doern, GB (eds) (2009) *Governing the Energy Challenge – Canada and Germany in a Multi-Level Regional and Global Context* (Toronto, University of Toronto Press).

Eberlein, B and Grande, E (2005) 'Beyond Delegation: Transnational Regulatory Regimes and the EU Regulatory State' 12(1) (February) *Journal of European Public Policy* 89–112.

Eberlein, B and Newman, A (2008) 'Escaping the International Governance Dilemma? Incorporated Transgovernmental Networks in the European Union' 21(1) (January) *Governance: An International Journal of Policy, Administration, and Institutions* 25–52.

Ebke, WF (2000) 'Centros- Some Realities and Some Mysteries' 48 *American Journal of Comparative Law* 623–60.

Edwards, T (2004) 'Corporate Governance, Industrial Relations and Trends in Company-level Restructuring in Europe: Convergence towards the Anglo-American Model?' 35 (6) *Industrial Relations Journal* 518–35.

Eichengreen, B (2008) 'Dix questions à propos de la crise des prêts subprime' Banque de France, 11 *Revue de la stabilité financière* (Numéro spécial liquidité — Février 2008).

Eliasoph, IH (2008) 'A "Switch in Time" for the European Community? Lochner Discourse and the Recalibration of Economic and Social Rights in Europe' 14 *Columbia Journal of European Law* 467–ff.

Elkin-Koren, N (2010) 'Governing Access to Users-Generated-Content: The Changing Nature of Private Ordering in Digital Networks' in E Brousseau, M Marzouki and C Méadel (eds), *Governance, Regulations, Powers on the Internet* (Cambridge, Cambridge University Press) (forthcoming).

Ellis, J (2006) 'All Inclusive Benchmarking' 14 *Journal of Nursing Management* 377.

Elster, J (1982) 'Sour Grapes – Utilitarianism and the Genesis of Wants' in AK Sen and B Williams (eds), *Utilitarianism and Beyond* (Cambridge, Cambridge University Press).

——(1983) *Sour Grapes: Studies in the Subversion of Rationality* (Cambridge, Cambridge University Press).

ERGEG (2007-a) 'Guidelines for Good Practice on Open Season Procedures (GGPOS)' (21 May).

——(2007-b) 'Conclusion Paper, Cross Border Framework for Electricity Transmission Network Infrastructure' (Ref: EO7-ETN-01–03).

——(2007-c) 'Treatment of New Infrastructure: European Regulators' Experience with Art. 22 Exemptions of Directive 2003/55/EC' (Ref: E07-TNI-01–04).

——(2009) 'ERGEG Recommendations on the 10-Year Gas Network Development Plan: An ERGEG Public Consultation Paper' (Ref: E08-GNM-04–03, 11 March).

Esty, DC and Geradin, D (2000) 'Regulatory Co-opetition' *Journal of International Economic Law* 235–55.

European Commission (2001) 'European Governance: a White Paper' (COM (2001) 428 final 25.7.2001).

——2004a) 'Proposal for a Directive on Services in the Internal Market' (COM (2004)2 final 13.1.2004).

——(2004b) 'Extended Impact Assessment of Proposal for a Directive on Services in the Internal Market' (SEC (2004) 21, 13.1.2004).

——(2009) 'Report on Progress in Creating the Internal Gas and Electricity Market' (COM (2009) 115 final).

Flam, H and Flanders, J (eds) (1991) *Heckscher-Ohlin Trade Theory* (Cambridge: MIT Press).

Flyvbjerg, B, Bruzelius, N and Rothengatter, W (2003) *Megaprojects and Risk: An Anatomy of Ambition* (Cambridge, Cambridge University Press).

Foray, D (2004) *The Economics of Knowledge* (Cambridge, MA, MIT Press).

Fowler C, Smale, M and Gaiji, S (2001) 'Unequal Exchange? Recent Transfers of Agricultural Resources and their Implications for Developing Countries' 19 *Development Policy Review* 181–204.

Francesco, F and Radaelli, C (2007) 'Indicators of Regulatory Quality' in C Kirkpatrick and D Parker (eds), *Regulatory Impact Assessment: Towards Better Regulation?* (Cheltenham, Edward Elgar).

Freeman, J (1997) 'Collaborative Governance in the Administrative State' 45 *UCLA Law Review* 1–98.

Fukuyama, F (1995) *Trust: The Social Virtues and the Creation of Prosperity* (New York, Free Press).

Ganesh, AR (2008) 'Appointing Foxes to Guard Henhouses: The European Posted Workers' Directive' 15 *Columbia Journal of European Law* 123–ff.

Gerstenberg, O and Sabel, CF (2002) 'Directly-Deliberative Polyarchy: An Institutional Ideal for Europe?' in J Christian and R Dehousse (eds), *Good Governance in Europe's Integrated Market* (Oxford, Oxford University Press) 289–342.

Gilardi, F (2005) 'The Institutional Foundations of Regulatory Capitalism: The Diffusion of Independent Regulatory Agencies in Western Europe' 598 *The Annals of the American Academy of Political and Social Science* 84–101.

Gilson, RJ, Sabel, CF and Scott, RE (2009) 'Contracting for Innovation: Vertical Disintegration and Interfirm Collaboration' 109 *Columbia Law Review* 431–502.

Glachant, JM (2002) 'Why Regulate Deregulated Network Industries?' 3 *Journal of Network Industries* 297–311.

——(2009) 'Creating Institutional Foundations Which Make Retail Markets Work: The Case of the Electrical Industry' in J Groenewegen and R Kunneke (eds), *Network Industry Competitive Arrangements* (Cheltenham (UK) and Northampton (USA, MA), Edward Elgar Publishing).

Glachant, JM and Finon, D (eds) (2010) 'Large Scale Wind Power in Electricity Market' (Special issue) *Energy Policy* (forthcoming).

Glachant, JM and Lévèque, F (2009) *European Union Electricity Internal Market: Towards an Achievement?* (Cheltenham (UK) and Northampton (USA, MA), Edward Elgar Publishing).

Glachant, JM and Perez, Y (2008) 'Institutional Economics and Network Industry Deregulation Policy', in E Brousseau and J-M Glachant (eds), *New Institutional Economics. A Guidebook* (Cambridge, University Press).

——(2009) 'The Achievement of Electricity Competitive Reforms: a Governance Structure Problem?' in C Ménard and M Ghertman (eds), *Regulation, Deregulation, Reregulation, Institutional Perspective* (Cheltenham (UK) and Northampton (USA, MA), Edward Elgar Publishing).

Glachant, J-M, Lévèque F and Ranci P (2008) Some Guideposts on the Road to Formulating a Coherent Policy on EU Energy Security of Supply 21(10) *Electricity Journal* 1040–61.

Goffman, E (1974) *Frame Analysis: An Essay on the Organization of Experience* (Cambridge, Harvard University Press).

Gospel, H and Druker, J (1998) 'The Survival of National Bargaining in the Electrical Contracting Industry: A Deviant Case?' 36 *British Journal of Industrial Relations* 249–267.

Grabosky, P and Braithwaite, J (1986) *Of Manners Gentle: Enforcement Strategies of Australian Business Regulatory Agencies* (Melbourne, Oxford University Press).

Grimshaw, D, Marchington, M, Rubery, J and Wilmott, H (2005) 'Fragmenting Work Across Organizational Boundaries' in Marchington, M, Grimshaw, D, Rubery, J and Willmott, H (eds), *Fragmenting Work: Blurring Organizational Boundaries and Disordering Hierarchies* (Oxford, Oxford University Press).

Gunningham, N (2009) 'Regulatory Reform and Reflexive Regulation: Beyond Command and Control' in E Brousseau, T Dedeurwaerdere, and B Siebenhüner (eds), *Reflexive Governance and Global Public Goods* (Cambridge, MA, MIT Press).

Gunningham, N and Grabosky, P (1998) *Smart Regulation: Designing Environmental Policy* (Oxford, Oxford University Press).

Gunningham, N and Sinclair, D (1999) 'Regulatory Pluralism: Designing Policy Mixes for Environmental Protection' 21 *Law and Policy* 49–76.

——(2002) *Leaders and Laggards: Next-Generation Environmental Regulation* (Sheffield, Greenleaf Publishing).

Haas PM (2004) Addressing the Global Governance Deficit 4(4) *Global Environmental Politics* 1–15.

Habermas, J (1996) *Between Facts and Norms: Contributions to a Discourse Theory of Law and Democracy* (Cambridge, Polity).

——(1988 (originally published in English 1976)) *Legitimation Crisis* (Oxford, Polity Press).

Hadfield, G (2000) 'Privatizing Commercial Law: Lessons from the Middle and the Digital Ages' Working Paper 195, JM Olin program in *Law & Economics*, (Standford, CA, Standford Law School).

Halewood, M (2009) 'Governing the Management and Use of Pooled Microbial Genetic Resources: Lessons from the Global Crop Commons' *International Journal of the Commons.*

Halewood, M and Nnadozie, K (2008) 'Giving Priority to the Commons: The International Treaty on Plant Genetic Resources for Food and Agriculture (ITPGRFA)' in G Tansey, and T Rajotte (eds), *The Future Control of Food* 115–140 (London, Earthscan).

Hall, C, Scott, C et al (2000) *Telecommunications Regulation: Culture, Chaos and Interdependence inside the Regulatory Process* (London, Routledge).

Hallström, KT (2004) *Organizing International Standardization: ISO and IASC in Quest of Authority* (Cheltenham, Edward Elgar).

Hancher, L and Moran, M (eds) (1989) *Capitalism, Culture and Regulation* (Oxford, Oxford University Press).

Hardin, G (1968) 'The Tragedy of the Commons' 162(3859) *Science* 1243–48.

Harty, C (2005) 'Innovation in Construction: A Sociology of Technology Approach' 33(6) *Building Research and Information* 512–522.

Harvey, D (2005) *A Brief History of Neoliberalism* (Oxford, Oxford University Press).

Hauteclocque (de), A and Rious, V (2009) 'Reconsidering the Regulation of Merchant Transmission Investment in the Light of the Third Package: The Role of Dominant Generators' *EUI Working Paper* RSCAS 2009/59.

Hawkins, K (2002) *Law as Last Resort: Prosecution Decision Making in a Regulatory Agency.* (Oxford, Oxford University Press).

HCHC, House of Commons Health Committee, *Patient and Public Involvement in the NHS*, Third Report of Session 2006–07, HC 278–1.

Heller, M and Eisenberg, R (1998) 'Can Patents Deter Innovation?' Anticommons in Biomedical Research 280 *Science* 698–701.

Heller, MA (1998) 'The Tragedy of the Anticommons. Property in the Transition from Marx to Markets' 111(3) *Harvard Law Review* 622–688.

Hemerijck, A and Visser, J (2006) 'How Europe's Semi-Sovereign Welfare States Learn' position paper 'Governance as Learning' (on file with the O De Schutter).

Hertting, N (2007) 'Mechanisms of Governance Network Formation: A Contextual Rational Choice Perspective' in E Sørensen and J Torfing (eds), *Theories of Democratic Network Governance* (Hampshire, Palgrave Macmillan) 43–60.

Hirsch, J (1995) *Der nationale Wettbewerbsstaat: Staat, Demokratie und Politik im globalen Kapitalismus (The Competitive National State: State, Democracy and Politics in Global Capitalism)* (Berlin and Amsterdam, Edition ID-Archiv).

HM Treasury (2009) 'Reforming Financial Markets' (London, HM Treasury).

Hodson, D and Maher, I (2001) 'The Open Method as a New Mode of Governance: The Case of Soft Economic Policy Co-ordination' 39 *Journal of Common Market Studies* 719–745.

Hogan (2002) 'Electricity Market Restructuring: Reforms of Reforms' 21(1) *Journal of Regulatory Economics* 103–32.

Hollis, M (1998) *Trust Within Reason* (Cambridge, Cambridge University Press).

Hood, C (1998) *The Art of the State* (Oxford, Oxford University Press).

Hood, C, Rothstein, H et al (2001) *The Government of Risk* (Oxford, Oxford University Press).

Hope, J (2008) *Biobazaar: The Open Source Revolution and Biotechnology* (Cambridge (MA), Harvard University Press).

Horn, M (1995) *The Political Economy of Public Administration* (Cambridge, Cambridge University Press).

Hughes, D and Vincent-Jones, P (2008) 'Schisms in the Church: NHS Systems and Institutional Divergence in England and Wales' 49 *Journal of Health and Social Behaviour* 400.

Improvement and Development Agency (I&DeA) (2008) *Shared Intelligence: Evaluation of the National Programme for Third Sector Commissioning Baseline Report* (Improvement and Development Agency, Cabinet Office of the Third Sector).

Innes, JE and Booher, DE (2003) 'Collaborative Policymaking: Governance through Dialogue' in MA Hajer and H Wagenaar (eds) *Deliberative Policy Analysis* 33–59.

Jaffe, AB and Lerner, J (2004) *Innovation and its Discontents: How our Broken Patent System is Endangering Innovation and Progress, and What to do About it* (Princeton, Princeton University Press).

Jensen, M (2000) *Theory of the Firm: Governance, Residual Claims and Organisational Forms* (Cambridge, MA, Harvard University Press).

Joskow, P (2003) 'Electricity Sector Restructuring and Competition: Lessons Learned' WP CEEPR 03–014 August.

——(2005) 'Regulation of Natural Monopolies' *WP CEEPR* 05–008, Apr .

Kahneman, D Diener, E and Schwarz, N (1999) *Well-Being: The Foundations of Hedonic Psychology* (New York, Russell Sage Foundation).

Kanie, N and Haas, PM (eds) (2004) *Emerging Forces in Environmental Governance.* (Tokyo, United Nations University Press).

Kennedy, I (2006) 'Of Regulation' in *Learning from Bristol: Are We?* (London, Healthcare Commission).

Kersley, B, Alpin, C, Forth, J, Bryson, A, Bewley, H, Dix, G and Oxenbridge, S (2006) *Inside the Workplace: Findings from the 2004 Workplace Employment Relations Survey* (London, Routledge).

Kersting, C and Schindler, CP (2003) 'The ECJ's Inspire Art Decision of 30 September 2003 and its Effects on Practice' 4 *German Law Journal* 1277.

Kessous, E (2000) 'L'objectivation des qualités industrielles en discussion. Les acteurs du marché européen confrontés à l'élaboration de normes communes' 18(102) *Réseaux* 91–117.

Kickert, W (1995) 'Steering at a Distance: A New Paradigm of Public Governance in Dutch Higher Education' 8(1) *Governance* 135–57.

Kingsbury, B, Krisch, N et al (2005) 'The Emergence of Global Administrative Law' 68 *Law & Contemporary Problems* 15–61.

Kirkpatrick, C and Parker, D (2004) 'Regulatory Impact Assessment and Regulatory Governance in Developing Countries' 24 *Public Administration and Development* 333–44.

Knill, C and Lenschow, A (2004) 'Modes of Social Regulation in the Governance of Europe' in J Jordana and D Levi-Faur (eds), *The Politics of Regulation* (Cheltenham, Edward Elgar).

Kolko, G (1965) *Railroads and Regulation* (Princeton, Princeton University Press).

Kooiman, J (1993) *Modern Governance: New Government-Society Interactions* (London, Sage).

——(2003) *Governing as Governance* (London, Sage).

Koppenjan, JFM (2007) 'Consensus and Conflict in Policy Networks: Too Much or Too Little?' in E Sørensen and J Torfing (eds), *Theories of Democratic Network Governance* (Hampshire, Palgrave Macmillan) 133–152.

Laffont, JJ and Tirole, J (1993) *A Theory of Incentives in Procurement and Regulation* (Cambridge, Mass, Mit Press).

Lane, C (1997) 'The Governance of Interfirm Relations in Britain and Germany: Societal or Dominance Effects?' in R Whitley and PH Kristensen (eds), *Governance at Work: The Social Regulation of Economic Relations* (Oxford, Oxford University Press).

Lenoble, J and Maesschalck, M (2010) *Democracy, Law and Governance* (Aldershot, Ashgate) (forthcoming).

Lenschow, A (1999) 'The Greening of the EU' 17(1) *Environment and Planning C* 91–108.

Lessig, L (1999) *Code: and Other Laws of Cyberspace* (New York, Basic Books).

Lessig, L (2000) *Code and Other Laws of Cyberspace* (New York, Basic Books).

——(2004) *Free Culture: How Big Media Uses Technology and the Law to Lock Down Culture and Control Creativity* (New York, The Penguin Press).

——(2006) *Code 2.0.* (New York, Basic Books).

Levi-Faur, D (2005) 'The Global Diffusion of Regulatory Capitalism' 598 *The Annals of the American Academy of Political and Social Science* 12–32.

Levitt, M (2003) 'Public Consultation in Bioethics. What's the Point of Asking the Public When They Have Neither Scientific nor Ethical Expertise?' 11(4) *Health Care Analysis* 15–25.

Levy, B and Spiller, P (eds) (1996) *Regulation, Institutions and Commitment* (Cambridge, Cambridge University Press).

Littlechild, S (1984) *Regulation of British Telecommunications Profitability* (London, Department of Industry).

Looijestijn-Clearie, A (2000) 'Centros-Ltd – A Complete U-turn in the Right of Establishment for Companies' 49 *International and Comparative Law Quarterly* 621–42.

Luhmann, N (1995) *Social Systems* (Stanford, CA, Stanford University Press).

——(2004) *Law as a Social System*, translated by K Ziegert, F Kastner, R Nobles, D Schiff and R Ziegert (eds) (Oxford, Oxford University Press).

Majone, G (1994) 'The Rise of the Regulatory State in Europe' 17 *West European Politics* 77–101.

Makkai, T and Braithwaite, J (1992) 'In and Out of the Revolving Door: Making Sense of Regulatory Capture' 12 *Journal of Public Policy* 61–78.

March, JG and JP Olsen (1995) *Democratic Governance* (New York, The Free Press).

Marchington, M and Rubery, J (2005) 'Worker Voice across Organisational Boundaries' *Reworking Work: Proceedings of the 19th Conference of the Association of Industrial Relations Academics of Australia and New Zealand* (Sydney, The University of Sydney).

Marchington, M, Grimshaw, D, Rubery, J and Willmott, H (2005) *Fragmenting Work: Blurring Organizational boundaries and Disordering Hierarchies* (Oxford, Oxford University Press).

Marengo, L and Dosi, G (2005) 'Division of Labor, Organizational Coordination and Market Mechanisms in Collective Problem-Solving' 58 (2) *Journal of Economic Behaviour and Organization* 303–26.

Martin, GP (2008) '"Ordinary People Only": Knowledge, Representativeness, and the Publics of Public Participation in Healthcare' 30(1) *Sociology of Health & Illness* 35–54.

Mayntz, R (1993) 'Governing Failure and the Problem of Governability: Some Comments on a Theoretical Paradigm' in J Kooiman (ed), *Modern Governance* (London, Sage) 9–20.

McAuslan, P (1980) *The Ideologies of Planning Law* (Oxford, Pergamon Press).

Mekouar, A (2002) 'A Global Instrument on Agrobiodiversity: The International Treaty on Plant Genetic Resources for Food and Agriculture' (Rome, FAO Legal Papers Online).

Mendrinou, M (1996) 'Non-Compliance and the Commission's Role in Integration' 3 *Journal of European Public Policy* 1–22.

Menger, C (1883) *1985 Investigations into the Method of the Social Sciences with Special Reference to Economics* (New York, New York University Press).

Menz, G (2003) 'Re-regulating the Single Market: National Varieties of Capitalism and their Responses to Europeanization' 10(4) *Journal of European Public Policy* 532–55.

Mirowski, P and Plehwe, D (eds) (2009) *The Road from Mont Pelerin: The Making of the Neoliberal Thought Collective* (Cambridge, Harvard University Press).

Monks, R and Sykes, A (2002) *Capitalism without Owners will Fail: A Policymaker's Guide to Reform* (London, Centre for the Study of Financial Innovation).

Moravcsik, A (1998) *The Choice for Europe. Social Purpose and State Power from Messina to Maastricht* (London and New York, Routledge).

Mullen, C (2008) 'Representation or Reason: Consulting the Public on the Ethics of Health Policy' 16(4) *Health Care Analysis* 397–409.

Murray, A and Scott, C (2002) 'Controlling the New Media: Hybrid Responses to New Forms of Power' 65 *Modern Law Review* 491–516.

Neale, A (1997) 'Organising Environmental Self-regulation: Liberal Governmentality and the Pursuit of Ecological Modernisation in Europe' 6(4) *Environmental Politics* 1–24.

Newbery, D (1998) 'Competition, Contracts and Entry in the Electricity Spot Market' 29 RAND *Journal of Economics* 726–49.

Newbery, D, Van Damme, V and Von der Fehr (2003) 'Benelux Market Integration: Market Power Concerns' *Report of the Market Surveillance Committee* (Dutch Competition Authorities).

Nobel Committee (2007) 'Mechanism Design Theory', Mimeo, Scientific background on the Sveriges Riksbank Prize in *Economic Sciences* in Memory of Alfred Nobel 2007, Stockholm.

Noll, R (1981) 'Regulation in Theory and Practice: An Overview' in G Fromm (ed), *Studies in Public Regulation* (Cambridge, Mass, The MIT Press).

Nonet, P and Selznick, P (2001 (originally published in 1978)) *Law & Society in Transition* (New Brunswick, Transaction Publishers).

Nooteboom, B (2000) 'Learning by Interaction, Absorptive Capacity, Cognitive Distance and Governance' 4 *Journal of Managament and Governance* 69–92.

Nooteboom, B, Van Haverbeke, WPM, Duijsters, GM, Gilsing, VA and Oord, A (2007) 'Optimal Cognitive Distance and Absorptive Capacity' 36 *Research Policy* 1016–34.

North, DC (1981) *Structure and Change in Economic History* (New York, Northern Press).

Northcott, D and Llewellyn, S (2005) 'Benchmarking in UK Health: A Gap Between Policy and Practice?' 12 *Benchmarking* 419.

Nussbaum, M (2000) *Woman and Human Development* (Cambridge, Cambridge University Press).

O'Neill, O (2002) *A Question of Trust* (Cambridge, Cambridge University Press).

Oates, WE (1999) 'An Essay on Fiscal Federalism' 37(3) *Journal of Economic Literature* 1120–49.

——(2005) 'Toward a Second-Generation Theory of Fiscal Federalism' 12 *International Tax and Public Finance* 349–73.

Ofgem (2009) *Addressing Market Power Concerns in the Electricity Wholesale Sector – Initial Policy Proposals* (London, Ofgem).

Ogus, A (1995) 'Re-Thinking Self-Regulation' 15 *Oxford Journal of Legal Studies* 97–108.

Ohlin, B (1933) *Interregional and International Trade* (Cambridge, Harvard University Press).

Ohlin, B et al (1956) 'Social Aspects of European Economic Co-Operation' Report by a Group of Experts, International Labour Office, Geneva (reproduced in 74 *International Labour Review* 99–ff.)

Orts, E (1995) 'Reflexive Environmental Law' 89 *Nortwestern University Law Review* 1227–1340.

Ostrom, E (1990) *Governing the Commons: The Evolution of Institutions for Collective Action* (Cambridge, Cambridge University Press).

——(2001) 'Decentralisation and Development: the New Panacea' in K Dowding et al (ed), *Challenges to Democracy: Ideas, Involvement and Institution* (New York, Palgrave Publishers) 237–56.

Parker, C (2002) *The Open Corporation: Self-Regulation and Democracy* (Melbourne, Cambridge University Press).

Parker, C and Braithwaite, J (2003) 'Regulation' in P Cane and M Tushnet (eds), *The Oxford Handbook of Legal Studies* (Oxford, Oxford University Press).

Peltzman, S (1976) 'Toward a More General Theory of Regulation' 19 *Journal of Law and Economics* 211–40.

Pendleton, A and Gospel, H (2005) 'Markets and Relationships: Finance, Governance, and Labour in the United Kingdom' in H Gospel and A Pendleton (eds), *Corporate Governance and Labour Management: An International Comparison* (Oxford, Oxford University Press).

Perez, O (2007) 'The New Universe of Green Finance: From Self-Regulation to Multi-Polar Governance' in O Dilling, M Herberg and G Winter (eds), *Responsible Business: Self-Governance in Transnational Economic Transactions* (Oxford, Hart Publishing).

Peschl, MF (2008) 'Triple-Loop Learning as Foundation for Profound Change, Individual Cultivation, and Radical Innovation: Construction Processes Beyond Scientific and Rational Knowledge' 9940 *Munich Personal RePEc Archive* (published in: 2–3 2 (2007) *Constructivist Foundations* 136–45).

Plant, R (2009) *The Neo-Liberal State* (Oxford, Oxford University Press).

Posner, RA (2005) 'Judicial Behavior and Performance an Economic Approach' 32 *Florida State University Law Review* 1259–79.

Presentation material from British Airways (BA), Department for Transport (DfT), Merrill Lynch, Peel Airports, and Strategic Aviation Special Interest Group (SASIG).

Prior, G (2008) 'Electricians Denied Pay Bonanza on 2012 Work' *Contract Journal* 27 February.

Propper, C and Bartlett, W (1997) 'The Impact of Competition on the Behaviour of National Health Service Trusts' in R Flynn and G Williams (eds), *Contracting for Health: Quasi-Markets and the National Health Service* (Oxford, Oxford University Press).

Prosser, T (1997) *Law and the Regulators* (Oxford: Oxford University Press).

——(1999) 'Theorising Utility Regulation' 62 (2) *Modern Law Review* 196–217.

Radaelli, C (2004) 'The Puzzle of Regulatory Competition' 24 *Journal of Public Policy* 1–23.

——(2007) 'Whither Better Regulation for the Lisbon Agenda' 14 *Journal of European Public Policy* 190–207.

Reason, P and Bradbury, H (eds) (2001) *The SAGE Handbook of Action Research: Participative Inquiry and Practice*, 1st edn (London, Sage).

Richards, S, and Rodrigues, J (1993) 'Strategies for Management in the Civil Service: Change of Direction' 13(2) *Public Money and Management* 33.

Richardson, B (2002) *Environmental Regulation through Financial Organisation: Comparative Perspectives on the Industrialised Nations* (The Hague, Kluwer Law International).

Roth, WR (2003) 'From Centros to Uberseering: Free Movement of Companies, Private International Law and Community Law' 52 *International and Comparative Law Quarterly* 177–208.

Ruggie, JG (1982) 'International Regimes, Transactions, and Change: Embedded Liberalism and the Postwar Economic Order' 36(2) *Int. Org.* 379.

Sabel, CF (1994) 'Learning by Monitoring. The Institutions of Economic Development' in NJ Smelser and R Swedberg (eds), *The Handbook of Economic Sociology* (Princeton, Princeton UP and Russell Sage Foundation) 137–65.

——(2004) 'Beyond Principal-Agent Governance: Experimentalist Organisations, Learning and Accountability', draft discussion paper prepared for WRR meeting, Amsterdam (10–14 May 2004) in Ewald Engelen & Monika Sie Dhian Ho (eds), *De Staat van de Democratie. Democratie voorbij de Staat*. WRR Verkenning 3 (Amsterdam, Amsterdam University Press).

——(2005) 'A Real Time Revolution in Routines' in C Heckscher and P Adler (eds), *The Firm as a Collaborative Community* (Oxford, Oxford University Press).

——(2005) 'Globalisation, New Public Services, Local Democracy: What's the Connection?' in *Local Governance and the Drivers of Growth* (Paris, Organisation for Economic Co-operation and Development (OECD)).

Sabel, CF and Cohen, J (1997) 'Directly-Deliberative Polyarchy' 3 *European Law Journal* 313.

Sabel, CF and Zeitlin, J (2008) 'Learning from Difference: The New Architecture of Experimentalist Governance in the EU' 14 *European Law Journal* 271–327.

——(eds) (2010) *Experimentalist Governance in the European Union: Towards a New Architecture* (Oxford, Oxford University Press).

Salais, R and Villeneuve, R (eds) (2004) *Europe and the Politics of Capabilities* (Cambridge, Cambridge University Press).

Samuelson, PA (1948) 'International Trade and the Equalisation of Factor Prices' 58 (230, June) *The Economic Journal* 163–184.

Schäfer, A (2006) 'A New Form of Governance: Comparing the Open Method of Coordination to Multilateral Surveillance by the IMF and the OECD' 13(1) *Journal of European Public Policy* 70–88.

Scharpf, F (1994) Games Real Actors Could Play: Positive and Negative Coordination in Embedded Negotiations 6(1) *Journal of Theoretical Politics* 27–53.

——(1997) 'Introduction: the Problem Solving Capacity of Multi-Level Governance' 4 *Journal of European Public Policy* 520.

——(1999) *Governing in Europe. Effective and Democratic?* (Oxford, Oxford University Press).

Schön, D (1983) *The Reflective Practitioner: How Professionals Think in Action* (London, Temple Smith).

——(1993) 'Generative Metaphor: A Perspective on Problem-Setting in Social Policy' in A Ortony (ed), *Metaphor and Thought* (Cambridge (UK), Cambridge University Press).

——(1996) *The Reflective Practitioner: How Professionals Think in Action* (Aldershot, Ashgate Publishing Ltd).

Schout, JA and Jordan, AJ (2005) 'Coordinated European Governance: Self-organizing or Centrally Steered?' 83(1) *Public Administration* 201–20.

Scott, C (2004) 'Regulation in Age of Governance: The Rise of the Post-Regulatory State' in J Jordana and D Levi-Faur (eds), *The Politics of Regulation* (Cheltenham, Edward Elgar) 145–74.

——(2006) 'Privatization and Regulatory Regimes' in M Moran, M Rein and RE Goodin (eds), *Oxford Handbook of Public Policy* (Oxford, Oxford University Press).

——(2006) 'Spontaneous Accountability' in MW Dowdle, *Public Accountability: Designs, Dilemmas and Experiences* (Cambridge, Cambridge University Press).

——(2007) 'How Reflexive is the Governance of Regulation?' Paper presented at the annual meeting of The Law and Society Association, TBA (Germany, Berlin).

——(2008) 'Reflexive Governance, Meta-Regulation and Corporate Social Responsibility: The Heineken Effect?' in N Boeger, R Murray and C Villiers (eds), *Perspectives on Corporate Social Responsibility* (Cheltenham, Edward Elgar).

Select Committee on Regulators (2006–07) *UK Economic Regulators* HL 189.

Selznick, P (1985) 'Focusing Organizational Research on Regulation' in R Noll, *Regulatory Policy and the Social Sciences* (Berkeley, University of California Press).

Sen, AK (1985) *Commodities and Capabilities* (Amsterdam, North Holland).

——(1987) *The Standard of Living* (G Hawthorn (ed)) (Cambridge, Cambridge University Press).

Serbruyns, I and Luyssaert, S (2006) 'Acceptance of Sticks, Carrots and Sermons as Policy Instruments for Directing Private Forest Management' 9(3) *Forest Policy and Economics* 285–96.

Shavell, S (1993) 'The Optimal Structure of Law Enforcement' 36 *Journal of Law & Economics* 255–87.

Shearing, C (1993) 'A Constitutive Conception of Regulation' in J Braithwaite and P Grabosky (eds), *Business Regulation in Australia's Future* (Canberra, Australian Institute of Criminology).

Shepsle, K (1992) 'Bureaucratic Drift, Coalitional Drift, and Time Consistency' 8 *Journal of Law, Economics, and Organization* 111–18.

Siebenhüner, B (2002) 'How Do Scientific Assessments Learn? Part1. Conceptual Framework and Case Study of the IPCC' 5 *Environmental Science and Policy* (October) 411–420.

Siems, M (2002) 'Convergence, Competition, Centros and Conflicts of Law: European Company Law in the 21st Century' 27 *European Law Review* 47–59.

Simmons, B, Elkins, Z and Guzman, A (2006) 'Competing for Capital: the Diffusion of Bilateral Investment Treaties, 1960–2000' 60(4) *International Organization* 811–46.

Sørensen, E and Torfing, J (ed) (2007) *Theories of Democratic Network Governance* (Hampshire, Palgrave Macmillan).

Starkie, D (2008) *Aviation Markets: Studies in Competition and Regulatory Reform* (Aldershot, Ashgate Publishing).

Steffen, W, Sanderson, A, Tyson, PD, Jager, J, Matson, PM, Moore, B, Oldfield, F, Richardson, K, Schnellnhuber, HJ, Turner, BL and Wasson, RJ (2004) *Global Change and the Earth System: a Planet under Pressure* (New York, Springer).

Streck, C (2002) 'Global Public Policy Networks as Coalitions for Change' in DC Esty and MH Ivanova (ed), *Global Environmental Governance: Options and Opportunities* (New Haven, Yale School of Forestry and Environmental Studies) 121–40.

Swieringa, J and Wierdsma, A (1992) *Becoming a Learning Organization* (Reading, MA, Addison-Wesley).

Takeover Panel (2006) *The City Code on Takeovers and Mergers*, 8th edn, May 2006.

Taylor, PL (2005) 'In the Market But Not of It: Fair Trade Coffee and Forest Stewardship Council Certification as Market-Based Social Change' 33 *World Development* 129–47.

Teschl, M and Comim, F (2005) 'Adaptive Preferences and Capabilities: Some Preliminary Conceptual Explorations' 63(2)(June) *Review of Social Economy* 229–47.

Teubner, G (1993) *Law as an Autopoietic System* (Oxford, Blackwell).

——(1998 (originally published 1987)) 'Juridification: Concepts, Aspects, Limits, Solutions' in R Baldwin, C Scott and C Hood (eds), *Socio-Legal Reader on Regulation* (Oxford, Oxford University Press).

Tiebout, CM (1956) 'A Pure Theory of Local Government Expenditure' 64 *Journal of Political Economy* 416–24.

Toledano, J (2010) 'Regulation: Enduring Questions and Some Lessons from Practice' in MA Crew Kleindorfer and PR Heightening (eds), *Competition in the Postal and Delivery Sector, Advances in Regulatory Economics Series* (Cheltenham, Edward Elgar Publishing).

Trachtman, Joel P (1993) 'International Regulatory Competition, Externalization, and Jurisdiction' 34(1) *Harvard International Law Journal* 48.

Trebilcock, MJ and Hrab, R (2006) 'Electricity Restructuring in Canada' in F Sioshansi and W Pfaffenberger (eds), *Electricity Market Reform – An International Perspective* (Oxford, Elsevier) 419–50.

Trebilcock, MJ and Prichard, JRS (1983) 'Crown Corporations: The Calculus of Instrument Choice' in JRS Prichard, *Crown Corporations in Canada* (Toronto, Butterworths).

Tritter, J, and McCallum, A (2006) 'The Snakes and Ladders of User Involvement: Moving Beyond Arnstein' 76 *Health Policy* 156–68.

Trubek, D and Trubek, L (2005) 'Hard and Soft Law in the Construction of Social Europe: The Role of the Open Method of Co-ordination' 11 *European Law Journal* 343–64.

Turner, BL, Kasperson, RE, Meyer, WB, Dow, KM and Golding, D et al (1990) 'Two Types of Environmental Change' 1 *Global Environmental Change* 14–22.

Tyler, TR (1998) 'Trust and Democratic Governance' in V Braithwaite and M Levi (eds), *Trust and Governance* (New York, Russell Sage Foundation) 269–94.

Van Gossum, P and De Maeyer, W (2006) 'Performance of Forest Groups in Achieving Multifunctional Forestry in Flanders' 5(1) *Small-scale Forest Economics, Management and Policy* 19–36.

Vaughan-Whitehead, D (2003) *EU Enlargement versus Social Europe? The Uncertain Future of the European Social Model* (Cheltenham, Edward Elgar).

Verheyen, K, Lust, N, Carnol, M, Hens, L and Bouma, JJ (2006) 'Feasibility of Forests Conversion: Ecological, Social and Economic Aspects (Fefocon)' Final Report of SPSD II MA/04 (Brussels, Belgian Science Policy).

Vincent-Jones, P (2006) *The New Public Contracting: Regulation, Responsiveness, Relationality* (Oxford, Oxford University Press).

Vincent-Jones, P, Hughes, D and Mullen, C (2009) 'New Labour's PPI Reforms: Patient *and* Public Involvement in Healthcare Governance?' 72 *Modern Law Review* 247.

Vitousek, PM, Mooney, HA, Lubchenco, J and Melillo, JM (1997) 'Human Domination of Earth's Ecosystems' 277 (5325) *Science* 494–99.

Voss, J-P, Bauknecht, D et al (eds) (2006) *Reflexive Governance for Sustainable Development* (Cheltenham, Elgar).

Waite, S and Nolte, E (2005) 'Benchmarking Health Systems: Trends, Conceptual Issues and Future Perspectives' 12 *Benchmarking* 436.

Weale, A (2006) 'What is So Good about Citizens' Involvement in Healthcare?' in E Andersson, J Tritter and R Wilson (eds), *Healthy Democracy: The Future of Involvement in Health and Social Care* (London, Involve and NHS National Centre for Involvement).

Weatherwill, S (2003) 'Competence' in B de Witte (ed), *Ten Reflections on the Constitutional Treaty for Europe* (Florence, European University Institute, Robert Schuman Centre for Advanced Studies and Academy of European Law).

Wedderburn, K (1973) 'Industrial Relations' in HR Hahlo, J Graham Smith and RW Wright (eds), *Nationalism and the Multinational Enterprise: Legal, Economic and Managerial Aspects* (A Leidenand W Sijthoff) (New York, Oceana Publications, Dobbs Ferry).

Wedderburn, Lord (1986) *The Worker and the Law*, 3rd edn (Harmondswoth, Penguin).

Weithölter, R (1985) 'Proceduralization of the Category of Law' in C Joerges and D Trubek (eds), *Critical Legal Thought: An American-German Debate* (Baden-Baden, Nomos).

Williamson, O (1985) *The Economic Institutions of Capitalism* (New York, Free Press).

——(1996) *The Mechanism of Governance* (Oxford, Oxford University Press).

Wolmar, C (2006) 'Project Management at Heathrow Terminal 5' *Public Finance* 22 April, available at http://www.christianwolmar.co.uk/2005/04/project-management-at-heathrow-terminal-5/

Wolstenholme, A, Fugeman, I and Hammond, F (2008) 'Heathrow Terminal 5: Delivery Strategy' 161 *Civil Engineering* 10–15.

Wouters, J and De Meester, B (2003) 'The Role of International Law in Protecting Public Goods. Regional and Global Challenges. Leuven Interdisciplinary Research Group on International Agreements and Development' Working Paper n°1.

Wymeersch, E (2003) 'The Transfer of the Company's Seat in European Company Law' 40 *Common Market Law Review* 661–95.

Young, AR (2005) 'The Single Market' in H Wallace, W Wallace and MA Pollack (eds), *Policy-Making in the European Union,* 5th edn (Oxford, Oxford University Press) chapter four.

Young, OR (2008) 'Navigating the Sustainability Transition: The Role of Governance' Paper for discussion at the Workshop on 'Which Governance for Which Environment?' (Cargèse, France, 4–8 February 2008).

Zumbansen, P (2006) 'Spaces and Places: A Systems Theory Approach to Regulatory Competition in European Company Law' 12 *European Law Journal* 503–33.

——(2008) 'Law after the Welfare State: Formalism, Functionalism and the Ironic Turn of Reflexive Law' 58 *American Journal of Comparative Law* 769–805.

——(2009) 'Post-Regulatory Law: Chronicle of a Career Foretold' Faculty Seminar (Montreal, McGill University).

Index